THIS IS

THIS IS

The Official Companion

BLOOMSBURY

First published 2000 by Bloomsbury Publishing Plc,
38 Soho Square, London, W1V 5DF

A CIP catalogue record for this book
is available from the British Library

ISBN 0 7474 4218 X

10 9 8 7 6 5 4 3 2 1

Typeset by Palimpsest Book Production Limited,
Polmont, Stirlingshire
Printed in the United States of America by
R.R. Donnelley & Sons Company, Harrisonburg, Virginia

CONTENTS

Prepilogue

By Michael McKean

When I am called upon to generate copy about the mostly fictional entity called Spinal Tap, I usually do so in the mostly fictional character of David St Hubbins, longtime guitarist/clothes-horse for said group. David can knock the piece off at one sitting, e-mail it to his manager, and be back in bed by ten a.m.

But the one thing David St Hubbins can't do for us is talk about a movie called *This Is Spinal Tap*. None of the band can give you a rundown on the odd genesis of this film, because it doesn't exist in their world. Nigel Tufnel can't tell you about casting Howard Hesseman in a role that didn't exist sixteen hours before we got him into make-up. Derek Smalls never even heard of June Chadwick.

So I'm filling in.

In 1978, Rob Reiner, fresh from a long distinguished stretch in series television, put together a special called *The TV Show*. It spooved (yes, that is the correct word) network and local television, satirising a full viewing day's worth of crap in one hour. It was very funny.

I knew Rob, mostly in non-working situations, and several of the writers were old friends of mine. One of the proposed pieces was a parody of a show called *Midnight Special*, a rock'n'roll concert/variety show, hosted by the late Wolfman Jack. Christopher Guest suggested that a pea-brained English rock band be featured in the sketch. Chris and I had played a couple of road-weary Britrockers in a short piece he had directed so I became involved in the project. Chris, Rob, the show's producer, Harry Shearer and I wrote the song 'Rock 'n' Roll Nightmare' and its accompanying visual foolishness. After some groping about for a suitably duff name, we settled on Spinal Tap.

About a year and a half later, Rob was looking to direct feature films, and the notion of doing a fake documentary about this awful band started to snowball. Rob pitched the idea and got a hearty 'maybe' from Sir Lew Grade's US wing, Marble Arch. In early 1980, the four of us began meeting daily to furnish Spinal Tap with a believable past from which we might extrapolate a sufficiently amusing present. We watched a lot of rock'n'roll concert and documentary film, and noted the recurrence of an interesting theme: the *survivor* – the yeoman road warrior who never says die, no matter how clearly the market suggests he do so.

We had no intention of writing a screenplay. The idea had always been to construct the history of the band and the characters, set the general story elements, and improvise the dialogue, having made sure to hire actors we knew could play the game. In lieu of said screenplay, we proposed making a short film which would give the boys at the studio an idea of what the hell we wanted to do.

We shot the demo in four days and Rob assembled the piece over the next few months. In the interim, Marble Arch had released *Legend of the Lone Ranger* and *Raise the Titanic* (right boat, wrong direction!) in rapid succession and slipped quietly out of the Big Tent. Not to worry: United Artists showed great interest in . . . no, they were absorbed by MGM, and the new boss gave *Tap* the old Pasadena.

We assumed it was not going to happen. We all went back to our day gigs and night sweats until Lindsay Doran, a fan of Rob's and a bright light at Embassy Pictures, creatively suggested they just *make* the damn thing already. Jerry Parenchio and Norman Lear, dean of Reiner's alma mater, *All in the Family*, were running Embassy at the time and things fell gradually into place. Somebody did some budgetary business in a field unrelated to mine, and we began writing, casting and crewing in earnest in the spring of 1982.

Peter Smokler's camera rolled late in that year. We had cast old buds like Paul Benedict, Billy Crystal, Ed Begley and Paul Shaffer along with new friends Fran Drescher, Dana Carvey, Patrick MacNee, Anjelica Huston, et al. Ric Parnell and David Kaff came aboard as drummer Mick Shrimpton and keyboardist Viv Savage, respectively. June Chadwick was cast as Jeanine, St Hubbins' ladylove. Tony Hendra became our manager, the faithless Ian Faith. We asked everyone to come and improvise with us. We'd made very few miscalculations: the actors got the joke and flew with it, and every day's shooting was at least as much fun as the day before.

Rob edited the film over the next year-and-change; hearts broke at necessary deletions, theories clashed in the mixing studio, everyone cringed at some of the proposed marketing ideas. And the film was released in March of 1984.

The critics liked us very much. The public that found us, either by fluke or in response to the 'trickle-down' theory of promotion, found us funny. But we were a modestly budgeted satirical film with a very specific voice; we gave the bigger spring releases no serious nightmares. It did play in one theatre in Boston for something like a year, and the fans we encountered were smart and funny and flattering in the extreme. *This Is Spinal Tap* made a lot of 'Best of the Year' lists; it just didn't crack 1984's top ten box office. But it was the movie we had wanted to make, and we were very happy with it.

Video release widened our circle of friends; bits of Tapspeak began finding their way into the language. We had achieved an important goal: *shelf-life* – the ability to stay fresh and crisp while other comedy around you gets stale and mouldy. When someone reports watching the movie regularly and finding new stuff to laugh at every time, it makes us very glad. Shelf-life, see?

Lots of other stuff has happened since. Rob, Harry, Chris and I have been thankfully busy most of the time, but for each of us, the making of this strange movie was a high point. We are pleasantly delighted that Karl French and the Bloomsbury people (who demonstrably know their onions) choose to bandy our work about in this manner. I know I speak for the rest of the guys, real (Christopher Guest, Harry Shearer, Rob Reiner) and imagined (Nigel, Derek, Marty DiBergi) when I say thanks for the ink.

And while we've got you, thanks to all the Tapheads, real and imagined, for being the small, sturdy target-audience we knew you'd be.

Michael McKean
May 2000

TAP'ISTORY

Tap'istory

1974: *Intravenus de Milo* released; keyboardist Ross MacLochness joins group; drummer Eric 'Stumpy Joe' Childs chokes to death on (someone else's) vomit

1975: Tap tours Far East, releases live *Jap Habit* and *The Sun Never Sweats*. Manager Glyn Hampton-Cross and keyboardist MacLochness leave to pursue other interests

1976: *Bent for the Rent* and *Tap Dancing* released; Tap sues Megaphone for back royalties, Megaphone countersues for 'lack of talent'; director Marco Zamboni casts Derek in his film *Roma 79*; Tap begins performing under the names Anthem and The Cadburys after settlement with Megaphone

1977: *Rock 'n' Roll Creation* released; Viv Savage comes aboard on keyboards as Tap regroups on strength of single 'Nice 'n' Stinky' and tours US to support *Bent for the Rent*; David meets future wife Jeanine Pettibone at a wake; drummer Peter 'James' Bond spontaneously combusts and is replaced by Mick Shrimpton

1978: Tap performs on ABC-TV variety show, *The TV Show*; backstage, Nigel is introduced to Marty DiBergi

1979: Nigel releases solo album, *Nigel Tufnel's Clam Caravan*

1980: Polymer signs Tap; *Shark Sandwich* released

1982: *Smell the Glove* released and supported by US tour and one Japanese date; Ian Faith takes hiatus as manager and is replaced by Jeanine Pettibone

1983: *Heavy Metal Memories* released

1984: *This Is Spinal Tap* released in cinemas (March); Tap performs on NBC-TV's *Saturday Night Live* (May); Tap's *Intravenus de Milo* goes bronze (1 million copies returned)

1985: An official band biography, *Inside Spinal Tap*, by rock journalist Peter Occhiogrosso, is published in the United States

1986: David marries Jeanine Pettibone

1988: Derek joins the Christian heavy metal band Lambsblood

1990: Ian 'dies', Tap regroups

1991: Tap begins search for new drummer; begins recording *Break like the Wind*; announces reunion during MTV Video Music Awards (September 5); performs first live set since botched Japan tour at *RIP* magazine party at Hollywood Palladium (October 6); conducts drummer auditions for upcoming tour (October 31)

1992: *Inside Spinal Tap* updated and published in Great Britain; Ric Shrimpton joins the band (January 30); Tap begins ten-day tour of the United Kingdom, Sweden, Norway and Germany (February 16); Tap begins eight-day tour of Australia and attends the Australian Record Industry Awards (March 2); *Break like the Wind* released (March 17); Tap appears on *Late Night With David Letterman* (March 27); episode of *The Simpsons* features Tap (April); Tap plays at the Freddie Mercury tribute at Wembley Stadium (April 20); Tap launches US tour at Arnold Hall, Air Force Academy, Colorado Springs (May 17); Tap causes controversy at Great Woods Center for the Performing Arts near Boston when two biker chicks appear topless on stage during 'Big Bottom' (June 26); Tap jets across five time zones to perform in St John's, Barrie and Vancouver as part of Much Music's 'Great Canadian Party' to celebrate Canada Day (July 1); Tap plays the Royal Albert Hall, London: concert is filmed for American television (July 7); Tap plays on ABC's *Halloween Jam at Atlantic Studios* (October 31); NBC airs *A Spinal Tap Reunion* (December 31)

1993: *The Return of Spinal Tap* released on home video; Tap takes part in a Voters for Choice benefit at the Civic Center in Santa Monica because 'we heard women would be there'

1994: Criterion releases enhanced laserdisc and CD-ROM reissues of *This Is Spinal Tap*

1996: Tap plays an ACLU benefit in Los Angeles (March 11); IBM commercial featuring Tap premiers on NBC-TV featuring a new song called 'Goat Boy'; official Spinal Tap site opens on the Web at <spinaltap.com>

1998: Tap agrees to present an award at the Brit Awards to The Eels, who won for Best International Newcomer. *Rolling Stone* reports that the exchange did not go well. 'They were bitter about being passed up as Best Newcomer for the past 35 years,' the Eels' lead singer said. 'Nigel had a particularly large amount of attitude.' (March); Criterion releases an enhanced DVD version of *This Is Spinal Tap* (July).

1999: Rumours swirl about possible Tap2K tour

2000: Tap performs live on VH1's *The List* with guest drummer Mick Fleetwood (June); a remastered and remixed version of *This Is Spinal Tap* is released in cinemas (September); MGM releases newly enhanced video and DVD versions of the rockumentary (September); Tap performs at the premiere of the remastered *This Is Spinal Tap* at the House of Blues in Los Angeles (September)

Timeline compiled by Chip Rowe of the Spinal Tap Fan Page <http://chiprowe.com/tap>

THIS IS SPINAL TAP

A Rockumentary by Martin DiBergi

Credits

Spinal Tap Productions for Embassy Pictures
Director: Rob Reiner
Producer: Karen Murphy
Production executive: Lindsay Doran
Production controller: Jeff Stott
Production co-ordinator: Margaret E. Fanin
Unit production manager: Gary Glieberman
Location manager: Douglas Evan Stoll
Post-production co-ordinators: Marsha Murphy, Cathy Rosenstein
Assistant directors: Donald Newman, Irwin Marcus
Screenplay: Christopher Guest, Michael McKean, Harry Shearer, Rob Reiner
Cinematography: Peter Smokler (Col: CFI)
Additional photography: Rod Blackie, Steve Green, James Quakenbush
Concert lighting designer: Richard Ocean
Additional camera operators: H. J. Brown, Ric Robertson, Hector Ramirez, Bob Carmichael, Tom Geren
Logo and album cover design: Gregory Boone
Additional album cover design: Will Weston
Photographic album stills: Susan Rogers
Supervising editor: Robert Leighton
Editors: Kent Beyda, Kim Secrist
Production designer: Bryan Jones
Additional assistant director: Stan Harris
Pop, Look and Listen assistant director: James Maher
Concert special effects: James Beauchamp
Music/lyrics: Christopher Guest, Michael McKean, Harry Shearer, Rob Reiner
Music performed by: Christopher Guest, Michael McKean, Harry Shearer, R.J. Parnell, David Kaff
Music editing: Kenneth Karman

Songs:
  'Heartbreak Hotel' by Mae Axton, Tommy Durden, Elvis Presley
  'Cups and Cakes' (arranger and copyist) Harlan Collins
Choreographer: Carol Kravetz
Costume stylist: Renee Johnston
Assistant wardrobe: Lesley Nicholson
Make-up supervisor: Michele Payne
Titles/opticals: CFI
Supervising sound editor: John Brasher
Sound editor: Beth Bergeron
Sound recordists: Bob Eber, (additional) Ocean Park Sound, (music)
  Patrick McDonald (Dolby Stereo)
Sound rerecording: John Reitz, Dave Campbell, Gregg Rudloff
Sound effects editor: Robert Doheny
Sound effects recording: Lars Nelson
Concert playback operator: Doug Arnold
Band road manager: Robert Bauer
Roadies: David Guerra, Ralph Lee Moss
Cast:
Christopher Guest (Nigel Tufnel)
Michael McKean (David St Hubbins)
Harry Shearer (Derek Smalls)
R.J. Parnell (Mick Shrimpton)
David Kaff (Viv Savage)
Rob Reiner (Martin DiBergi)
June Chadwick (Jeanine Pettibone)
Tony Hendra (Ian Faith)
Bruno Kirby (Tommy Pischedda)
Ed Begley Jr (John 'Stumpy' Pepys)
Paul Benedict (Tucker 'Smitty' Brown)
Zane Busby (*Rolling Stone* reporter)
Billy Crystal (Morty the Mime)
Howard Hesseman (Terry Ladd)
Patrick MacNee (Sir Denis Eton-Hogg)
Paul Shaffer (Artie Fufkin)
Fred Willard (Lieutenant Hookstratten)
Fran Drescher (Bobbi Flekman)

Joyce Hyser (Belinda)
Vicki Blue (Cindy)
Anjelica Huston (Polly Deutsch)
Kimberley Stringer, Chazz Dominguez, Shari Hall (heavy metal fans)
Jean Cromie (ethereal fan)
Danny Kortchmar (Ronnie Pudding)
Julie Payne (mime waitress)
Sandy Helberg (Angelo DiMentibello)
Robin Mencken (Angelo's associate)
Jennifer Child (limo groupie)
J.J. Barry (rack jobber)
George McDaniel (Southern rock promoter)
Annie Churchill (Reba)
Paul Shortino (Duke Fame)
Cherie Darr, Lara Cody (Fame groupies)
Andrew J. Lederer (student promoter)
Russ Kunkel (Eric 'Stumpy Joe' Childs)
Diana Duncan, Gina Marie Pitrello (*Jamboreebop* dancers)
Gloria Gifford (airport security officer)
Archie Hahn (room-service guy)
Charles Levin (Disc 'n' Dat manager)
Wonderful Smith (janitor)
Chris Romano, Daniel Rodgers (little druids)
Fred Asparagus (Joe 'Mama' Besser)
Rodney Kemerer (Los Angeles party guest)
Robert Bauer (Moke)

The Transcript

Film Studio

Marty: Hello. My name is Marty DiBergi. I'm a film maker. I make a lot of commercials. That little dog that chases the covered wagon underneath the sink? That was mine. In 1966, I went down to Greenwich Village, New York City, to a rock club called The Electric Banana . . . Don't look for it, it's not there any more.

But that night I heard a band that for me redefined the word 'rock and roll'. I remember being knocked out by their . . . their exuberance, their raw power – and their punctuality. That band was Britain's now-legendary Spinal Tap. Seventeen years and fifteen albums later, Spinal Tap is still going strong, and they've earned a distinguished place in rock history, as one of England's loudest bands. So in the late fall of 1982, when I heard that Tap was releasing a new album called *Smell the Glove*, and was planning their first tour of the United States in almost six years to promote that album, well needless to say I jumped at the chance to make the documentary – the, if you will, rockumentary – that you're about to see. I wanted to capture the, the sights, the sounds, the smells, of a hard-working rock band on the road. And I got that. But I got more, a lot more. But hey – enough of my yakkin'.

Whaddaya say, let's boogie!

Outside concert venue

Fan 1: Gives me a lot of energy, makes me happy.
Fan 2: Heavy metal's deep, you can get stuff out of it.
Fan 3: The way they dress, the leather.

JFK Airport, New York

David: Which one is this? Is this La Guardia or is this—?
Ian: No, this is J.F.K.

David: Oh yes.

Ian: New York, New York.

Back outside the venue

Roadie: Watch it now, watch it now.

Ethereal fan:
It's like you become one with the guys in the band. I mean there's . . . there's no division, you just . . . the music just unites . . . people . . . with the players.

Onstage

New York MC:
You want it live, direct from hell – Spinal Tap!

SPINAL TAP PERFORMS 'TONIGHT I'M GONNA ROCK YOU TONIGHT'

David: We are Spinal Tap from the UK, you must be the USA!

Garden Interview I

Marty: Let's . . . uh, talk a little bit about the history of the group. I understand, Nigel, you and David . . . originally started the band wuh . . . back in . . . when was it . . . 1964?

David: Well before that we were in different groups. I was in a group called The Creatures which was a skiffle group.

Nigel: I was in Lovely Lads.

David: Yeah.

Nigel: And then we looked at each other and said, well we might as well join up you know and uh . . .

David: So we became, uh, The Originals.

Nigel: Right.

David: And, uh, we had to change our name, actually . . .

Nigel: Well there was, there was another group in the East End called The Originals and we had to rename ourselves.

David: The New Originals.

Nigel: New Originals and then, uh, they became . . .

David: The Regulars, they changed their name back to The Regulars and we thought, well, we could, we could go back to The Originals but what's the point?

Nigel: We became The Thamesmen at that point.

THE THAMESMEN PLAY 'GIMME SOME MONEY' ON *POP, LOOK & LISTEN* 1965

Marty: Your first drummer was, uh . . .

Nigel: The peeper . . .

David: John, 'Stumpy' Pepys . . . great great . . . uh . . . tall blond . . . geek . . . with glasses uh . . .

Nigel: Uh . . . good drummer.

David: Great look, good drummer, yeah.

Nigel: Good, good drummer . . .

David: Fine drummer . . .

Marty: What happened to him?

David: He died, he, he died in a bizarre gardening accident some years back.

Nigel: It was really one of those things . . . it was . . . you know . . . the authorities said . . . you know . . . best leave it . . . unsolved, really . . . you know.

Marty: And he was replaced by . . . uh . . .

David: Stumpy Joe – Eric 'Stumpy Joe' Childs.

Marty: And what happened to Stumpy Joe?

Derek: Well, uh, it's not a very pleasant story . . . but, uh . . .

David: He's passed on.

Derek: He died, uh . . . He choked on . . . the ac – the official explanation was he choked on vomit.

Nigel: It was actually, was actually . . . someone else's vomit. It's not . . .

David: It's ugly.

Nigel: You know. There's no real . . .

Derek: Well they can't prove whose vomit it was . . . they never – they don't have facilities at Scotland Yard . . .

David: They don't print, there's no way of . . . with spectrum-photographing

Nigel: You can't really . . . dust for vomit.

Opening Night Party, New York

Ian: Here we go . . . SoHo, they call this, SoHo . . .

David: 'So' what?

Ian: SoHo. SoHo.

Bobbi: How *are* you? Ian! Hi fellas, how you doin' . . . Come over here. I want you to meet everybody.

Derek: Who is that?

Ian: Bobbi Flekman.

Derek: Who's that?

Ian: Bobbi Flekman.

Derek: Who is it . . . with the record company?

Bobbi: Yes, Bobbi Flekman – the hostess with the mostest. You know, you know. Hi, handsome. How you doing? Alright, listen, I want you to all meet Sir Denis Eton-Hogg, now he's the head of Polymer.

Band: We know, we know.

Bobbi: (*To Nigel*) You don't talk so much – just smile and look smart.

David: Oh, she knows . . .

Bobbi: Denis, come here . . . come here. I want you to meet Spinal Tap, our guests of honour.

Sir Denis: How very nice to meet you!

Bobbi: Kids, this is Sir Denis Eton-Hogg . . . this is Nigel.

David: Hello, David St . . .

Sir Denis: Oh, so this is Nigel!

Nigel: Thanks a lot for letting us, uh . . .

Bobbi: Let's go over here and we'll all take a picture together. Where's Christine? Where's my photographer? Come over here honey. What's your name? Christine? OK, right over here . . . good, *good*!

Reporter: Guys, you look great. I mean you look fantastic. You would never know that you are almost forty. I mean if I looked this good; from the stage too, it's amazing you know . . .

Morty the Mime: I did the bird, do the dead bird . . . change this, get the dwarf cannoli, the little ones . . .

Mime: I did the bird . . .

Morty the Mime: C'mon, don't talk back, huh . . . mime is money, let's go. Come on, move it!

Sir Denis: Now, we here at Polymer, we're all looking forward to a long and . . . and . . . and fruitful relationship with Spinal Tap.
We wish them great success on their North American tour and so say all of us . . . Tap into America!
Bobbi: Yeah!

Limo

Driver: Excuse me . . . are you reading *Yes I Can*?
Groupie: Yeah, have you read it?
Driver: Yeah, by Sammy Davis Jr?
Groupie: Yeah.
Driver: You know what the title of that book should be? 'Yes I Can if Frank Sinatra Says it's OK'. 'Cause Frank calls the shots for all of those guys. Did you get to the part yet where uh . . . Sammy is coming out of the Copa . . . it's about three o'clock in the morning and, uh . . . he sees Frank. Frank's walking down Broadway by himself . . . (*Limo window raised by Nigel*) Fuckin' limeys.
Marty: Well, you know . . . they're not uh . . . they're not used to that world –
Driver: Yeah yeah. Yeah I know. That's right.
Marty: Frank Sinatra, it's a different world that they're in.
Driver: You know, it's just – people like this . . . you know . . . you know, they get all they want so they don't . . . really understand, you know . . . about a life like Frank's, I mean when, you know when you've, when you've loved and lost the way Frank has, then you, uh . . . you know what life's about.

Ian: *The Times* may even do something.
Nigel: Really?
David: The *New York Times*?
Ian: Uh-huh. The *New York Times*.
David: The bump we've got to iron out here is when do we get the album released. I mean it doesn't matter how good the press is or what the stringers . . .

Ian: Well, as I explained last night, you know, we're not, we're not gonna saturate . . . the New York market. Now Philly, now that's a real rock and roll town.

David: Oh, Philly's a great town.

Ian: Be assured that the album will be available all through the Philadelphia metropolitan area.

David: So you are hitting that market regardless of how we're selling in New York?

Ian: We're certainly, uh, we're certainly doing . . . *I'm* doing everything I can.

David: That's right. We are not blaming you. You *know* that we're not blaming you.

Marty: But you don't feel that these guys have an effect on an audience, I mean . . . kids go to their concert, they have a great time, uhh . . .

Driver: But it's . . . it's a passing thing . . . it's uh . . . I mean I would never tell them this but this is, uh . . . this is a fad.

SPINAL TAP PLAYS 'BIG BOTTOM' AT FIDELITY HALL PHILADELPHIA

Garden interview II

Marty: Let's talk about your reviews a little bit . . . regarding *Intravenus de Milo*: 'This tasteless cover is a good indication of the lack of musical invention within. The musical growth rate of this band cannot even be charted. They are treading water in a sea of retarded sexuality and bad poetry.'

Nigel: That's, that's nit picking, isn't it?

Marty: *The Gospel According to Spinal Tap*: 'This pretentious ponderous collection of religious rock psalms is enough to prompt the question: "What day did the Lord create Spinal Tap and couldn't he have rested on that day too?"'

David: Never heard that one!

Derek: That's a good one, that's a good one!

Marty: The review you had on *Shark Sandwich* – which was merely a two-word review – just said 'shit sandwich'. Umm . . .

Derek: Where'd they print that, where'd they print that?

David: Where did that appear?

Nigel: That's not real, is it?

Derek: You can't print that!

Recording Industry Convention, Atlanta, Georgia

Derek: Y'know, all those arguments about touring and not touring and all that, I mean it's obvious we belong on tour, you know . . .

Ian: I couldn't agree more. I mean, all that stuff about you being too old and you being too white but . . .

Derek: But what about the album, Ian?

David: Well that's the real problem, there's no way to promote something that doesn't exist, you know . . .

Ian: It's a very unimportant reason, it's just that they're just experimenting with, uh, with some new, uh . . . packaging materials. Let me get the door.

Derek: What kind of experimenting? They got monkeys opening it or what?

Ian: Oh there's, uhh . . . the other thing is that the, uh . . . the Boston gig has been cancelled.

Nigel: What?

Ian: Yeah. I wouldn't worry about it though, it's not a big college town.

Polymer Records Hospitality Suite

Promoter: I heard you boys got an album coming out.

David: Yeah, it's called *Smell the Glove* . . . it should be out now, yeah . . . yeah, yeah . . .

Promoter: *Smell the Glove*?

Rep: It's a provocative title.

David: Well, wait till you see the cover, wait till you see the cover, very provocative indeed.

Ian: Bobbi, Bobbi, can I tear you away from all of this?

Bobbi: Do you have a drink? Everything OK?

Ian: No, I don't, I don't really need one. But, um, listen, I really, I really do have to talk to you a bit about this, uh . . .

Bobbi: Ian, come on, whatever's on your mind . . .

Ian: . . . this whole issue of the, uh . . . the issue of the cover.

Bobbi: Yeah.

Ian: . . . Um, we, uh, I mean, we feel . . . and it seems to be facts that, uh
. . . the company's rather down on the cover, is that the case?

Bobbi: Yes.

Ian: You can give it to me straight, you know.

Bobbi: Listen umm . . . they don't like the cover. They don't like the cover.

Ian: Uh huh, well that's certainly straight.

Bobbi: They find it very offensive and very sexist.

Ian: Well what exactly . . . do you find offensive? I mean, what's offensive?

Bobbi: Ian, you put a greased naked woman . . .

Ian: Yes . . .

Bobbi: . . . on all fours . . .

Ian: Yes.

Bobbi: . . . with a dog collar around her neck . . .

Ian: . . . with a dog collar . . .

Bobbi: . . . and a leash . . .

Ian: . . . and a leash . . .

Bobbi: . . . and a man's arm extended out up to here holding on to the leash
and pushing a black glove in her face to sniff it. You don't find that offensive,
you don't find that sexist?

Ian: No I don't, this is 1982, Bobbi, come on.

Bobbi: That's right, it's 1982, get out of the sixties, we don't have this mentality
any more.

Ian: Well you should have seen the cover they wanted to do. It wasn't a glove,
believe me.

Bobbi: I don't care what they wanted. Now see, this is something, Ian, that
you are going to have to talk to your boys about.

Ian: We're certainly not laying down any conditions . . .

Bobbi: And I don't think that a sexy cover is the answer for why an album
sells or doesn't sell because you tell me . . . the *White Album*, what was that?
There was nothing on that goddamn cover. Excuse me, the phone's ringing.
Ian, we'll talk about this after.

Ian: OK, bye bye.

Bobbi: Hello. Oh, hi Denis. Uh oh, OK. Why don't you tell him? OK, hold
on one minute. Ian? It's Eton-Hogg, he wants to talk to you.

Ian: OK. Thank you darling.

Bobbi: You're welcome . . . dear.

Ian: Hello Sir Denis. Hi, how are you? (*away from mouthpiece*) Oh, fucking old poofter! (*to phone*) But it's really not that offensive, Sir Denis, come on. OK. I'll call you absolutely first thing in the morning. (*slams phone*) Ah, shit. They are not gonna release the album . . . Because they have decided that the cover is sexist.

Nigel: But what's wrong with being sexy? I mean there's no . . .

Ian: Sex–ist.

David: –ist. More than sexy.

Bobbi: OK, listen. I wanted to tell you this and, and . . . I was holding back because I didn't know what Denis's decision was going to be . . . but at this point both Sears and K-Mart stores have refused to handle the album.

Ian: That old one, huh?

Bobbi: They're boycotting the album only because of the cover. If the first album had been a hit . . .

Ian: If the company is behind the album it can shove it right down their throats.

Bobbi: Money talks and bullshit walks and if the first album was a hit *then* we could have pressed on them, then we could have told them yes . . .

Ian: The music . . . every cut on this album is a hit.

Bobbi: Let's . . . I don't give a shit what the album's . . .

Nigel: It's a matter of compromise, we made a joke, and it was a long time ago, they're making it like a big deal.

David: That's true. You know, if we were serious and we said this . . . 'yes she should be forced to sn . . . smell the glove' then you'd have a point, you know, but it's all a joke, innit. I mean we're making fun – we're making fun of that sort of thing, you know?

Nigel: Well, it is and it isn't. She *should* be made to smell it, but not . . .

David: Not, you know, over and over again.

Bobbi: You know, we can probably work something out. I'll talk to Denis and maybe we can come up with a compromise – a new design concept that we can all live with.

Interview in restaurant

Marty: You guys were school mates?

Nigel: We don't . . . we, we, we're not . . . university material.

David: What's that on your finger?

Nigel: That's my gum!

David: What are you doing with it on your finger?

Nigel: I might need it later.

David: Put it on the table, that's terrible.

Nigel: Well . . . I might forget it on the table.

David: You can't take him anywhere.

Marty: How old were you guys when you met?

David: About eight years old. Eight or nine.

Nigel: You were eight and I was seven.

David: That's right, yeah.

Marty: Do you remember the first song you guys ever wrote together?

David: 'All the Way Home', probably.

Marty: 'All the Way Home'?

David: Yeah.

Marty: Can you remember a little bit of it? I'd love to hear it.

David: Christ. Some black coffee, maybe we could do it.

Nigel: How's it go?

Nigel and David:

   I'm standing here beside the railroad track . . .

   and I'm waiting for that train to bring you back . . .

   (bring you back)

   if, if, if, if, if she's not on the, the 5:19

   then I'm gonna know what sorrow means . . .

   and I'm gonna cry cry cry all the way home . . .

   all the way home . . . all the way home . . .

   all the way home . . . all the way home . . .

Nigel: Cry, cry, cry all the way home . . .

David: . . . Fairly simple . . . there's about six words in the whole song, you know.

Marty: Sounds like a big hit.

David: Just repeat them over and over again.

Marty: Let's talk about your music today . . . uh . . . one thing that puzzles me . . . um . . . is the make up of your audience seems to be . . . uh . . . predominantly young boys.

David: Well it's a sexual thing, really, isn't it. Aside from the identifying that the boys do with us, there's also like a re . . . a reaction to the female . . . of the female to our music. What was it, the way you . . . ?

Nigel: Really they're quite fearful – that's my theory. They see us on stage with tight trousers, we've got, you know, armadillos in our trousers, I mean it's really quite frightening . . .

David: Yeah.

Nigel: . . . the size . . . and, and they, they run screaming.

Vandermint Auditorium

Nigel: Ian, can I have a word with you for a minute?

Ian: Yes, of course.

Nigel: . . . Um, a couple of problems with the, uh . . .

Ian: What?

Nigel: . . . arrangements backstage . . .

Ian: What exactly?

Nigel: Well, uh . . .

Ian: What, I mean . . .

Nigel: Well, no, there's some problems here, uh, I don't even know where to start. Alright – this, uh . . .

Ian: Soundcheck? What's, what's, what's wrong?

Nigel: No, no, no, no this . . . look, look, look, there's a little problem with the . . . look this, this miniature bread. It's like . . . I've been working with this now for about half an hour. I can't figure out . . . let's say I want a, a bite, right, you've got this . . .

Ian: You'd like bigger bread?

Nigel: Exactly! I don't understand how . . .

Ian: You could fold this though.

Nigel: Well, no, then it's half the size.

Ian: No, not the bread, no, you could fold the meat.

Nigel: Yeah, but then it, then it breaks up, breaks apart like this.

Ian: No, no, no, you put it on the bread like this, see.

Nigel: But then, if you keep folding it, it keeps breaking . . .

Ian: Why would you keep folding it?

Nigel: And then you . . . everything has to be folded, and then it's this, and I don't want this. I want large bread so that I can put this . . .

Ian: Right.

Nigel: . . . so then it's like this, but this doesn't work because then . . . it's all . . .

Ian: 'Cause it hangs out like that?

Nigel: Look . . .

Ian: Yeah.

Nigel: Would you . . . be holding this?

Ian: No, I don't want to eat . . . I wouldn't want to put that in my mouth, I must say. No, you're right, Nigel, you're right, you're right . . .

Nigel: No, alright, 'A', exhibit, exhibit 'A'. And now we move on to this – look, look, who's in here? No one! And then in *here* there's a little guy, look! So it's, it's a complete catastrophe!

Ian: No, you're right, Nigel, Nigel, but calm down, calm down.

Nigel: Calm . . . ? Look, no it's no big deal, look it's a joke, it's really, it's . . .

Ian: I'm sorry. It's, it's just, it's just some crappy university, you know.

Nigel: I know. Yeah, right, it's a joke, it's all a . . .

Ian: I mean I really . . . I don't want it to affect your performance.

Nigel: It's not going to affect my performance, don't worry about it, alright? Just hate it, it really . . .

Ian: Well, it won't happen again.

Nigel: It does disturb me.

Ian: It's disgusting.

Nigel: But I'll rise above it, I'm a professional, right?

Ian: Alright.

SPINAL TAP PERFORMS 'HELL HOLE'

Guided tour of Nigel's guitar collection

Marty: Do you play all . . . I mean do you actually play all these or . . . ?

Nigel: Well, I play them and I cherish them.

Marty: Mmm–hmm . . .

Nigel: This is the top of the heap right here. There's no question about it. Look at the, look at the flame on that one . . .

Marty: Yes.

Nigel: I mean, it's just . . . it's quite unbelievable. This o– this one is just, uh . . . it's perfect . . . 1959 . . . uh . . . you know, it just, you can, uh . . . listen!

Marty: How much does this . . .

Nigel: Just listen for a minute . . .

Marty: I'm not . . .

Nigel: The sustain . . . listen to it . . .

Marty: I'm not hearing anything.

Nigel: You would, though, if it were playing, because it really . . . it's famous for its sustain . . . I mean, you can just hold it . . .

Marty: Well I mean so you don't . . .

Nigel: Aaaaaaaaaaaaaaa . . . You can go, go and have a bite an' . . . aaaaaaaaa . . . you'd still be hearin' that one. Could you hold this a sec?

Marty: Sure.

Nigel: This one . . . this 'course is a custom three-pickup −'Paul. This is my radio . . . unit . . .

Marty: Oh, I see . . .

Nigel: So I strap this . . . this piece on, you know, right down in here when I'm on stage and . . .

Marty: It's a wireless.

Nigel: Wireless, exactly. And . . . uh, I can play without all the mucky-muck.

Marty: You can run anywhere on stage with that.

Nigel: Exactly. Now this is special, too, it's a . . . look . . . see . . . still got the uh . . . the ol' tagger on it . . . see . . . never even played it . . . see . . .

Marty: You just bought it and . . .

Nigel: Don't touch it! Don't touch it! No one . . . no! Don't touch it.

Marty: Well, uh, I wasn't . . . uh, I wasn't gonna touch it . . . I was just pointing at it . . . I . . .

Nigel: Well, don't point, even.

Marty: Don't even point?

Nigel: No. It can't be played . . . never . . . I mean I . . .

Marty: Can I look at it?

Nigel: No.

Marty: Don't look at it.

Nigel: No, you've seen enough of that one. This is a top to a, you know, what we use on stage, but it's very . . . very special because if you can see . . .

Marty: Yeah . . .

Nigel: . . . the numbers all go to eleven. Look . . . right across the board.

Marty: Ahh . . . oh, I see . . .

Nigel: Eleven . . . eleven . . . eleven . . .

Marty: . . . and most of these amps go up to ten . . .

Nigel: Exactly.

Marty: Does that mean it's . . . louder? Is it any louder?

Nigel: Well, it's one louder, isn't it? It's not ten. You see, most . . . most blokes, you know, will be playing at ten. You're on ten here . . . all the way up . . . all the way up . . .

Marty: Yeah . . .

Nigel: . . . all the way up. You're on ten on your guitar . . . where can you go from there? Where?

Marty: I don't know . . .

Nigel: Nowhere. Exactly. What we do is if we need that extra . . . push over the cliff . . . you know what we do?

Marty: Put it up to eleven.

Nigel: Eleven. Exactly. One louder.

Marty: Why don't you just make ten louder and make ten be the top . . . number . . . and make that a little louder? . . .

Nigel: . . . These go to eleven.

Hotel Lobby, Memphis, Tennessee

Smitty: Are you, uh – are you Spinal Tap?

Ian: Spinal Tap – this is Spinal Tap.

Smitty: Welcome to Memphis, gentlemen. We have a slight problem with your reservation. Nothing serious, I'm afraid.

Ian: How slight?

Smitty: You wanted seven, uh, suites.

Ian: Seven. Seven suites.

Smitty: Yes w-we-he mistakenly put you on the seventh floor with one suite.

Ian: That's considerably more than minor.

Smitty: Well, it's a good-sized room, sir. It's a, it's a 'King Leisure'. We can get you a – something.

Ian: How are we going to get fourteen people in a 'King Leisure' bed, Tucker?

Smitty: Oh-ho-ho don't – don't tempt me, sir.

David: Have a good time, will you – take care.

Ian: I will, I'll take care of it.

Smitty: Welcome, gentlemen – and very attractive they are, too.

Ian: Hey! Hey! Listen to me: we want these suites, and we want them now! OK? These people are tired, we have soundcheck in an hour.

Smitty: Yes, sir. We can't help you out – Reba – perhaps you can help here.

Reba: What's the problem, Smitty?

Smitty: Can you give me a hand, please?

Ian: Yeah. I'll tell you what you can do. OK? This – twisted old fruit here – tells me that *you* have not got my reservations.

Smitty: I'm just as God made me, sir.

David: What's the difference between golf and miniature golf?

Derek: I think, uh . . .

Mick: The walls. (*Crazed female fans shriek.*)

David: Uh-oh – look out, here they come . . .

Fan: Duke! Duke! Can I have your autograph?

Nigel: It's Duke.

David: Duke! Duke!

Terry: Get your hands back.

David: That's OK, we know him, it's Spinal Tap. Spinal Tap.

Terry: Sure.

David: David St Hubbins, Spinal Tap; Derek Smalls, Spinal Tap.

Terry: Look, we gotta get going here.

David: Listen, uh . . . uh . . . where you playing in town? You playin' here?

Terry: We're doin' the . . . uh . . . Enormodome, whatever it is. It's terrific, it's a good house. We sold it out.

David: Oh yeah big place, outside of town.

Terry: Very nice.

David: That's a big place. You sold it out?!

Nigel: What's that, twenty thousand seats?

Terry: We really should run, you know . . .

Ian: Good heavens. How are you, Laddy?! Great to see you, Ter! Terrific to see you.

Terry: Uhhhhm . . . Liam!

Ian: Ian. Ian.

Terry: Ian. Yeah, listen, we'd love to stand around and chat, but we've gotta . . . sit down in the lobby and wait for the limo.

Derek: OK.

David: OK. Great. Duke, great to see you. Great to see you again, Terry.

Derek: We'll catch up with you on the road.

Duke: Cheers.

David: Duke! Great to see you. See ya. See you, Duke. Good days. Good days!

David: Fuckin' wanker.

Nigel: What a wanker.

David: What a wanker.

Derek: Total no talent sod.

Nigel: He's got this much talent – this much if he's lucky.

David: We carried him. We had to apologise for him with our set.

Derek: That's right.

Mick: That's right, yeah.

David: People were still booin' 'im when we were on. It's all hype. It's all hype.

Ian: Yep. We got our rooms, big fat suites.

David: Can I ask you something – can I ask you something?

Ian: What?

David: Have you seen Duke Fame's current album?

Ian: Um . . . yes, yes.

David: Have you seen the cover?

Ian: Um . . . no, no, I don't think I have.

David: It's a rather lurid cover, I mean . . . ah, it's, it's like naked women, and, uh . . .

Nigel: He's tied down to this table.

Ian: Uh-huh.

Nigel: And he's got these whips and they're all . . . semi-nude.

David: Knockin' on 'im and it's like much worse . . .

Ian: What's the point?

David: Well the point is it's much worse than *Smell the Glove* . . . he releases that and he's number three.

Ian: Because he's the victim. Their objections were that *she* was the victim. You see?

Derek: I see . . .

Nigel: Oh . . .

David: Ah . . .

Ian: That's alright, if the singer's the victim, it's different. It's not sexist.

Nigel: He did a twist on it. A twist and it's . . .

Derek: He did, he did. He turned it around.

Ian: We shoulda thought of that . . .

David: We were so close . . .

Ian: I mean if we had all you guys tied up, that probably woulda been fine.

All: Ah . . .

Ian: But it's . . . it's still a stupid cover.

David: It's such a fine line between stupid an' . . .

Derek: And clever.

David: Yeah, and clever.

Nigel: Just that little turnabout . . .

Ian: I have a small piece of bad news. Although it may not be that bad.

Mick: For a change, you mean?

Ian: We're – uh. We're cancelled here.

Derek: At the hotel?

Ian: No, we're cancelled – the gig is cancelled.

Derek: Fuck!

Ian: Uh . . . it says 'Memphis show cancelled due to lack of advertising funds' . . .

Ian's office

Marty: The last time Tap toured America, they were, uh, booked into ten-thousand-seat arenas, and fifteen-thousand-seat venues, and it seems that now, on the current tour, they're being booked into twelve-hundred-seat arenas, fifteen-hundred-seat arenas, and uh, I was just wondering, does this mean, uh . . . the popularity of the group is waning?

Ian: Oh, no, no, no, no, no, no . . . no, no, not at all. I, I, I just think that the . . . uh . . . that their appeal is becoming more selective.

Marty: Uh-huh. Now, I notice this here, you've got this cricket bat here . . .

Ian: Yes.

Marty: Do you play?

Ian: Um . . . no. I carry this partly out of, uh, I don't know, sort of sort of, uh, I suppose, uh, what's the word . . . uh . . .

Marty: Affectation?

Ian: Yes, I mean it's, it's a, it's a kind of *totemestic* thing, you know, but to be quite frank with you, it's come in useful in a couple of situations. Certainly in the topsy-turvy world of heavy rock, having a good solid piece of wood in your hand is quite often . . . useful.

Marty: Mhmh.

Hotel room, Memphis, Tennessee

David: I miss you too, darling . . . um, not too well, actually . . . well, we've got some cancellations, that's all, we got to Memphis, and there's no gig in Memphis, and we find out this, this promoter in the Mid-West, uhh, has pulled out of St Louis, and Kansas City, and uh . . . oh, Des Moines . . . I don't know, it's in Indiana or something . . . I thought . . . oh don't tease me, that's not until April, great! We'll do it, oh good, oh, fucking great. . . Milwaukee . . . Milwaukee, Wisconsin . . . I've no idea, you might have to take the plane to New York, and then get, and then go to, uh, to Milwaukee from there . . . . . . oh, good I love you too . . . OK, bye . . . Ah, well, my problems are solved, mate!

Nigel: Who's that?

David: Jeanine, she's going to come meet us. She was supposed to do this, uh, window layout for Neil Kite's Boutique, but it's not until April.

Nigel: Is she coming to drop some stuff off, you know, and then . . .

David: No.

Nigel: . . . go right back?

David: No, she's coming on the road, she's going to travel with us, she's gonna go on the road with us.

Derek: Turn it up, turn it up!

David: She says she can hear that I'm eating too much sugar on the phone. She says my larynx is fat.

Derek: You, uh, might want to come next door. The radio is playing a bit of your past.

David: Ohooow . . . I don't believe it!

DJ: Oh, yeah, going *all* the way back to 1965 that one . . .

DJ: Don't it feel good, with The Thamesmen and 'Cups and Cakes'.

Derek: You're an oldie . . . you're an oldie!

DJ: When The Thamesmen later changed their names to Spinal Tap, they had a couple of nice-sized hits. They are currently residing in the 'where are they now' file. Johnny Q with you on Golden 106 and right after we . . .

Derek: Fuck you!

Elvis's grave, Graceland, Memphis, Tennessee

David: I'm not really sure this was such a great idea, I mean I don't feel any better than I did at the hotel.

Derek: He was going to do a TV special from here, before he died.

David: Yeah, that's right, a musical version of 'Somebody Up There Likes Me' . . . (*Sings:*) Well since my baby left me, I found a new place to dwell well, it's down at the end of Lonely Street, at Heartbreak Hotel.

Nigel: Do it, do it with the harmony parts.

David: Alright.

David and Nigel: Well since my baby . . .

David: The same key, though, I think.

David and Nigel: Well since my baby left me . . .

Nigel: If I'm going: since my baby left me, meeee . . .

David: No, you can't hit *that* note!

Derek, David and Nigel: Mmmmm . . . since my baby left me, well, I found a new place to dwell . . .

Nigel: That's alright.

Derek: Not really, not really . . . voice down . . .

David: Well it sounds raga, don't want to go raga on this stuff.

Nigel: No, not with this you don't. Well since my baby left me . . .

David: It sounds . . . fuckin' barbershop . . .

Derek: Hey!

David: Barbershop raga. A new hybrid.

Derek: Hey, watch the, watch the language, you're paying homage to the King!

David: Oh sorry . . . well this is thoroughly depressing.

Nigel: It really puts perspective on things, though, doesn't it?

David: Too much. There's too much fucking perspective now.

Garden interview III

Marty: In 1967, uh, you . . . that was the first time Spinal Tap came into existence?

Derek: Well, the whole world was changing in those days.

David: And, and also we had the world's ear.

Derek: We were changing the world.

David: Because we had just released an *enormous*-selling single: '(Listen to the) Flower People'.

Nigel: Flower People!

David: We toured the world, we toured the States . . .

Derek: We toured the world and elsewhere.

David: It was, it was a dream come true.

Marty: Now, during the Flower People period, who was your drummer?

David: Stumpy's replacement, Peter 'James' Bond. He also died in mysterious circumstances . . . We were playing a . . .

Nigel: Festival . . .

David: Jazz-blues festival, where was that?

Nigel: Blues-jazz really.

Derek: Blues-jazz festival . . .

Nigel: It was the, uh, it was in the Isle . . .

Nigel and Derek: Isle of Lucy.

Nigel: Isle of Lucy.

David: The Isle of Lucy Jazz-Blues Festival . . .

Nigel: And . . . it was tragic really . . . he exploded on stage.

Derek: Just like that . . .

David: He just went up . . .

Nigel: He just was like a flash of green light . . . and that was it. Nothing was left . . .

David: Look at his face . . . It's true, this truly did happen.

Nigel: Well, there was a little green globule on his drum seat.

David: Like a stain, really.

Nigel: More of a stain than a globule, actually, and . . .

David: You know several . . . you know dozens of people spontaneously combust each year, it's just not really widely reported.

Nigel: Right.

Soundcheck, Shank Hall, Milwaukee, Wisconsin

Nigel: Hello, hello, hello, hello.

David: Testin', test, test, test. This is mike number one, this is mike number one, isn't this a lot of fun?

Nigel: Two, two.

David: OK, got the mikes . . .

Nigel: Let's do G. S. M, alright . . . G. S. M.

SPINAL TAP PLAYS 'GIMME SOME MONEY'

Jeanine: Hello, darling, hellooo, got a surprise for you.

David: Hey! Where'd you come from?

Jeanine: Where do you think I came from? Bloody airplane, didn't I? Right? . . . Oh, god that feels good, oh I've been wanting to do that for the longest time.

David: . . . Carry you about with me . . .

Jeanine: What's . . . tell me . . .

David: Wh . . . that's the film crew. I told you about this . . . the film crew: Ma . . . Mart'n . . .

Jeanine: Hi, Martin.

David: This is Jeanine.

Marty: Hello.

Jeanine: Hello.

Ian: Here it is!

Derek: Visitor's Day, isn't it?

Ian: Here it is, lads! *Smell the Glove* me old beauties . . . gather round . . . Where's David? . . . David, David, get up here!

Derek: David, *Smell the Glove* is here. Hello, Jeanine.

Ian: The moment we've all been waiting for . . . Here we go. Plenty for everybody . . .

David: I never thought I'd see . . . I never thought I'd live to see the day.

Ian: So what do you think?

Derek: This is the test pressing?

Ian: No, this is it. Yes, that's right . . .

David: This is *Smell the Glove* by Spinal Tap . . .

Ian: That's *Smell the Glove*. That's, that's the jacket cover. It's going out across the country in every store.

David: This is the compromise you made . . . ?

Ian: Yes.

Derek: Is it going to say anything here, or on the spine here?

David: It doesn't even say anything here.

Ian: Nope, it's not going to say anything.

Nigel: So it's just going to be like this, all black . . .

Ian: No, it's going to be that simple, beautiful, classic!

Derek: You can see yourself in . . . both sides.

David: I feel so bad, I feel so bad about this . . .

Nigel: It's like a black mirror.

David: Well, I think it looks like death . . . it looks like mourning. I mean it looks . . .

Ian: David, David, every, every movie, in every cinema is about death. Death sells!

Nigel: I think he's right, there is something about this that's, that's so black, it's like, 'How much more black could this be?' and the answer is: 'None, none . . . more black.'

David: I think, like you're, like, rationalising this whole thing, like into something you did on, on purpose. I think we're stuck with a very, very stupid and a very, and a very dismal-looking album, this is depressing.

Nigel: David!

David: This is something you wear around your arm, you don't put this on your fucking turntable.

Nigel: David, it's a choice.

Ian: I frankly think that this is the turning point, OK? I think, I think this is . . . we're on our way now.

Nigel: I agree, I agree . . .

Ian: It's time to, it's time to kick arse!

SPINAL TAP PERFORMS 'ROCK AND ROLL CREATION'

Mick Shrimpton in bathtub

Marty: Given the history of Spinal Tap drummers, uh, in the past, do you have any fears, uh, for your life?

Mick: When I did join, you know, they did tell me, they kind of took me aside and said, 'Well, Mick, ah, it's, you know, it's like this,' and it did kind if freak me out a bit, but it can't always happen to every . . . can it?

Marty: Right . . . right, the law of averages says . . .

Mick: The law of averages . . .

Marty: . . . says you will survive.

Mick: Yeah.

Tour Bus

Viv: Ohh, quite exciting, quite exciting this computer magic, wheeeee . . .

Ian: How many, uh, planets have you destroyed, Viv?

Viv: Well, fourth or fifth time round I think . . . I think really five. Few galaxies gone, you know . . .

Derek: This is Cindy's first moustache.

Ian: Is it?

David: Can I take it off now?

Jeanine: Why? Too hot in here?

David: No, it's . . . um, I thought I might go back to see what they're up to back there you know, I don't think they really need to see this until you've finished with it, you know . . .

Jeanine: Well, you were reading, you can, you can read here . . .

David: Yeah, but . . . they, they've got the game back there, thought I'd maybe have a look at the new game, it's like a submarine thing.

Jeanine: You've got, you've got all stuff over you again.

David and Jeanine interview

David: Before I met Jeanine, my life was cosmically a shambles, it was, uh . . . I was using bits and pieces of whatever Eastern philosophies happened to drift through my transom and, uh, she sort of sorted it out for me, straightened it out for me, gave me a path, you know, a path to follow.

Marty: I wonder if you have as much influence over his musical expression?

Jeanine: Oh, yeah, I mean I listen to him when he's experimenting, and things like that, don't I? He's, uh, he plays things to me sometimes when he's worked out he's got a new bit that he wants to tell me about, you know, and I say, 'Yeah, that's good', or 'that's bad', or 'that's shit' or whatever, you know.

David: Yes, she is very honest, she's brutally frank.

Marty: Well, how does that go over with the other band members? I mean, you . . .

David: Well, what happens is she gives me the brutally frank version and I sort of tart it up for them.

Jeanine: Yes.

David: And of course it's, you know, it's so strange because Nigel and Jeanine are *so* similar in so many ways, but they just can't, they don't dislike each other at all . . .

Jeanine: No.

David: . . . and there's great *love* between the two of them . . .

Jeanine: Oh, yes . . .

David: . . . but, they just, there's some sort of communication that's just not . . . it's just blocked or something . . .

Nigel plays piano

Marty: It's pretty.

Nigel: Yeah, I like it, just been fooling about with it for a few months now, very delicate . . .

Marty: It's a, it's a bit of a departure from the kind of thing you normally play.

Nigel: Yeah, well it's part of a . . . a trilogy really, a musical trilogy that I'm doing . . . in D minor, which I always . . . find is really the saddest of all keys, really. I don't know why, but it makes people weep instantly. You play a – baaaaa . . . baaaaaa . . . it's a horn part.

Marty: It's very pretty.

Nigel: . . . baaaa, baaaaa. Yeah, just simple lines intertwining, you know very much like, I'm really influenced by Mozart and Bach, and it's sort of in between those, it's really, it's like a Mach piece really, it's . . .

Marty: What do you call this?

Nigel: Well, this piece is called 'Lick My Love Pump'.

Marty: Hmm.

Airport security

ASO: Excuse me, sir, do you have any metal objects in your pockets?

Derek: Yeah.

ASO: Take them out and put them in the bucket.

Derek: Coins, keys . . . tuning fork. Musician – I have to stay in tune, you know. Be a moment.

David: One more.

ASO: OK. Would you take this jacket off please?

Derek: Oh, it's the zipper . . . settin' off the machine.

David: Let's go then, let's go, hurry up.

ASO: Step over here, please . . .

David: Troublemaker!

ASO: Raise your arms . . . Do you have any artificial plates or limbs?

Derek: Not really, no . . .

ASO: Uh . . . would you umm . . .

David: Do it.

Nigel: Do it.

SPINAL TAP PLAYS 'HEAVY DUTY'

Holiday Inn, Chicago, Illinois

Artie: Hi, Artie Fufkin.

Viv: Hi, Artie . . .

Artie: Polymer Records, how are you? Hey, how ya doin' — you are . . . Derek?

Derek: Derek. Yeah.

Artie: Artie Fufkin, Polymer Records, how are you. I'm your promo man here in Chicago.

Nigel: Wow, that's great.

Artie: I love you guys.

Nigel: Yeah.

Artie: And of course, Nigel.

Nigel: Nigel.

Artie: I love you, Nigel Tufnel.

Nigel: Right.

Artie: I love your stuff, I go back with you guys . . . boy do I. Artie Fufkin, Polymer Records. I love you.

Nigel: Right, yeah.

Artie: And who are you, darlin'?

Derek: Oh, this is my special new friend, Cindy.

Artie: Hello, Cindy.

Nigel: And this is Belinda.

Artie: Hello, Belinda . . .

Belinda: Hi. Nice to meet you.

Artie: Artie Fufkin, Polymer Records, promo . . . and I'm . . . oh . . . what's going on here . . .

Derek: They're making a . . .

Artie: . . . hi, hi guys, Artie Fufkin, Polymer Records, nice to see you. And where is David? . . . David, hi, Artie Fufkin, how are you?

David: It's nice to see you . . .

Artie: We've got something exciting happening tomorrow . . .

Mick: The food! The food! . . . Ahhhhh . . . owwww . . . ohhhh.

RSG: Oh, thank god, civilisation! Where do I put this?

Disc an' Dat autograph session

Artie: What are you doing to me here?

RO: I'm not doing anything.

Artie: I thought we had a relationship here . . . I don't know what happened?

RO: Business is terrible, Artie, what can I tell you . . . this is the truth.

Artie: I know business is terrible, but what happens with the, with the record store, with the promotion, and nobody shows up!

RO: This isn't a personal thing, Artie, nobody's coming in the store to –

Artie: Forget personal thing. We had a relationship here, forget about personal, what about a relationship? . . . I feel like a shlub. And I don't know what's happening. It's me, that's what is happening. It's me, I did it, it's my fault.

Nigel: We were told massive radio support.

Artie: We did! We did massive.

Nigel: *Vast* . . . they said *vast* radio support.

Artie: We did massive, we saturated, we oversaturated. That's what it is. It's me, I did it, I fucked up. I fucked up the timing, that's all, I fucked up the . . . I got no timing, I got no timing, I got NO timing. You know what I want you to do? Will you do something for me?

Nigel: What?

Artie: Do me a favour, just kick my ass, OK? Kick this ass for a man, that's all, kick my ass, enjoy! C'mon, I'm not asking, I'm telling with this. Kick my ass!

Xanadu Star Theater, Cleveland, Ohio

Crowd: C'mon . . . c'mon!

Derek: Well, we've kept 'em waiting long enough. Let's do it to them.

Nigel: Let's go Mr Shrimpton!

Derek: Let's rock'n'roll!

Crowd: C'mon. Let's hear some rock'n'roll!

Derek: Rock'n'roll!!!

Nigel: Let's go then!!!

Viv: Yeah. Yeah mate!!!

Derek: Going to be a hot one isn't it?

Nigel: It's going to be a great show.

Derek: No it's not an exit. Not an exit.

David: We don't want an exit.

Derek: No, that's true.

David: Try this way.

Derek: I hope so. This way . . .

David: Wait, this looks familiar, though . . . it really does.

Derek: Listen.

Crowd: Tap! Tap! Tap! . . .

David: Shit.

Derek: Let's not lose it though! Let's not lose it . . . Where the *fuck* is Ian? You know he should be here.

Crowd: Tap! Tap! Tap! . . .

Derek: We got to get to it some way. We've been on stage right?

David: We're in the group. We're in the group that's playing tonight.

Janitor: You go right straight through this door here, down the hall . . .

David: Yeah.

Janitor: . . . turn right . . .

David: Yeah.

Janitor: . . . and then there's a little jog there, about thirty feet.

Derek: A jog?

Janitor: . . . jog to the left . . .

David: A jog?

Derek: We don't have time for that.

Janitor: . . . go straight ahead . . .

David: We trust you. We trust you.

Janitor: . . . go straight ahead, go straight ahead, turn right the next two corners, and the first door, the sign 'Authorized Personnel Only' . . .

David: Yeah.

Janitor: Open that door, that's the stage!

David: You think so?

Janitor: You're authorized. You're musicians aren't you?

David: We've got guitars, yeah.

Janitor: It's on the . . .

David: Alright! Thank you. Thank you very much. *Rock*'n'roll! *Rock and roll!!!*

Viv: Let's get it! Let's get it!

David: This way?

Derek: No, this way.

David: I see, this way.

Derek: Straight through. Rock'n'roll! Hello Cleveland! Hello Cleveland!!!

Nigel: Let's go!

David: Fuck!

Janitor: You must've made a wrong turn.

Derek: We gotta go another way.

David: Other way. Other way. Other way.

Derek: Other way. Other way.

Seasons Restaurant

David: I hate to keep harping on this, but I think that the notion of a black album has really *cursed* us, in a way.

Ian: Believe me, we're getting some very substantial reports of airplay. I don't think we have to worry about that.

Jeanine: You know, it might have been better if the, uh, album had been mixed right.

David: Well it's no use crying over that, but of course that's true. I mean, well, it's true.

Jeanine: It wasn't . . . it was mixed all wrong, wasn't it?

Nigel: It was mixed wrong?

Jeanine: Yeah . . .

Nigel: Were you there?

Jeanine: . . . you couldn't hear the . . .

Nigel: How do you know it was mixed—?

David: But she's . . . she's heard the . . . she's heard the record.

Jeanine: No, but I've heard the album.

Nigel: Oh, so your judgment is it was mixed wrong.

Jeanine: You couldn't hear the lyrics on all of it.

David: You don't agree that you can't hear the vocals?

Nigel: No, I don't. I do not agree. No.

David: Well I think maybe—

Nigel: It's interesting that she's bringing it up.

David: Well she'd like to hear the vocals.

Nigel: I mean it's like me saying, you know, you're using the wrong conditioner for your hair, you know. It looks sort of . . . uh frizzy.

David: Don't be stupid.

Jeanine: You don't, you don't do heavy metal in dobly, you know, I mean . . . it's

Nigel: In what? In what?!

Jeanine: In dobly . . .

Nigel: In doubly? What's that?

David: She means Dolby, alright? She means Dolby. You know perfectly well what she means.

Jeanine: Oh . . . Dolby.

Nigel: . . . Ha ha . . .

David: We shan't recover from this one. We shan't recover from this one.

Ian: Oh, come on.

David: Can I have . . . can I have the floor for just one moment because I've got, you know, something I'd like to show you. These, uh, Jeanine's been working on these very hard. These are a new direction . . .

Jeanine: Got a new idea for a new presentation.

David: . . . the stage look . . . of the band fashioned after . . .

Jeanine: The signs of the zodiac.

David: . . . the, uh, signs of the zodiac.

Jeanine: We needed a new presentation.

David: This is a look for Viv: he's a Libra. There's sort of the yin[g] . . . yang . . .

Jeanine: . . . yin[g] and the yang . . .

David: . . . sort of look. This is Nigel: he's . . . he's uh . . . Capricorn. Sort of a goat look.

Jeanine: I've given you a little bib.

Nigel: Is this a joke?

David: . . . this is the . . .

Nigel: Excuse me, is this a joke?

Jeanine: A joke?!

David: Just bear with us for one moment please. This . . . I love this. I wish I were the . . .

Nigel: That's attractive.

David: This is your crab face. Give it a chance! Give it a chance . . . and this is a . . .

Jeanine: David's a lion.

Ian: David. David. David. Wait, please, wait a minute. Have you any idea what it will cost . . . to dress up the band as animals?

Jeanine: Oh, it don't cost nothing. It really doesn't.

David: They're not animals, they're signs of the zodiac.

Ian: They're animals.

David: It's a way to fight the drabs. You know we've got the drabs.

Nigel: Well that's true. I think mine would look better in doubly. If it was done in doubly . . .

Jeanine: Oh shut up!

David: I knew it wouldn't be easy. Not quite open-minded enough.

Derek: David. No, no, David, you know there are solutions to our problems. I think we know what they are.

David: I've yet to hear them. I've yet to hear them from another quarter besides this one . . .

Derek: We can take the *rational* approach; we can say . . .

Nigel: May I make a suggestion? May I make a suggestion? I've got one other suggestion.

David: Well let's hear yours. Let's hear your suggestion.

Nigel: Stonehenge! Stonehenge. It's the best production value we've ever had on stage.

David: But we haven't got the equipment. We haven't *got* Stonehenge.

Nigel: Not *yet* we don't. Let's start . . .

David: We haven't got . . .

Nigel: Please, please, just a moment. Musically, musically we all know it.

Ian: We know it works . . . I don't think it's a bad idea.

Nigel: Musically we all know it. Right? No problems musically. We go right on stage. And it's quite simple. This is, you know . . . Ian can take care of this . . . it's . . .

David: I know what the Stonehenge monument looks like. We don't have that piece of scenery any more.

Nigel: I *know*, so we build a new one . . . And this is it, look!

Ian: Consider . . . consider it done.

David: So you're just going to take care of it like that. You're going to find someone to design it . . . using that as a plan?

Ian: Let's try. Let's try.

David: If you can do it, I'll do the number.

Interview in Nigel's guitar room I

Marty: Do you feel that *in* collaboration with David, that you are afforded the opportunity to express *yourself* musically the way you would like to?

Nigel: Well, I think I do, you know, in my solos. My solos are my trademark.

Room in Austin, Texas

Ian: This looks absolutely perfect. I mean it's, uh, it's the right proportions. It'll be this colour, right?

Artist: Yeah. Yeah.

Ian: Yeah. That's . . . that's . . . that's just terrific. I mean, it almost looks, uh, looks like the real thing.

Artist: You got it.

Ian: Yeah. When we get the actual, uh, set, when we get the piece, it'll . . . it'll follow *exactly* these specifications. I mean even these contours and everything?

Artist: Um, I'm not understanding. What do you mean, 'the actual piece'?

Ian: But I mean . . . well, when we, mean when, when you build the actual piece.

Artist: But this is what you asked for, isn't it?

Ian: What?

Artist: Well this is the piece.

Ian: *This* is the piece?

Artist: Yes.

Ian: Are you telling me that this is it? This is scenery? Have you ever been to Stonehenge?

Artist: No, I haven't been to Stonehenge.

Ian: The triptychs are . . . the triptychs are twenty feet high. You can stand four men up them!

Artist: Ian, I was . . . I was . . . I was supposed to build it eighteen inches high.

Ian: This is, this is insane. This isn't a piece of scenery.

Artist: Look, look. Look, this is what I was asked to build. Eighteen inches. Right here, it specifies eighteen inches. I was given this napkin, I mean . . .

Ian: Forget this! Fuck the napkin!

SPINAL TAP PERFORMS 'STONEHENGE'

Hotel room

David: I do not, for one, think that the problem was that the band was down. I think that the problem may have been . . . that there was a Stonehenge monument on the stage that was in danger of being crushed . . . by a dwarf. Alright?

That tended to understate the hugeness of the object.

Ian: I really think you're just making a . . . much too big thing out of it.

Derek: Making a big thing out of it would've been a good idea.

Ian: Nigel gave me a drawing that said eighteen inches. Alright?

David: I know he did, and that's what I'm talking about.

Ian: Now, whether he knows the difference between feet and inches is not my problem. I do what I'm told.

David: But you're not as confused as him are you? I mean it's not your job to be as confused as Nigel is.

Ian: It's my job to do what I'm asked to do by the creative element of this band. And that's what I did. C'mon . . .

Jeanine: The audience were laughing.

Ian: So it became a comedy number.

David: Yes it did! Yes it fucking well did, and it was not pleasant to be part of the comedy on stage. Backstage, perhaps, it was very amusing.

Derek: Maybe we just fix the choreography. Keep the dwarf clear.

David: What do you mean?

Derek: So he won't trod upon it.

David: I don't think that's the issue. I think it's symptomatic that maybe you're taking on more than you can . . . uh . . . uh . . . uh . . . handle.

Jeanine: It's not exactly the first time you've messed things up, is it?

David: I mean there have been some, uh, gaping holes in the business end of this, of this, uh . . .

Ian: 'Not the first time' . . . Excuse me just a minute. Excuse me. This is a band meeting. Right? Are you here for some reason?

David: Don't worry about it. Don't worry about it. She's, you know she's with me.

Ian: No, but is she now in the band. I mean, is she singing backup or something?

Jeanine: I *care* what happens to the band.

David: She's with me alright?

Ian: David, whenever a single bump or a ruffle comes into this little fantasy, adolescent fantasy world that you guys, you guys have built around yourselves . . .

David: Hey don't knock it mate. Don't knock it mate.

Ian: . . . you start screaming like a bunch of poncy hairdressers. I mean it's just a *problem* you know. It gets solved . . .

Jeanine: It doesn't.

Ian: . . . you can't . . . you can't live in a bubble.

Jeanine: If it got solved, that would be alright, but it *doesn't* get solved. I mean, what do you think happened out there? What got solved tonight?

Ian: For one thing that goes wrong . . . one . . . one single thing that goes wrong, a hundred things go right. Do you know what I spend my time doing? I sleep two or three hours a night. There's no sex and drugs for Ian, David. Do you know what I do? I find lost luggage. I locate mandolin strings in the middle of Austin!

David: Yes. We've seen you. We've seen you do that.

Ian: You know? I prise the rent out of the local Hebrews. That's what I do.

Jeanine: Well maybe you should get someone else to find the lost luggage, and you should concentrate on what's going on on stage!

David: Yes, yes. That's what we're talking about.

Ian: You mean you want me to be the road manager?

David: All bad . . . *No*, all bad ba . . . uh, could we . . .

Jeanine: What David's trying to say, if you'd let him get a word through, is . . . you could maybe . . . do with some help . . .

Ian: Some help?

Jeanine: . . . managing the band.

David: It's very simple, it's very simple.

Jeanine: It's that clear.

David: Maybe there's someone already in the organisation. We don't have to pay insurance. We don't have to pay extra room, etc. Since she's already here, she's already among us, and, uh, and she can . . . she is perfectly capable of taking over . . .

Ian: She? She? Wait a minute! Wait a minute!

David: Well who do you think I'm talking about? Who do you think I'm talking about?

Ian: I would . . . I would have never dreamed in a million years that it was her you were talking about!

David: Why not?

Jeanine: I am offering to help out here.

Ian: No, you're not offering to help out. You're offering to co-manage the band with me. Is that it?

David and Jeanine: Yes!

Ian: Let's get straight.

David: In so many words, that is exactly it.

Jeanine: Exactly!

Ian: I'm certainly not going to co-manage with some . . . some . . . some girl just because she's your girlfriend . . .

David: Don't call her my girlfriend!

Ian: Alright, she's not your girlfriend. I don't know . . .

Jeanine: Oh girlfriend is it? You couldn't manage a classroom full of kids! I don't know what you're doing managing a band!

David: Why don't we just . . .

Jeanine: Oh shut up!

Ian: Look, look . . . I . . . I . . . this is . . . this is my position OK? I am not managing it with you or any other woman, especially one that dresses like an Australian's nightmare. So fuck you!

Jeanine: Fuck you too!

Ian: And fuck all of you . . . because I *quit*! Alright? That's it! Good-night! . . .

Derek: Can I raise a practical question at this point?

David: Yeah.

Derek: We gonna do 'Stonehenge' tomorrow?

David: No we're not gonna fucking do 'Stonehenge'!

Airport

Jeanine: OK, we're all set, thank you. Alright fellows, we've got the tickets. We're on the 3.10 flight at gate 24, alright? And it arrives at four o'clock in Colorado, and then we've got a limo to take us to the lodge.

David: That's about a hundred yards from Rainbow Trout Studio.

Jeanine: Uh, what I've done . . . is, uh, to arrange a whole load of charts.

David: Wait till you see this, wait till you see this, this is so great.

Jeanine: Now we know that the band's sign is Virgo, and we see it's Saturn in the third house, alright, and it's a bit rocky. But, because Virgo is one of the most highly intelligent signs of the zodiac, we're gonna pull through this with great aplomb.

David: Yeah. It is so clear, it really is, it's so clear . . .

Jeanine: Nigel hasn't got one. Nigel, Nigel, we've got, uh, pages for you here . . .

David: No, he's got one, he's got it . . . you know, if you think about the jumble that a tour usually is . . .

Jeanine: If you have a look at this . . . He doesn't want it – Oh, right.

David: No, he's got one, he's got one.

Jeanine: Now, what I want to explain to you here is that Denver . . .

Interview in Nigel's guitar room II

Marty: How would you characterise your relationship with David over the years. Has it changed in any way?

Nigel: Not really, I mean, you know, they go, we've grown up . . . but really it's not, no, not really . . . we, we feel like children . . . much of the time, even when we're playing. We're closer than brothers . . . Brothers always fight, sort of disagreements, and all that. We really have a relationship that's way, way past that.

Rainbow Trout Studio

David: Ahhhhhhh . . .

Nigel: He can't play the fucking guitar any more.

Derek: You know the part, you did it this morning.

Nigel: No, he doesn't know the fucking . . . if he knew the fucking part he'd play it, wouldn't he? . . . Are you walking out? Are you walking out?

Derek: Fuck!

Nigel: Great, great. Just tell me what I'm supposed to do, alright?

David: Well we're supposed to play the fucking thing, aren't we. We have no choice, we spent an hour and a half . . .

Nigel: Look, I'm doing my part . . . do you know what would make this a lot simpler, I mean I hate to cut right to it here. Why don't you play this alone, without some fucking angel hanging over your head, you know what I mean?

Derek: Jesus Christ, this is fucking all we need!

Nigel: You can't fucking concentrate, because of your fucking wife, simple as that, alright, it's your fucking wife!

David: She's not my wife!

Nigel: Whatever fuck she is, alright, you can't concentrate, we can't fucking do the track.

David: This is unbelievable! This is unbelievable!

Nigel: No, it's not unbelievable at all . . . it all leads up to this . . . it all leads up to this

David: This is unbelievable. Will you check me on this? Am I losing my fucking mind? Could you check me on this, am I losing my mind? I-I-I-I don't understand what this has to do with *anything*.

Derek's office

Derek: We're very lucky in a sense that . . . we've got two visionaries in the band.

Marty: Right.

Derek: You know, David and Nigel are both like, uh, like poets, you know, like Shelley or Byron, or people like that. The two totally distinct types of visionaries. It's like fire and ice, basically, you see, and I feel my role in the band is to be kind of in the middle of that, kind of like lukewarm water, in a sense.

Limo

Jeanine: Listen, I don't think we've got time to go to the hotel, I think we better go straight to the base.

Nigel: To the what?

Viv: Base?

David: The gig.

Derek: To the Civic Arena, right?

David: No.

Jeanine: No.

David: It fell through.

Nigel: Wait a sec, wait a sec, hold it, hold it! Do you know about this, and
we don't know about this? What are you talking about?

Jeanine: We are going to the air force base.

Nigel: Why are we going to an air force base?

Jeanine: 'Cause the original gig fell through . . .

Lindberg Air Force Base, Seattle, Washington

Jeanine: Lieutenant Hookstrat . . .

Hookstratten: Ahh . . . Hookstratten . . . and you are Spinal Tarp?

Jeanine: I'm Jeanine Pettibone, and this is Spinal *Tap*.

Hookstratten: Spinal *Tap*, my mistake. I'm Lieutenant Bob Hookstratten.
Welcome to the Lindberg air force base. This is you gentlemen's first visit
to a military facility?

Derek: Yeah . . .

Hookstratten: Fine, may I start by saying how thrilled we are to have you
here, we are such fans of your music, and all of your records.

Derek: That's great

Hookstratten: I am not speaking of yours personally, but the whole genre of
the rock and roll . . .

David: I can understand that.

Derek: It's a great genre.

Hookstratten: . . . and of the exciting things that are happening in the music
today. Let me explain a bit about what's going on. This is our monthly
'at-ease weekend' – gives us the chance to kind of let down our hair,
although I see you all have a head start on that. These haircuts wouldn't
pass military muster, believe me. Although I shouldn't talk, I . . . my hair's
getting a little shaggy too. Better not get too close to you, they'll think I'm
part of the band. I'm joking, of course. Shall we go in and I'll show you
around. Walk this way, please, right through here. Did you ever run into
a musical group works out of Kansas City call themselves 'Four Jacks and

a Jill'? They've been at a Ramada Inn there for about eighteen months. If you're ever in Kansas City and want to hear some good music, you might want to drop by. I would like to get the playing on about 1900 hours, if that's satisfactory?

Derek: When will that be?

Hookstratten: I make it now, it's about 1830 hours.

Derek: So that's what? 50 hours?

David: 120 hours?

Hookstratten: That's actually about thirty minutes, about a half hour, give or take just a few minutes, I don't want to rush you. The idea is that we get it on and we get it over with and I have just one request, would you play a couple of slow numbers so I can dance.

SPINAL TAP PERFORMS 'SEX FARM'

Jeanine: He totally ruined the gig, there. He walks off and then, you know, I mean he can't be expected to sit home and get money, as we've got to get someone else in there.

Hotel lobby

Marty: Has he ever done this before? Has he ever . . .

David: Well, no.

Marty: . . . quit the band before?

David: No, but it's . . . you've got to understand that, like, in the world of rock and roll there are certain changes that sometimes occur, and you've just got to, sort of, roll with them, you know. I mean this . . . you read . . . you read that . . . you know, you saw exactly how many people have been in this band over the years. Thirty-seven people have been in this band over the years. I mean it's like, you know, six months from now, I can't see myself missing Nigel any more than I . . . I might miss, uh, Ross MacLochness, or Ronnie Pudding, or Denny Upham, or Little Danny Schindler, or any of those, you know, it's . . .

Marty: I can't . . . I can't believe that. I can't believe that, you know, you're lumping Nigel in with, uh, you know, these people you've played with for a short period of time . . .

David: Well, I'm sure I'd feel much worse if I weren't under such heavy sedation, but still, in all, I mean you've got to be realistic about this sort of thing, you know . . .

Marty: So what happens to the band now?

David: What do you mean?

Marty: He's not coming back, on . . . ?

David: No. We, we shan't work together again.

Themeland Amusement Park, Stockton, California

Jeanine: Oh, no! If I told them once, I told them a hundred times: put Spinal Tap first and puppet show last.

Derek: It's a morale builder, isn't it?

Jeanine: We've got a big dressing room, though.

David: What?

Jeanine: Got a big dressing room . . .

David: Oh, we've got a bigger dressing room than the puppets? Oh, that's refreshing . . .

Viv: I've got some of this Mendocino Rocket Fuel that's supposed to be really amazing . . .

David: Can you play . . . excuse me, Viv, can you play a bassline, uh, like Nigel used to on 'Big Bottom'? can you double that? You recall the lines in fifths?

Viv: Oh, yeah. Yeah. I've got two hands here, I can do it.

David: So, that's good, we can play that one.

Derek: 'Hole' is out, 'Heavy' is out . . .

David: 'Heavy-Hole, Heavy-Hole.'

Derek: Right, right, right, right . . . 'America' is out . . .

David: 'America' we can't do, it's Nigel's tune, it's not my tune.

Derek: We know, we know, we know, we know . . . That's a nice little set, isn't it, that's a cosy ten minutes.

David: What are we going to do, we've got nothing to play here . . .

Derek: I'll tell you what we're gonna have to do . . .

David: What?

Derek: 'Jazz Odyssey'!

David: We're not going to do a free-form jazz, uh, exploration in front of a festival crowd!

End of Tour Party, Los Angeles

Reporter: So tonight's the last show of the tour. How's that feel? You know, is, like, this your last waltz, are we talkin' the end of Spinal Tap, or are you gonna try to milk it for a few more years in Europe, I mean . . .

David: Well, I don't, I don't really think that the end can be assessed . . . uh, as of itself as being the end because what does the end feel like, it's like saying when you try and extrapolate the end of the universe you say the . . . if the universe is indeed infinite then how, what does that mean? How far is it . . . is all the way and then if it stops, what's stoppin' it and what's behind what's stoppin' it, so 'what's the end?', you know, is my . . . question to you . . .

Bearded Man: 'S a good crowd. Good crowd.

Jeanine: It is, isn't it?

Bearded Man: Yeah, it really is. I mean, you know, some of these things just, you know, don't mean much.

Jeanine: It was hard to get at the last minute, you know, you can't arrange it all overnight.

Derek: David, we had a fifteen-year ride, mate. 'Mean, who wants to be a fuck'n forty-five-year-old rock'n'roller farting around in front of people less than half their age? . . .

David: That is . . . that is so true, that is so true, yeah . . .

Derek: . . . cranking out some kind of mediocre head-banging bullshit, you know, that we've forgotten . . .

David: It would b . . . it's beneath us . . . who wants to see that . . . not me.

Derek: That's right . . . absolutely right. I mean, we could take those projects that we thought, you know, we didn't have time for . . .

David: Oh, there's dozens, there's so many dozens of projects.

Derek: You know, we didn't have time for 'em because of Tap, and bring 'em back to life maybe.

David: Do you remember what we were . . . do you remember the time? . . .

Derek: At the Luton . . . at the Luton Palace . . .

David: Yes.

Derek: We were talking about a rock musical based on the life of Jack the Ripper . . .

David: Yeah, 'Saucy Jack'.

Derek: Right. 'Saucy Jack'. Now's the time to do that.

David: 'Saucy Jack, you're a naughty one, Saucy Jack, you're a haughty one, Saucy Jack.'

Derek: Right . . .

David: It's a freein' up, innit?

Derek: Yeah.

David: It's all this free time, it's suddenly time is so elastic . . .

Derek: It's a gift, it's a gift of freedom. You know.

David: I've always, I've always wanted to do a collection of my acoustic numbers with the London Philharmonic as you know.

Derek: We're lucky.

David: Yeah.

Derek: I mean people . . . people should be envying us. You know.

David: I envy us.

Derek: Yeah.

David: I do.

Derek: Me too.

Dressing Room, last gig of the tour

Derek: We'll make 'em miss us.

Viv: Last stop.

David: I'm in, I'm in tune . . . the last tuning.

Derek: Last tuning . . .

Jeanine: Time to go . . . shall we go . . . I think it's time to go.

Derek: Yeah. We're gonna do a good show, we'll do a dynamite show.

David: Come to see the show?

Nigel: Yeah. Hi, Mick!

Mick: Nige.

David: So did you just come here to hang around backstage like a real rock and roller? Is that what you're doing?

Nigel: I . . . I'm really a messenger . . .

David: Oh, a messenger . . .

Nigel: Yeah. I bumped into Ian, and . . .

David: Ian . . . Ian? . . . Oh, the other dead man, yeah.

Nigel: Seems that 'Sex Farm' is . . . on the charts in Japan . . .

Derek: Spinal Tap's recording of 'Sex Farm'?

Nigel: It's number five, last week, actually. And so, he, he, he, um he asked me, to ask you, Tap, if you would be interested in reforming and, uh, doing a tour. Japan.

David: So you've come back to replug our life-support systems in? Is that it? By the grace of your, of your, uh, by the stroke of your hand . . . you . . . is that what you're gonna do? . . . you're gonna bring us back to life? Is that what you've come here for?

Nigel: No, I've come . . .

David: I mean it's . . . I don't . . . you've a fucking . . . nerve that you display in com—

Nigel: No that's, it's, I'm just passing on information, really . . .

Jeanine: Yeah, I think it's time to go in, we haven't got time to discuss this now . . .

Nigel: David, do a good show, alright

David: Yeah, OK.

SPINAL TAP PERFORMS 'TONIGHT I'M GOING TO ROCK YOU TONIGHT'

Closing credits

Marty: Do you feel that playing rock'n'roll . . . music keeps you a child? That is, keeps you in a state of arrested development?

Derek: No . . . no . . . no, I feel, it's like, it's more like going, going to a national park or something, and there's, you know, they preserve the moose . . . and that's, that's my childhood up there on stage is that moose, you know, and . . . and—

Marty: So, when you're playing you feel like a preserved moose on stage?

Derek: Yeah.

David: I've been listening to the classics, I belong to a . . . great series, um . . . It's called the 'Namesake Series' of cassettes.

Marty: Uh huh . . .

David: And they send you the works of famous authors, done by actors with the same last name. So I've got Denholm Elliot reading T.S. Eliot on this one . . .

Marty: Yeah . . . well, that's interesting . . .

David: I've go . . . Yes, I've got Danny Thomas doing *A Child's Christmas in*

Tonight we're gonna rock you.

Nigel Tufnel (lead guitar).

David St Hubbins
(lead guitar).

Derek Smalls (bass guitar).

Marty DiBergi with Viv Savage (keyboards).

Mick Shrimpton (drums).

The band with manager, Ian Faith (left), and Sir Denis Eton-Hogg,
President of Polymer Records (centre).

Bobbi Fleckman (Artists Relations,
Polymer Records).

Tap into America.

Tap photo shoot.

'(Listen to the) Flower People', *Jamboree Bop*, 1967.

Tap visit Graceland.

The majesty of rock.

Wales by Dylan Thomas, and . . . next month it's Mclean Stephenson reads Robert Louis Stevenson. *Treasure Island* I believe.

Marty: That's interesting . . . It's fascinating.

David: Yeah . . . There's also something . . . there's, uh, shorter works of Washington Irving, read by someone called Dr J.

Marty: Oh, that's Julius Irving . . . Julius Irving . . .

David: Oh!

Marty: The basketball player.

David: There you go, in keeping with the series, yes. I didn't know that, yeah.

Nigel: You like this?

Marty: It's very nice . . . it looks like Halloween . . .

Nigel: This is exact . . . my exact inner structure, done in a T-shirt. Exactly, medically accurate, see.

Marty: So, in other words, if we were to take all your flesh and blood and every . . .

Nigel: . . . take them off . . .

Marty: . . . and you'd see . . . exact . . .

Nigel: This is what you'd see . . .

Marty: It wouldn't be green, though?

Nigel: It is green. You know, see, see how your blood looks blue?

Marty: Yeah, well, that's just the vein, I mean the colour of the vein, the blood is actually red . . .

Nigel: Oh, maybe it's not green then . . . Anyway, this is what I sleep in sometimes.

Marty: Yeah.

Marty: Denis Eton-Hogg, the president of Polymer Records . . .

Ian: Yes.

Marty: . . . was recently knighted. What were the circumstances surrounding his knighthood?

Ian: The specific reason why he was knighted was, uh, for the founding of Hogwood, which is um, a summer-camp for pale, young boys.

Marty: David St Hubbins . . . I ne . . . I must admit I've never heard anybody with that name . . .

David: It's an unusual name, well, he was an unusual saint, he's not a very well known saint.

Marty: Oh, there actually is, uh . . . there was a Saint Hubbins?

David: That's right, yes.

Marty: What was he the saint of?

David: He was the patron saint of quality footwear.

Marty: You play to predominantly, uh, predominantly a white audience. Do you feel your music is racist in any way?

David: No!

Nigel: No, no, of course not . . .

David: We pro . . . we say, we say 'love your brother'. We don't say it, really, but . . .

Nigel: We don't *literally* say it.

David: No, we don't say it . . . at all.

Nigel: No, we don't really literally *mean* it. But we're not racists.

David: No, we don't believe it either, but . . . that message should be clear anyway.

Nigel: We're anything but racists.

Derek: You know, we've grown musically . . . I mean you listen to some of the rubbish we did early on, it was stupid . . .

Marty: Yeah.

Derek: . . .you know. Now, I mean a song like 'Sex Farm', we're taking a sophisticated . . . view of the idea of sex, you know, and music . . .

Marty: And putting it on a farm?

Derek: Yeah.

Marty: If I were to ask you what your philosophy of life, or your creed . . . what would that be?

Viv: 'Have . . . a good . . . time . . . all the time.' That's my philosophy, Marty!

David: I believe virtually everything I read, and I think *that* is what makes me *more* of a selective human, than someone who doesn't believe anything.

Marty: Do you have a philosophy, or creed that you live by?

Mick: Well . . . personally, I like to think about sex and drugs and rock'n'roll, you know, that's my life . . .
Marty: Yeah.

Marty: If you were to have something written as your epitaph . . .
David: 'Here lies . . . David St Hubbins . . . and why not?'
Marty: You feel that sums up your . . . your life?
David: No, 's the first thing I could think of.
Marty: Oh, I see . . .
David: It doesn't sum up anything, really.
Marty: Yeah.

Nigel: I'm a real fish nut. I really like fish . . .
Marty: What kind of fish?
Nigel: Well, in the United States, you have cod . . . I like cod. And I love tuna . . . those little cans you've got here . . . tuna fish . . .
Marty: Yeah.
Nigel: . . . no bones!
Marty: Yeah.

Marty: If you could not play rock'n'roll, what would you do?

David: Be a full-time dreamer!

Viv: I'd probably get a bit stupid and start to make a fool of myself in public, 'cause there wouldn't be a stage to go on.

Derek: Probably work with children.

Mick: As long as there is, you know, sex and drugs, I can do without the rock'n'roll.

Nigel: Well, I suppose I could, uh, work in a shop of some kind or . . . or do, uh . . . freelance . . . selling of some sort of . . . uh . . . product, you know . . .
Marty: A salesman, you think you . . .
Nigel: A salesman, like, maybe in a haberdasher, or maybe like a . . . uh, a

chapeau shop, or something . . . you know, like: 'Would you . . . what size do you wear, sir?' and then you answer me.

Marty: Uh . . . seven and a quarter.

Nigel: 'I think we have that . . .' You see, something like that I could do.

Marty: Yeah . . . you think you'd be happy doing something like—

Nigel: 'No! We're all out, do you wear black?' See, that sort of thing, I think I could probably muster up.

Marty: Yeah, do you think you'd be happy doing that?

Nigel: Well, I don't know, wh-wh-what are the hours?

The Out-takes

On the balcony at the opening tour-date party

David: Well, cool, this is certainly the best place to contemplate, it really is, y'know.

Nigel: Yeah.

David: 'Cause it's like you're on the top of the world here, y'know, you really are. It's like the pinnacle. Y'know it's like when Dalglish is really on his game and he's away down the field and you know he's going to take them all away, 'cause he's on top of his game, y'know. That's how I feel.

Nigel: It's like the unisphere, for us right now. It's our own. Nothing can go wrong, everything can go right if given the chance.

David: I feel . . . I don't know . . . it's like the stars are just right or something, y'know, some sort of magnetic thing happening, it just seems to . . . (*laughs*) I don't know. It's good.

Nigel: I know that, I know, I'm feeling the same exactly.

David: Exactly. It's this country, y'know. It's a great, it's a great country.

Nigel: You know what this country is doing for us? It's giving us a . . . um . . . a rebirth, really, innit?

David: That's what it's like, yeah.

Nigel: It's like everything is conspired to make this the perfect timing for us. Yeah. Musically and as far as friendship goes, y'know, it couldn't be much higher.

David: A lot of groups don't have what we have. A lot of groups don't really care about the other guy. They don't even know them. They look them in the eye, 'Who are you?'

Nigel: Right.

David: But we know.

Nigel: It really feels great, dunnit? Our writing is like a triangle and it's at the top of the little . . .

David: That's where I feel we are now.

Nigel: We're at the pointy top.

David: We're at the apex.

Nigel: The apex.

David: We're at the apex of the pyramid.

(*They do their 'squatney handshake'*)

Nigel: You know I've been thinking of doing a special tune, another suite, but really dedicated to this country.

David: Well there's certainly no dearth of material, it's an incredible land, it really is.

Nigel: I'd like a crack at it myself and then of course defer to your wonderful words.

David: Well count me in, count me in. A song about America? OK.

Nigel: You know what the title is?

David: What?

Nigel: America.

David: So you're calling it 'America'? Well it better be pretty fucking profound then, hadn't it?

Nigel: Well, I do like to think it will be.

David: It's certainly a fascinating subject.

Nigel: When you think about a country like this – how old is it?

David: Two . . . seventeen . . .

Nigel: Fifty-six . . .

David: Seventeen fifty-six, right?

Nigel: And the Dutch people came over and they had to strangle all those Indians.

David: No, first it was the Spaniards looking for the fountain of youth.

Nigel: The Spaniards came over and they strangled the Dutch.

David: No, no, Spaniards came over first.

Nigel: No, the Spaniards came over with the Dutch, that was it, and they fought, and that's why they named it Man-Hat-Tan. It was a Dutch/Spanish sort of retreat, and then the Indians bludgeoned all these . . .

David: How do you know all this?

Nigel: I read a bit.

Marty and the Head Mime Waiter

Marty: Hi, I'm Marty DiBergi, nice to meet you. I was just watching the . . .

Waiter: It's a kick isn't it?

Marty: . . . people working for you. It's amazing.

Waiter: It's a kick isn't it?

Marty: Yeah, it's like, what a concept. I mean the whole mime idea of, y'know, mixing food with mime. It's just sensational.

Waiter: Well, y'know, I used to be an actor.

Marty: Oh yeah?

Waiter: But I could never remember my lines. My father sort of started this because at home, every day, he used to say the same thing to me: 'Shut up and eat'. So that's what we do.

Marty: I see.

Waiter: It's the name of the company.

Marty: Oh yeah?

Waiter: 'Shut Up and Eat', yeah.

Marty: It's incredible.

Waiter: It's good. They're very good. There's some new people, y'know. We teach them that basically food . . . you get them to eat . . . because of guilt. That's what we do . . . walking along . . . by the time we get across the floor, they think. He came a long way, I better eat that. Y'know, you manipulate them because the food's not all that good.

Marty: It's a show.

Waiter: It's a show. But I tell you, I enjoy it. Like today, I made some of the food myself. I get a kick when I see a big fat guy sitting back with half a dozen of the things. Made my day.

Marty: That's nice.

Waiter: Yeah.

Marty: Nice talking to you.

Waiter: You too. Good luck with this movie.

Marty: Thanks.

Waiter: What channel is it going to be on?

Marty: No, it's a feature film. It's in the theatres.

Waiter: Oh boy.

Marty: Five dollars it'll cost you.

During an interview with Marty DiBergi, the band bring the history of their drummers up-to-date

Derek: Then we got Mick . . .

David: Mick came in . . .

Derek: Mick came in . . . not dead yet.

　(*All laugh except drummer.*)

In a New York hotel

Bobbi: Now, one of the most important things we do. You're going to be plugging 'Hell Hole', the single that's going to come off the album. But you've got to do this and you've got to do it good otherwise, y'know . . . (*looks at David's groupie*) Honey, you're not going to be able to talk during the fill OK. You're going to have to be real quiet. I'm going to need your attention . . .

Nigel: Excuse me, can I make a quick announcement? My little sweetheart here has lost a lens, her contact lens, and she can't find it.

Derek: Awwww.

Nigel: What shall we do?

Groupie: You never helped me find it.

Nigel: Well, let me do this first, alright?

Bobbi: Did she leave it by her clothes or something?

Derek: It's not in there . . .

Nigel: If you go I'll help you in a minute. (*Kisses her*)

Bobbi: Please, try and keep your hormones in your hip pocket for a while and let's get on with this. The sooner we get started with this, the sooner I can be on my way.

David: No we're not stalling, we're not stalling.

Derek: No, we're trying to get this done.

Bobbi: OK, this is our read: 'Hi, we're Spinal Tap and New York's no hell-hole as long as you keep rocking with the Big Six.'

Later

Derek: The one question: two dozen people came up to me after the show last night and said, 'Where's the record? I thought there was going to be a record with the tour,' and I said, 'Well, there's supposed to be a record, but . . .'

Ian: We decided basically not to use New York as a place to break the record.

Derek: What do you mean? Not to sell it here?'

Ian: We'll sell it. No, obviously it'll get released here. We've pinpointed various markets and we decided that New York wasn't one of them because we wouldn't be able to get any meaningful . . .

David: Oh, is this why the record isn't in New York?

Ian: That's right.

Derek: Is this that stuff about the shot-gun and the rifle?

David: The shot-gun effect and the rifle effect.

Ian: Well, yeah, we hope it'll be more like a machine gun.

In the limo

Tommy: I'll tell you a great story. Frank's walking down Broadway one night so he sees there two cops and they're hassling a prostitute and they say, 'Hey, sweetheart, what are you doing?' She says, 'Well, I'm waiting for my boyfriend,' and the cops say, 'Oh yeah, sure, sure sweetheart,' and they get ready to take her in. And Frank overhears her saying that so he says, walking over, 'I'm sorry I kept you waiting, darling.' Just like that.

Marty: I see.

Tommy: He takes her, he gets her away from the cops, he takes her to a bar, he buys her a drink and he says, 'Here's a hundred dollars, I don't want you working for the rest of the night.'

Marty: He went to bat for her.

Tommy: He went to bat for her.

Marty: Unbelievable.

Tommy: This is a man who's the most written-about human being in the history of the world, more written about than Kennedy, than Stalin . . . um, speaking of Stalin, in Russia a Sinatra album goes for a hundred dollars. This is a place where they don't have any money, they don't have any . . . er, y'know. Russia. They want to pay a hundred dollars.

Marty: That's amazing that a guy like that . . . uh, I mean all he does is sing.

Tommy: No, he does a lot more than sing. We're talking about a man who does . . . he probably does more for charity than any other human being in the United States. I mean he just did a concert down in Brazil . . . um, a hundred and fifty thousand people showed up and he got to meet this foster-child down there that he's been supporting for the kid's whole life.

Marty: Yeah . . .

Tommy: He's that kind of a person. I tell you the kind of love people have.

Everybody knows about this relationship he had with Ava Gardner and how
much . . . y'know, he loved, he really loved. But, y'know, it didn't work
out, people change, they go their separate ways, one thing leads to another,
y'know, it's life.

Marty: Yeah . . .

Tommy: But . . . a while back Ava Gardner was in this club and in the lobby
of the club was a life-size picture of Frank. And she goes up to this picture of
Frank and she kisses it full on the mouth. And she turns to the owner of the
club and she says to him, 'Take care of him. He still belongs to me.' (*Hits his
horn twice at another motorist*) WAKE UP!

Marty: Did you ever drive Frank?

Tommy: No, I never drove him, but I did pick up a car one day that he'd been in
the night before, and, I swear to God, the essence, the magic, was still there.

Marty: In the car?

Tommy: Yep.

Marty: You could feel it?

Tommy: I swear to God.

In the limo – after the pod fiasco

Nigel: Can you explain the pods? Can we get them to function without any
question?

Ian: Well, either the pods got damaged in transit or the workmanship is simply
shoddy, I really can't tell you. It's as simple as that.

Derek: Look, it's no fucking effect if two of them open and one of them
doesn't.

David: It's no effect if two of the pods open and one of them doesn't.

Derek: I just told him that, David.

Ian: Well, frankly, I think you should just forget about the pods. The next pod
is shunned . . .

Derek: No!

Nigel: We can't kill them . . . it's half the show down the dump. Really. We
can't do that.

Derek: That's what they're paying to see, innit?

Nigel: If you're listening to the record you want to know what that song is,
what in your mind you've got to visualize what is happening. And it's pods.
It's obvious that we're in some sort of pod.

Ian: On the album it's obvious you're in pods?

Nigel: Of course.

Ian: You can't hear a pod.

Nigel: You can't hear it but you can imagine it. That's the whole point of our making records.

Derek: It's a conceptual pod.

Nigel: Exactly.

Ian: But what I'm saying is why don't we simplify the conception for stage presentation.

Derek: You're cheating the people!

Ian: They don't know . . . only you know we've got pods.

Derek: You're cheating the people if you do that!

The band are lost backstage in Philadelphia

Nigel: Which way now? Logically we should say . . .

Derek: Look logic tells us . . .

Nigel: . . . have we tried all the ways possible . . .

Derek: Yes, yes . . .

Nigel: . . . to get where we're going?

Derek: Yes, we have.

Nigel: So we should be there.

Derek: We're there now. Logically.

Nigel: Logically we're playing but we're not.

Derek: Logically we're onstage now.

Nigel: But we're not.

Derek: We're not. So fuck logic, let's go.

Viv has a coldsore

Mick: That's horrible. No, I never had one.

Viv: I feel sure you told me about someone who did and how they got rid of it.

Mick: What I've been told is . . . uh . . . that a megadose of, like, y'know, kelp juice and, uh . . . Vitamin J, like, in a blender . . . about half a pound . . . like, you have to make a big lot otherwise it doesn't work.

Viv: Blimey. Oh . . .

Mick: I mean I've never tried it so I wouldn't know if it works.

Viv: Right . . .

Mick: But it's worth a try.

Bobbi and Ian discuss the *Smell the Glove* artwork

Bobbi: The first album that they had . . . what the hell was that? Shark Salad or
  something?

Ian: Sandwich, sandwich.

Bobbi: See how memorable it was?

Ian: Well . . .

Bobbi: Came out with a bullet . . . lay flat and dropped down.

Ian: That's why we need a sexy cover!

And so do Nigel and David

Nigel: But the fact that we've not made the choice to do this, the choice has
  been made for us. It's like if we'd made a choice like this, people will say,
  'They made that choice.'

David: We didn't do that.

Nigel: No, we didn't and yet we did because here it is. This is our choice.

In the lobby of a Memphis hotel

Ian: Are you going to be in New York at all in the near future?

Terry: No, no.

Ian: You're not?

Terry: We're on our way to Hawaii and Atlanta.

Ian: Uh-huh. Because I'd really like to talk to you about a couple of things.

Terry: Call the office.

Ian: The girl will know where you are?

The band watch television in a Memphis hotel room

Nigel: Ooh, look at that. Italian movies . . . they're always so . . . they're
  always in bed.

Derek: Yeah, they're great. I worked on one . . .

Nigel: I know.

Derek: Yeah, I mention that from time to time just to keep your awareness up.

Nigel: Well, I love the Italian movies because they're so . . . it's roma . . . it's romantic but it's so smutty.

Derek: Well, Roma is the root of the word romantic.

Nigel: Well, Roma – Love. It means love.

Derek: Right.

Backstage, Nigel and Jeanine recline on some cushions

Jeanine: Looks like you've really got your act together up there.

Nigel: What do you mean?

Jeanine: Well, you've kind of got that airy aggro look, y'know, very sort of . . . um . . . neanderthal, y'know.

Nigel: Who me?

Jeanine: Yeah . . . sort of . . . coming over really well.

Nigel: Oh yeah?

Jeanine: Yeah . . . sort of nocturnal glow in your eyes.

Nigel: I wasn't trying to do a large thing, I was trying to make it sort of a subtle thing.

Jeanine: Well, it was subtle.

Nigel: But you noticed it?

Jeanine: I did notice it.

Nigel: That's what's important, I suppose.

Jeanine: I'm not saying it was caveman time but it was sort of . . .

Nigel: I'm not really striving for caveman, I'm trying for an overall sort of strength move really, y'know. It's playing off David, y'know, and he's sort of lean, sort of a lean machine.

Nigel and Derek lag behind David into the lobby of their hotel

Derek: Proper dump.

Nigel: Is Jeanine becoming a bit of a pain in the arse for you?

Derek: Not my arse fortunately . . . but, uh . . .

Nigel: She's really busting my balls.

Derek: I don't understand it. I feel for you.

(*David reappears, Derek and Nigel spot two girls at the bar.*)

David: I've been running the harmony parts to Stone.

Nigel: What do you think about this? She's unbelievable.

Derek: She's a certain likely.

Nigel: Very likely. (*To David*) Will you hold the lift for us?

David: Can't hold the lift . . .

Derek: One second, one second.

Nigel: Just a minute. Like this . . . (*Walks over to girls*). Hello.

Girl 1: Hi.

Nigel: How are you doing?

Girl 1: Oh, good.

Derek: Don't like to be repetitive but how are you doing?

Girl 2: Great.

Girl 1: And how are you?

Nigel: Having some drinks, yeah?

Girl 1: Yeah.

Nigel: I love having drinks, don't you?

Derek: Oh, it's the best.

Nigel: We were just thinking of having some drinks. Maybe . . . uh . . .

Girl 1: Well, you can join us.

Derek: Well, there's a little party going on upstairs.

Nigel: Would you be interested in . . . um . . . making a foray to the upper floors?

David: Look, I can't hold the elevators forever.

Derek: One second, it's one second, mate.

David: I'm not going to hold the lift indefinitely. People want to use it OK?

Nigel: Were you at the show tonight?

Girl 1: Yeah.

Nigel: You liked it?

Girl 1: Great show. I loved it.

Nigel: Great.

Girl 1: I had a great time.

Nigel: Would you do me a favour?

Girl 1: Well, depends what it is . . .

Nigel: I have a small favour. Would you marry me?

Girl 1: I hardly know you.

Nigel: That's the whole point.

David: I just had to give the lift up to a load of folding chairs.

Derek: Punch another one would you?

David: There's some sort of celebration in the ballroom or something. There's a very busy lift, OK? People are sick. They're sicking up waiting to get into the ballroom.

Nigel: We can go to the room. We'll be there in ten minutes, come up and we'll . . .

Derek: You're going to like it.

Girl 1: OK.

Nigel: If we're being too forward just, uh . . .

Girl 1: Well, we'll just sit down here and finish our drinks.

Derek: Don't forget. (*Holds out hand*) Derek.

Nigel: Nigel. Nice to meet you.

Derek: Nice to meet you.

Nigel: And you . . .

    (*Nigel and Derek walk away from bar.*)

Girl 1: (*in hysterics*) Oh my God . . .

Derek walks into David's dressing room holding a dry-cleaning bag filled with bondage gear

Derek: Look at this, back from the hotel valet.

David: (*reading from the label*) 'We are sorry but stains on this garment cannot be removed without possible damage to the colour . . .'

Derek: '. . . or fabric.' It's fucking metal, isn't it? Damage to the fucking fabric?! It wasn't such a bad stain either.

David: This is just rust.

On the tour bus, David tries on a jumper with sewn-on planets and stars on its front – a gift from Jeanine

Jeanine: I like it.

David: Well, if you like it, I like it.

Jeanine: I think I'll put some on the back though too . . . it's just ordinary on the back, innit? There's nothing here.

David: Can't make my mind up about that.

Jeanine: There's a little hole in it.

David: You're not going to do it now are you?

Jeanine: No, no, no.

David: Sticking your nails in my back.

Jeanine: Is that a nail . . .

David: No, I've got sort of a spot back there.

Jeanine: Got a pimple?

David: Well, yeah, don't spread it all round the bus.

Jeanine: I'll do that tonight.

David: Just don't pick at it, OK?

Jeanine: Got to let the stuff out of it.

David: Well, don't do it into your new shirt unless you want to work it into the motif.

Jeanine: What?

David: Don't get spots on the shirt unless you're going to work them in in someway design-wise, y'know. All I need is a stain back there.

Jeanine: I'm not getting it on the shirt. I'm getting the pus out of the spot. Well hold still. Won't hurt, I promise. Did that hurt?

David: Yeah.

A few minutes later

Jeanine: It's not *that* pretty. It's only got two bits of pink on it.

David: I think it's just a bit flashy, y'know . . .

Jeanine: Well that's what you want . . .

David: It's like maybe flashy in the wrong way. I mean the Saturn is nice but this Pluto bit . . .

Jeanine: That's Venus, not Pluto. Pluto's way off.

David: Well, the sleeves are what bothers me. Maybe a bit short aren't they?

Jeanine: That's bracelet length, that.

David: Well, I don't wear bracelets, y'know.

Jeanine: Oh, you must like that. I didn't want to make it too cosmic.

David: It's not too cosmic, I mean, the very cushiony quality makes it go cosmic in a way, very . . . yeah. It's a yielding universe, it's not that, I've got nothing against it mystically but it's . . .

Jeanine: Well, you told me you wanted something glittery.

David: Well, it's nice, yeah, it's nice, I really like it, y'know, I like the purple one and . . .

Jeanine: I can put some more sparkles on it.

David: No, I think we've got enough sparkles.

Jeanine: I love sparkles.

It is the flower power era and the band are holding a press conference

David: I really think that too much stress can't be placed on the dictum that one must follow one's own star.

Derek: Y'know, cigarettes are a drug.

David: It's true, so we all use.

Derek: Water's a drug.

David: It's true – hydrogen, oxygen, it's that simple.

Nigel: 'Cause you know, you get up in the morning and you put water on your face, and that's a drug. That's the strongest drug of all – it wakes you up, dunnit?

David meets his punk son backstage

David: Last time I saw you you had shoulder-length blond hair and you looked great, you looked like a fucking angel. I'm not saying you've gotta look like an angel or anything else. But I just don't get it, I just don't get it. You look like Walter Brennan after a scalping.

On the tour bus

Ian (*to Viv while playing a video game*): You don't think this kind of game tends to make you feel more violent?

Viv: I think it gets rid of a bit but there's always a little spare for whatever you want to put it out on.

Ian: It might be much better if they were non-violent.

Viv: Maybe, I dunno.

Ian (*turning to Derek*): Hey, Derek, we're going to be bubbling under next week in *Billboard*.

Derek (*busy with a groupie*): I'm bubbling under right now.

Ian: You're bubbling over, mate.

Derek: What does that mean, bubbling under?

Ian: It means you're not dead in the water.

Derek: That's what happens before you drown, isn't it?

Backstage – after a triumphant gig

Ian: For once at least, we made our guarantee.

Mick: Plus a little more.

David: A bit more, I should think.

Ian: No, well, no, well, we made the guarantee, come on, that's pretty good. We didn't make any more than that.

Derek: The place was full. They was dropping from the rafters.

David: Those were fans out there.

Ian: They were let in free is the point.

Derek: Whose idea was that?

Ian: It was the promoter's.

Nigel: All those people did not pay?

Ian: So when they leave – this is good – when they leave, we ask them to pay. They've seen the show and they liked the show. It's a great idea. Right?

The band meet Scott, their Number One Fan . . .

Derek: Why do we always have to pander to people?

David: It's not pandering, you're badgering. Y'know there's a difference between pandering and badgering.

Derek: We're expanding.

David: No, we're not, we're groping.

Derek: We're growing.

David: Or groping.

For more out-takes, see *A–Z*:

'All the Way', 'All the Way Home', Armpit Farting, Bass, Cricket Bat, Divorce, The Dose, Far-Eastern Music, Bobbi Flekman, Flower People Press Conference, Artie Fufkin, Graceland, Guitars, Lost Backstage, Tommy Pischedda, Signings, Slime-Moulds, Tennis, *Troggs Tapes*, VD, Western Music, 'Where Are They Now?', and Zucchini.

TAP LYRICS

The Returning

. . . THE KNOCK OF BONEWHITE KNUCKLE ON THE
DREAMDOOR . . .
. . . THE HELLHOWL FROM THE WELL OF THE FORGOTTEN . . .
. . . THE SPINNING COIN HEADTAILHEADTAILHEADTAIL . . .
. . . THE SUDDEN SHOUT THE MISREMEMBERED VOICE . . .

. . . WE HAVE RETURNED . . .

. . . THE DARKYEARS SET ABLAZE WITH SOUNDFIRE . . .
. . . THE DEATHPONY TOSSES ITS BLOODY MANE . . .
. . . SHATTERED SLEEP AND FANTASY MADE FLESH . . .
. . . THE CROWS THE CROWS . . .

. . . WE HAVE RETURNED . . .

. . . WHEN THE DAEMON DANCES . . .
. . . WHEN THE KRAKEN WAKES . . .
. . . WHEN THE HILL AND GLEN SWARM WITH DOOMLOCUSTS . . .
. . . AND ALL ELSE IS EMPTINESS . . .

. . . WE HAVE RETURNED . . .

Hell Hole

The window's dirty, the mattress stinks,
This ain't no place to be a man.
Ain't got no future, I ain't got no past
And I don't think I ever can.

The floor is filthy, the walls are thin,
The wind is howling in my face.
The rats are peeling I'm losing ground,
Can't seem to join the human race.

I'm living in a hell hole.
Don't want to die in this hell hole.
Don't want to die in this hell hole.
Girl, get me out of this hell hole.

I rode the jetstream, I hit the top,
I'm eating steak and lobster tails.
The sauna's drafty, the pool's too hot,
The kitchen stinks of boiling snails.

The taxman's coming, the butler quit,
This ain't no way to be a man.
I'm going back to where I started,
I'm flashing back into my pan.

It's better in a hell hole.
You know where you stand in a hell hole.
Folks lend a hand in a hell hole.
Girl, get me back to my hell hole.

Tonight I'm Gonna Rock You Tonight

Little girl, it's a great big world
But there's only one of me.
You can't touch 'cause I cost too much but
Tonight I'm gonna rock you
Tonight I'm gonna rock you
Tonight!

You're sweet but you're just four feet
And you still got your baby teeth,
You're too young and I'm too well hung but
Tonight I'm gonna rock you
Tonight I'm gonna rock you
Tonight!

You're hot to take all we got,
Not a dry seat in the house.
Next day, we'll be on our way but
Tonight I'm gonna rock you
Tonight I'm gonna rock you
Tonight!

Little girl, it's a great big world
But there's only one of me—

Heavy Duty

No light fantastic ever crosses my mind.
That meditation stuff can make you go blind.
Just crank that volume to the point of pain.
Why waste good music on a brain.

Heavy, duty,
Heavy duty rock and roll.
Heavy duty
Brings out the duty in my soul

I see you dancing there in front of the band.
You're playin' no solos with no guitar in your hand.
I don't pull no punches, I wouldn't waste your time.
And just 'cause it pays, that ain't no crime.

Heavy, duty,
Heavy duty rock and roll.
Heavy duty
Brings out the duty in my soul.

I don't need a woman, I won't take me no wife.
I got the rock and roll and that'll be my life.
No page in history, baby – that, I don't need.
I just want to make some eardrums bleed.

Heavy, duty,
Heavy duty rock and roll.
Heavy duty
Brings out the duty in my soul.

Rock and Roll Creation

When there was darkness and the void was king and ruled the elements,
When there was silence and the hush was almost deafening,
Out of the emptiness
Salvation, rhythm and light and sound,
'Twas the rock and roll creation,
'Twas a terrible big bang,
'Twas the ultimate mutation,
Yin was searching for his yang
And he looked and he saw that it was good.

When I'm alone beneath the stars and feeling insignificant,
I turn within to see the forces that created me.

I look to the stars and the answer is clear,
I look in the mirror and see what I fear,
'Tis the rock and roll creation,
'Tis the absolute rebirth,
'Tis the rolling of the ocean and the rocking of the earth
And I looked and I saw that it was good.

America

We came like babies
From a home across the sea
To see America.
And the people opened up their arms to welcome us
To America.

We came like children
From a far and distant land
To see America.
And the golden sun, the freedom filtered down to us
In America.

And the people stood and stared,
Loved us more than we had dared to
In America.

Superhighways here and there.
Pretty women everywhere.
Brady Buck and Smoky Bear.

Buildings reaching to the sky.
Appleseed and apple pie.
PTA and FBI.

Jumbo Jet begins to rise,
A joyful nation waves its byebyes.

Each religion, race and creed
Gets exactly what it needs;
God bless Johnny Appleseed.

Cups and Cakes

Cups and cakes,
Cups and cakes,
Oh what good things mother makes.
You've got to take tea, won't you take it with me,
What a gay time it will be.

Cups and cakes,
Cups and cakes,
Please make sure that nothing breaks.
The china's so dear and the treacle so clear
And I'm glad that you are here.

Milk and sugar,
Bread and jam,
Yes please, sir and thank you, ma'am,
Here I am.

Cups and cakes,
Cups and cakes,
I'm so full my tummy aches.
How sad it must end
But I'm glad I'd a friend
Sharing cups and cakes with me
And cakes with me . . .

Big Bottom

The bigger the cushion, the sweeter the pushin',
That's what I said.
The looser the waistband, the deeper the quicksand,
Or so I have read.
My baby fits me like a flesh tuxedo.
I like to sink her with my pink torpedo.

Big bottom,
Big bottom,
Talk about bum cakes,
My girl's got 'em.
Big bottom,
Drive me out of my mind.
How could I leave this behind?

I saw her on Monday, 'twas my lucky bun day,
You know what I mean.
I love her each weekday, each velvety cheekday,
You know what I mean.
My love gun's loaded and she's in my sights,
Big game is waiting there inside her tights.

Big bottom,
Big bottom,
Talk about mud flaps
My girl's got 'em.
Big bottom,
Drive me out of my mind.
How could I leave this behind?

Sex Farm

Working on a sex farm
Trying to raise some hard love
Getting out my pitchfork
Poking your hay

Scratching in your henhouse
Sniffing at your feedbag
Slipping out your back door
Leaving my spray

Sex farm woman
I'm gonna mow you down
Sex farm woman
I'll rake and hoe you down
Sex farm woman
Don't you see my sallow eyes
I – I – I'm

Working on a sex farm
Hosing down your barn door
Bothering your livestock
They know what I need

Working up a hot sweat
Crouching in your pea patch
Ploughing through your beanfield
Planting my seed

Sex farm woman
I'll be your hired hand
Sex farm woman
I'll let my offer stand
Sex farm woman
Don't you hear my tractor rumbling
By – by – byyyy

Stonehenge

SPOKEN:
In ancient times, hundreds of years before the dawn of history, lived a strange race of people – the druids. No one knows who they were, or what they were doing, but their legacy remains, hewn into the living rock – of Stonehenge.

> Stonehenge, where the demons dwell,
> Where the banshees live and they do live well.
> Stonehenge,
> Where a man is a man and the children dance
> To the pipes of pan.

> Stonehenge,
> 'Tis a magic place where the moon doth rise
> With a dragon's face.
> Stonehenge,
> Where the virgins lie
> And the prayers of devils fill the midnight sky.

> And you my love, won't you take my hand.
> We'll go back in time to that mystic land
> Where the dew-drops cry and the cats meow,
> I will take you there,
> I will show you how.

SPOKEN:
And oh how they danced, the little children of Stonehenge, beneath the haunted moon, for fear that daybreak might come too soon . . .

. . . And where are they now, the little people of Stonehenge? And what would they say to us, if we were here . . . tonight.

Gimme Some Money

Stop wasting my time.
You know what I want.
You know what I need
Or maybe you don't.
Do I have to come right flat out and tell you everything? –

Gimme some money
Gimme some money.

I'm nobody's fool.
I'm nobody's clown.
I'm treating you cool.
I'm putting you down
But baby I don't intend to leave empty-handed –

Gimme some money
Gimme some money.

Gimme some money
Gimme some money.

Don't get me wrong.
Try getting me right.
Your face is OK
But your purse is too tight.
I'm looking for pound notes, loose change, bad cheques, anything –

Gimme some money
Gimme some money
Gimme some money
Gimme some money.

(Listen to the) Flower People

Listen to what the flower people say
Aahhh—
Listen, it's getting louder every day
Listen, it's like a bolt out of the blue
Aahhh—
Listen, it could be calling now for you.

Flower people walk on by
Flower people don't you cry, it's not too late
It's not too late.

Listen, it's like a Mozart symphony
Listen, it's something just for you and me
Listen, to what the flower people say
Aahhh—
Listen it's getting truer every day
Aahhh.

Bitch School

You been bad.
Don't do what I say.
You don't listen.
And you never obey.
I try to teach you.
But you just won't be good.
You won't behave the way
A big girl should.
It's time to give that whip a crack.
I'm gonna have to send you back to
Bitch school.
Bitch school.

You're a beauty.
You're the best of your breed.
You're a handful.
And I know what you need.
You need training.
Gonna bring you to heel.
I'm gonna break you with my will of steel.
Discipline's my middle name.
And no one comes back the same from
Bitch school.
Bitch school.

No more sniffing strangers, or running free at night.
You think my bark's bad, honey – wait till you feel my bite.
Wait till you feel my bite.

You got problems.
You whine and you beg.
When I'm busy,
You wanna dance with my leg.
I'm gonna chain you.
Make you sleep out of doors.
You're so fetching when you're down on all fours.
And when you hear your master,
You will come a little faster, thanks to
Bitch school.
Bitch school.
Bitch school.
Gonna have to take you back to
Bitch school.

The Majesty of Rock

There's a pulse in the new-born sun;
A beat in the heat of noon;
There's a song as the day grows long,
And a tempo in the tides of the moon.
It's all around us and it's everywhere,
And it's deeper than Royal blue.
And it feels so real you can feel the feeling!

And that's The Majesty of Rock!
The Fantasy of Roll!
The ticking of the clock,
The wailing of the soul!
The prisoner in the dock,
The digger in the hole,
We're in this together . . . and ever . . .

In the shade of a jungle glade,
Or the rush of the crushing street,
On the plain, on the foamy main,
You can never escape from the beat.
It's in the mud and it's in your blood
And its conquest is complete.
And all that you can do is just surrender.

to The Majesty of Rock!
The Pageantry of Roll!
The crowing of the cock,
The running of the foal!
The shepherd with his flock,
The miner with his coal,
We're in this together . . . and ever . . .

When we die, do we haunt the sky?
Do we lurk in the murk of the seas?
What then? Are we born again?
Just to sit asking questions like these?
I know, for I told me so,
And I'm sure each of you quite agrees:
The more it stays the same, the less it changes!

And that's The Majesty of Rock!
The Mystery of Roll!
The darning of the sock,
The scoring of the goal!
The farmer takes a wife,
The barber takes a pole,
We're in this together . . . and ever . . .

Diva Fever

Can't go back
To London,
Can't go back
To Swindon,
Can't go back
To Waterloo.
Can't go back
To Debra,
Can't go back
To Sheila,
Can't go back
To girls like you.

Here she comes,
Lovely,
Here she comes,
Deadly,
Here she comes,
Big as life.
There she goes,
Snubs me;
There she goes,
Cuts me,
There she goes,
Like a knife.
I got . . .

Diva Fever
It's staying on me
Diva Fever
And it's preying on me.
Diva Fever
She was born to thrill me;
Diva Fever
And it's gonna kill me.

And yet I would gladly die screaming, in insufferable agony, if it meant I could spend my last few moments gazing into her eyes . . .

Can't go back
To London,
Can't go back
To Swindon,
Can't go back
To Waterloo.
Can't go back,
It's too late,
Can't go back,
She's too great,
Can't go back,
I can't deny.
There she goes,
Love her,
There she goes,
Hate her,
There she goes,
Want to die
Of . . .

Diva Fever
They'll never cure me,
Diva Fever
They won't insure me.
Diva Fever
My demon lover
Diva Fever
And I shan't recover . . .

Just Begin Again

When the game has just been lost.
When the race has all been run.
When the storm has left your ship well-tossed . . .
Ignore the cost.
Get your stars uncrossed.
Back at Square One.

Just begin again.
You can always find a way.
Just begin again.
No matter what they say.
Life is just a wheel, if it's even real,
You can rest another day.
Life is just a meal, and you never say when.
Just begin again.

People say enough is enough.
And people say you can't undo what's done.
People say the road is just too rough.
But what do they know?
Life is just a show.
Go re-load your gun.
Just begin again.

Just begin again.
Make the bastards eat their words.
Just begin again.
Like bumblebees and hummingbirds.
Life is just a dream, an unconscious stream,
A picture worth five hundred words.
Rise! for you are cream.
And you can have the strength of ten.
Don't hope to win.
Losing is no sin.
So just dig in . . .
Just begin again.
Begin again.
Begin again.

Cash On Delivery

Well, you got the eyes, and you got the lips,
With your long blonde hair and your wild young hips;
You look like a million, including tips . . .
Well, I'm a busy man, baby, can't you see?
And I got no time for coquetry,
But I'm willing and able to pay the fee if it's

Cash On Delivery
So make it cash on delivery if you're gonna do business with me.
Let's keep it strictly C.O.D.

Well, I love you, baby, but why take a chance?
I don't want to be a victim of circumstance,
So don't be looking for no big advance, it's . . .

Cash On Delivery
now, you got the style and you got the look,
and you got a big hole in your pocketbook,
and you gotta buy groceries before you can cook . . .

Cash On Delivery
So make it cash on delivery, that's the way it should be.
Let's make it cash on delivery
If you wanna close a deal with me.
Let's keep it strictly C.O.D.

So if you wanna man that's good and true,
Who's gonna love you no matter what you do,
I'd look somewhere else if I were you . . .

Cash On Delivery
But when the deed is done and the lights are low,
You can count your gold in the afterglow;
Love's like money, gotta spend it slow . . .

Cash On Delivery
So make it cash on delivery, I know nothing is free,
Just make it cash on delivery if you wanna do business with me.
Let's keep it strictly C.O.D.
Just make it cash on delivery with me . . .

The Sun Never Sweats

Bolder than the pirates who used to rule the sea,
Braver than the natives, who never heard of tea.
They never knew what hit them, said the Spaniards later on.
Empire. It was here and now it's gone.
Even the biggest elephant never forgets
And the sun never sweats. No, the sun never sweats.

You were younger than a virgin, and older than the sea.
You were angel, you were devil, and I was all of me.
You knew you met your master, when I made you stay at home.
Woman. Whatever made you roam.
Even the hardest concrete never quite sets.
And the sun never sweats. No, the sun never sweats.

Losing is for losers, and winners play to win.
Always love the sinner, you might even like the sin.
The door that used to open has now closed without a crack.
Woman, you're like the Empire and I still want you back.
We may be gods or just big marionettes.
But the sun never sweats.
Life is a gamble and we're all placing our bets.
And the sun never sweats.
No the sun never sweats.

Rainy Day Sun

Here she comes, that Rainy Day Sun,
Peeking in and out the falling raindrops;
Smiling down on everyone.

In her golden, gossamer gown,
And a necklace of the finest rainbows;
Drying out this rainy day town.

Good-bye, Cloudy Skies!
Here she comes! Here she comes to . . .
Cut them down to size,
And dry the tears in my eyes.

Here she comes that Rainy Day Sun,
Like a moppet at a birthday party;
Rainy day's not spoiling her fun.

Open up the top of your mind;
Catch the water in your magic paint-box,
Oh, the many colours you'll find!

Good-bye, Cloudy Skies!
Here she comes! Here she comes to . . .
Cut them down to size,
And dry the tears in my eyes . . .

Break like the Wind

We are the children who grew too fast
We are the dust of a future past
We raise our voices in the night
Crying to heaven
And will our voices be heard
Or will they Break Like The Wind

We are the footprints across the sands
We are the thumbs on a stranger's hands
We made a promise in the night
Swearing to heaven
Is this a promise we keep
Or one we Break Like The Wind

We are the guests who have stayed too long
We are the end of the endless song
We send our hearts into the night
Soaring to heaven
And will our hearts still beat on
Or will they Break Like The Wind
Ooh, Break Like The Wind?

Stinkin' up the Great Outdoors

Late afternoon in the open air;
A human sea made out of mud and hair.
Ain't nothing like a festival crowd:
There's too many people so we play too loud.
Touch down, the plane's on the ground,
Look for the drummer and he's nowhere around.
We're running late, at least an hour,
No time to rest, no time to shower now we're

Stinkin' up the great outdoors
We're stinkin' up the great outdoors
We're stinkin' up the great outdoors
But the kids don't mind!

We had a drink going up in the plane,
We had another coming down again.
We got more at the airport bar,
And then some home-brewed stuff in the promoter's car.
Here we go, on with the show,
We're bubblin' under and we're ready to flow,
Wound up! Turned loose!
Ain't got the power but we sure got the juice and now we're

Stinkin' up the great outdoors
We're stinkin' up the great outdoors
We're stinkin' up the great outdoors
But the kids don't mind!

We hit the stage, with rock and rage
And do our best to earn the maximum wage.
The lights are bullshit, the sound's for the birds,
Don't know the music and we don't know the words but now we're

Stinkin' up the great outdoors
We're stinkin' up the great outdoors
We're stinkin' up the great outdoors
Where the kids don't mind!

Springtime

Springtime is on my mind
Flowers blooming, all the time
Smell the roses
Smell the grass
Old man winter can kiss my arse

Don't you think that it's a pity?
Don't you think that it's a shame?
Don't you wish that
Every season was the same

Time for loving in the park
Wear a jumper when it gets dark
Mind the prickles
Mind the dew
Wash your willie when you're through

Don't you think that it's a pity?
Don't you think, that it's a shame?
Don't you wish that
Every season was the same

Springtime, enough's enough
Tired of flowers and all that stuff
Want some drizzle
Want some sleet
Want some wellies on my feet

Don't you think that it's a pity?
Don't you think that it's a shame?
Don't you wish that
Every season was the same?

Clam Caravan

I ride 'cross the desert on my camel
Over hills of sand
(Hills of sand).
What's that I see in the distance?
Only hills of sand
(Hills of sand).
There is no oasis in sight;
I'll have to ride through the night
If I'm to make Baghdad by light
Of dawn.

The sun's not your friend in the desert
Like he is at home
(Is at home).
The wind has a name in the desert
(Sirocco!)
But it's barely known
(Rarely known).
It's only the heartiest bloom
That can blossom in darkest Khartoum;
So I will just stay in my room
Tonight.

The desert isn't free with her secrets:
She's a silent bird
(Quiet bird).
I asked the Sphinx for the answer,
It said, 'Mum's the word'
(Mum's the word).
So, I'll catch the Zanzibar train
And sleep till I'm wakened by rain
And I'm back in Olde Englande againe
Once more.

Christmas with the Devil

The elves are dressed in leather
And the angels are in chains
(Christmas with the Devil)

The sugar plums are rancid
And the stockings are in flames
(Christmas with the Devil)

There's a demon in my belly
And a gremlin in my brain
There's someone up the chimney hole
And Satan is his name

The rats ate all the presents
And the reindeer ran away
(Christmas with the Devil)

There'll be no Father Christmas
'cause it's Evil's holiday
(Christmas with the Devil)

No bells in Hell
No snow below –
Silent Night, Violent Night

So come all ye unfaithful
Don't be left out in the cold
You don't need no invitation, no . . .
Your ticket is your soul

All The Way Home

Well, I'm sittin' here beside the railroad track,
And I'm waitin' for that train to bring her back.
If she's not on the five-nineteen,
Then I'm gonna know what sorrow means,
And I'm gonna cry, cry, cry,
All the way home.

All the way home,
All the way home.
Yes, I'm gonna cry, cry, cry,
All the way home.

Now, her daddy never liked me, this he said.
And he could not get it through his old grey head
That I loved his daughter so,
I did not mean to see her go.
Now I'm gonna cry, cry, cry,
All the way home.

All the way home,
All the way home.
Yes, I'm gonna cry, cry, cry,
All the way home.

Let Him Go

In a hospital bed
On the outskirts of town
Lay an old grey man
In a soiled white gown

His hair was all wispy
His eyes were a blank
His breath came in spurts
From an oxygen tank

The nurse hovered near
And so did the reaper
But which had the number
To his private beeper?

Shall he lie there for ever
With a tube up his nose
And his pee-pee and poo-poo
Slipping out through a hose?

Or shall he be released
To float towards the light
Like a wee baby doveling
Or a really good kite?

Let him go. Let him go.
It's too late for healing
Put an end to the pain
That we know he is feeling

His life is a burden
His death is his right
Let's send him off gently into that good

Night.

Rock'n'Roll Nightmare

I been a rocker since I don't know when,
I been a roller since way back then,
Oh, yeah.
But late at night when the boogie's through,
I go to bed same as you,
Oh, yeah.

But when the rock'n'roll nightmare comes,
the Devil's gonna make me eat my drums!

I try to fight it, but I just can't win;
I chase it out, but it comes back in
Again—
It's like a weight pressing on my brain;
If I were smart, I would go insane,
Oh, yeah.

'Cause when the rock'n'roll nightmare's here,
I start to worry 'bout my whole career!

And when the rock'n'roll nightmare's gone,
I jump about with my pyjamas on!

Just Spell My Name

You can say what you want about the way I dress
You can say that my room's a bloody mess
You can say that my songs all sound the same

Just spell my name
Just spell my name
Any way you write it
Just spell my name

You can say I may sing like a cat in heat
You can say that the birds only want my meat
You can say I'm too wild, you can say that I'm too tame

Just spell my name
Just spell my name
Put it in the headlines.
Just spell my name.

Never cared what anyone said
Say I was living, say I was dead
Never cared what anyone thought
Couldn't sell out, 'cause nobody bought
You can say as a lover I'm better than none
You can say I'm not new under the sun
You can say I was broken by the breaks of the game

Just spell my name
Just spell my name
One way or another
Just spell my name

Celtic Blues

When I first laid eyes on County Dunne,
I was green as the hills so high.
But in later years the streets ran red
With blood 'neath the violet sky.

I loved me a lass whose hair was long
And brown as the finest stew
And she swore by the stars in the jet-black night
She'd be true as the sky so blue.

As I look back on the colours of me life,
I see them in faded hues.
The red of the blood of the orange and the green,
The grey of the sky and the moon's silver sheen
all give me the Celtic blues . . .

Back In Harness

Back in harness, it's been so long since we been around.
Back in harness, we got lost and now we got found.
Back in town – you can't keep a good band down.
Back in harness, at one time we said never again.
Back in harness, but rock and roll is our only friend.
Back in town – you can't keep a good band down.

We've been away,
But not to stay,
Like pigs in a blanket,
We've come to lay.
You got to be strong
To last this long,
It even takes guts
Just to sing this song.
May not be young,
But we're still well strung.

Back in harness, we're glad you're along for the ride.
Back in harness, the sores have healed, the vomit has dried.
Back in town, swim or drown, where's the crown?
You can't keep a good band down.

A–Z

by Karl French

Introduction

To me Tap represented the ultimate rebellion. You know, rebellion not just against authority, but against taste and standards. – Derek Smalls

On its release in 1984, *This Is Spinal Tap* was only a modest commercial success, although it was almost universally well received by the critics. In the past fifteen years it has become a major cult success. It is enormously popular among musicians, and indeed anyone who likes or is interested in pop music. *This Is Spinal Tap* is a great rock and roll film – without great rock. It both blatantly and subtly evokes dozens of bands, songs, individuals, rumours and incidents. It is to some degree informed by countless other films. *Spinal Tap* is in fact a product of at least three cinematic traditions – the rock and roll film, the rockumentary/mock-rockumentary, and the music/rock and roll parody.

Cinema has always been intimately connected to music. Films were there at the birth of rock and roll, and cinema and rock have enjoyed a synergistic if not always entirely healthy relationship ever since. When, in the mid-1950s, the idea of the teenager was born as a subject for films and a crucial market to be exploited by the movie business, films reflected and shaped the look and attitude of youth rebellion that would always be at the heart of rock and roll. From formative influences on, and icons of, youth style like Marlon Brando in *The Wild One* (1954) and James Dean, especially in *Rebel Without a Cause* (1955), and the first true sound of rock and roll in a film – with Bill Haley and the Comets' 'Rock Around the Clock' playing over the opening credits of *The Blackboard Jungle* (1955) – the presentation of rock music, of rock or proto-rock stars on screen, in however conservative a form, gave film makers instant access to a vast audience of what became the crucial constituency of film goers: the sixteen to twenty-five-year-olds.

Elvis Presley, who idolised Dean and was inspired by him to act, was an immediate film star. He paved the way (in fact continuing the tradition of popular singers establishing themselves as film stars – Al Jolson, Rudy Vallee, Bing Crosby, Frank Sinatra, Dean Martin, *et al.*) that would lead countless rock and pop stars to make the transition from stage to screen. A near-random selection of notable pop stars on celluloid includes Mick Jagger (*Performance*, 1969), David Bowie (*The Man Who Fell to Earth*, 1976), Jimmy Cliff (*The Harder They Come*, 1972), John Lennon (*How I Won the War*, 1967) and Ringo Starr (*That'll Be the Day*, 1973), Paul Simon (*One Trick Pony*, 1977, featuring *Spinal Tap*'s Harry Shearer) and Art Garfunkel (*Bad Timing*, 1980), Bob Dylan (*Pat Garrett and Billy the Kid*, 1973), James Taylor and Dennis Wilson (*Two-Lane Blacktop*, 1971), Joe Strummer (*Mystery Train*, 1989), Tom Waits (*Ironweed*, 1987), Sting (*Radio On*, 1979), Debbie Harry (*Videodrome*, 1983). Rock stars have the attitude and the ability to perform and, or so the logic goes, should bring their fans with them.

The concept of building a film around an individual rock band began with The Beatles, who established the template for the packaging, style, behaviour and career of the rock and roll band with their star vehicle, *A Hard Day's Night* (1964). The genre continued to thrive throughout the 1960s and 1970s, with films created around the talents of The Dave Clark Five (*Catch Us If You Can*, 1965), The Monkees – a group manufactured for a musical comedy TV show inspired by The Beatles' success – (*Head*, 1968), Slade (*Flame*, 1974), and The Sex Pistols (*The Great Rock 'n' Roll Swindle*, 1979). While these tell the bands' story in a semi-biographical style, there is the parallel genre of the entirely fictional rock and roll story, such as *Stardust* (1974) and *Eddie and the Cruisers* (1983). Somewhere between the two are the rock/pop films *à clef* – thinly disguised biopics of real music stars, like the leading lights of the country music scene in *Nashville* (1975), in which all the actors wrote and performed their own songs, the treatment of Janis Joplin in *The Rose* (1979), and the glam generation in *Velvet Goldmine* (1998).

There is a further genre, the rock biopic and historical rock film, with movies being built around the lives and careers of Alan Freed (*American Hot Wax*, 1977), Buddy Holly (*The Buddy Holly Story*, 1979), Elvis Presley (*Elvis – The Movie*, 1979), The Beatles (*The Birth of the Beatles*, 1979, and *Backbeat*, 1993), and The Doors (*The Doors*, 1991).

The rockumentary emerged at the same time as The Beatles, with the Maysles brothers recording their first experiences of America in *What's*

Happening! The Beatles in the U.S.A. (1964) which, like the infamous *Cocksucker Blues* (1973) – the story of the Rolling Stones on their 1972 tour of America – retains a certain cult cachet for having been withdrawn from circulation. There are films that capture the spirit of live performances, like *Woodstock* (1970), and *Monterey Pop* (1969), and the The Maysles also went on to co-direct with Charlotte Zwerin the brilliant *Gimme Shelter* (1970), one of the key influences on the look of *This Is Spinal Tap*. Other notable films within the genre which directly or indirectly fed into *Spinal Tap* are *Don't Look Back* (1967), *The Last Waltz* (1978) and *The Kids Are Alright* (1979).

Martin Scorsese, director of *The Last Waltz* and an editor on *Woodstock*, was one of the first film makers to understand that rock music was serving as the soundtrack to people's lives. *The Graduate* (1967), *Easy Rider* (1969), *American Graffiti* (1973) and *Mean Streets* (1973) set the fashion for using rock and roll as a convenient and instantly evocative source of film soundtrack music.

A sub-genre of the rockumentary is the film that intersperses fictional or fantasy material with live footage of the starring band, as in *Abba – The Movie* (1977), Bob Dylan in *Renaldo and Clara* (1977), and the Led Zeppelin vehicle *The Song Remains the Same* (1976), the latter of which was one of the major influences on the look and atmosphere of *This Is Spinal Tap*.

The mockumentary could be said to have been launched by the fake newsreel footage in *Citizen Kane* (1941). It is a convenient form for satire, pastiche and technical virtuosity, as exemplified by the likes of Woody Allen's *Zelig* (1983), the brilliant post-modernist films of Nanni Moretti, such as *Dear Diary* (1994), and Abbas Kiarostami's *Close-Up* (1990). The tiny sub-genre of the mock-rockumentary sees *This Is Spinal Tap* sitting alongside Eric Idle's *The Rutles – All You Need is Cash* (1979) and the Comic Strip's *Bad News* (1982) and *More Bad News* (1986).

This Is Spinal Tap is also part of the tradition of improvised or semi-improvised cinema of the kind developed by Ken Loach, Mike Leigh and John Cassavetes, with whom Kent Beyda, one of the editors on *This Is Spinal Tap*, worked.

'Trumpet Volunteer', a classic parody of an interview with a British rock star conducted by a BBC reporter, performed by Peter Sellers and produced by George Martin in the late 1950s, was a key influence on the creators of the band and film. The characters and the group itself evolved over a number of years. Christopher Guest and Michael McKean had been writing together since the late 1960s. Guest, McKean and Harry Shearer were at least competent musicians, talented and experienced improvisers, busy character actors, voice-artists and comedians. The three worked together and separately on a variety of satirical music projects throughout the 1970s, during which time they gradually developed the characters that would be fully formed by the time the film was made. The band proper was born in the 1978 programme *The TV Show*. In the preparation for the show they were forced by a technical problem (hot oil dripping on to them on stage) to further improvise the characters in the band, which had by then been christened Spinal Tap.

After successive attempts to persuade investors and production companies that their idea was a viable project, *This Is Spinal Tap* was finally shot over a five-week period in 1983. The film was built around a prearranged skeletal plot, but individual scenes, which themselves often had established themes and ideas or were working towards prepared punchlines ('Stonehenge', the title of 'Lick My Love Pump'), would be improvised as the camera ran. The camera movements, under the control of director Rob Reiner and accomplished documentary cinematographer Peter Smokler, were determined by the actions and words of the characters as they went along. Rob Reiner, who collaborated in the composition of the band's songs and is himself a keen musician and improviser, is the son of Carl Reiner, one of America's most accomplished comedy actors, writers, directors and improvisational performers, celebrated for his off-the-cuff 'Thousand Year Old Man' sketch performed with Mel Brooks.

After a painstaking collaborative editing process, paring down more than 100 hours of footage, the final film was released in the United States and Britain in 1984. The success it gradually achieved was due to the wholly unpredictable power of word of mouth. It is a film that requires the repeated viewings allowed by video, and has become a staple of the video collection on bands' tour buses. It has launched a dozen or so catch-phrases and captured and created archetypal rock-band moments. The actors are steeped in the traditions of rock music. Before filming, Harry Shearer went on the road with Saxon to perfect the nuances required for Derek Smalls' rounded character. All three actors playing the band had toured extensively in various comedy and spoof rock acts in the 1970s. The film is simultaneously an expression of the creators' love of rock and an acknowledgment of the absurdity of the rock music world.

Surveying the uneven history of the rock movie, Charles Shaar Murray in the *Guardian* on 4 August 1990 wrote: 'The movie which most rock musicians accept as the most accurate portrayal of their existence is the mock-rockumentary *This Is Spinal Tap*.' It is this quality that makes the film so unusual and enduringly popular. In an interview in the *NME* in 1984, Harry Shearer said: 'Well, one of the things which made it troublesome at every turn was that we wanted to make a comedy that was capable of working on many different levels. Rather than there's one joke at a time and all the resources of the material are marshalled towards smashing the joke into your face. We wanted jokes people might or might not get, depending on how much they know about the business, then other things going on simultaneously: sight gags, dialogue, cameo roles. It's all layered.'

In his essay 'Rock and Roll Creation: an examination of the Mock Rock Documentary *This Is Spinal Tap*', Justin Meadows writes: 'An advance screening of the feature *This Is Spinal Tap*, a film that follows the British heavy metal band Spinal Tap on their first US concert tour, *sic*, plays to an audience in Dallas, Texas. When polled afterward, over half of the audience wondered why the film maker would want to make a "serious" documentary about a terrible band that no one had ever heard of.'

Spinal Tap were born twice. First as the fake band in the late seventies and captured in *This Is Spinal Tap*, but in a parallel universe Spinal Tap were also formed in December 1966, crawling from the wreckage of the various incarnations of Originals, New Originals, Thamesmen, and Dutchmen. They have continued to exist since the film in the collective imagination of the Tap's many devoted fans.

Christopher Guest has said: 'Generally we haven't spoken out of character about the film or the parts. We have spent hundreds and hundreds of hours in motel and hotel rooms talking to journalists about the film.' By their own reckoning Michael McKean, Christopher Guest and Harry Shearer have conducted more than 500 interviews in costume and character.

When they go on tour, not only is the audience real, but the group also attracts the same hangers-on as legit rock acts. Christopher Guest told me: 'The Spinal Tap tours were incredibly surrealistic. Here we were playing live shows to an audience who behaved as if they were in the film. It seemed as if it was all just a continuation in real time. This extended to the groupies who showed up backstage. Did they know we were actors? This was all made more confusing by the fact that we were an actual band actually playing, as opposed to some of the quite famous acts that we shared the stage with who in many cases were miming to a DAT. The ultimate irony, I suppose.'

The *Wall Street Journal* ran a front-page story on the continuing phenomenon of the Tap under the headline: 'It Sings Like a Band, Gyrates Like a Band, But Is It a Band?' Reporting on the band members' (actors') intentions for their upcoming tour, the article discusses how they 'wanted to prove that only their characters, not their musical proficiency, were make-believe'.

Rock stars and music business people boast that they are the source for characters or incidents in the film. The group have inspired a devoted following, a number of websites and, inevitably, a tribute band. They have advertised a spoof greatest hits collection, but their music has been included on bona fide heavy metal compilation albums. In the fictional world of the band, Spinal Tap have released fifteen albums, recorded a further three that were never officially released, and had numerous group and solo projects that have never come to fruition. In the real world Spinal Tap have released two albums and several singles. Their songs have been covered, and real rock stars continue to prove eager to collaborate with the group on record and in their live tours. They have toured successfully in the past and are planning to do so again.

Perhaps fundamentally *This Is Spinal Tap* is one of the great films about failure. Noddy Holder recalls meeting Bob Geldof in the early 1980s. At the time, the latter was at the height of his success with the Boomtown Rats and Slade were suffering from a dip in popularity and were slogging it out on relentless tours of minor venues. Geldof pitied Holder, but said that he could never cope with such a slump. Of course, in the nature of such things, within a couple of years, before the dramatic revival of his fortunes inspired by his involvement with Band Aid and Live Aid, Geldof had suffered a similar fate. And as a performer he had lost his audience and would never again come close to the success of his early days. There is a story – surely apocryphal – that in 1977, at the height of punk, Marc Bolan attended a punk concert and for some reason decided to stand up in a lull between bands and announce to the audience: 'Hi, I'm Marc Bolan.' Naturally, there followed a profoundly embarrassed silence, punctuated by a wit in the crowd shouting out something along the lines of: 'Fuck off, grandad.'

One of the cruellest moments in Michael Hutchence's troubled final year was at the Brit Awards ceremony. As Hutchence handed a prize to Oasis, Noel Gallagher (an avowed Taphead) loudly pointed out to the man who was the lead singer of what had recently been one of the top rock acts in the world that he was a has-been and had no business handing out awards to the young, hip and happening.*

One of the most fascinating and perhaps inevitable facts of artistic creativity is the loss of the golden touch. Rock music is about sex and rebellion and youth. At one stage Spinal Tap had been big, and we see at the end of the film that they briefly have the chance to be big again – in Japan, of course. But the central theme of the film is the idea that they have no sense of their own badness, that they are deceiving themselves that they are still a potent force. There is the one poignant moment that they can't ignore, when they are confronted with the reality of being regarded as 'currently residing in the "Where are they now?" file'.

The tour is an extended exercise in self-deception. The band are reduced to appearing at small-scale venues, and even then more and more gigs get cancelled. Ian disguises their tour of diminishing returns with one of the film's best lines, in a wonderfully euphemised justification: 'I just think that their appeal is becoming more selective.'

They still behave and babble like big stars, complaining about the backstage refreshments, the incompetently handled album release, the unattended record signing. The film, which begins as a series of comic sketches on the absurdity of the band's behaviour, the pomposity of their stage act, the stupidity of their philosophies, the crassness of their lyrics, gradually develops a narrative. It is about the refusal to give up or grow up. It is about the great subject of losing it.

The film – and its attendant mythology – touches on the entire history of popular music in the UK and America, from blues, jazz and folk to disco and punk, Sinatra and Sammy Davis, rock and roll, skiffle and heavy metal to dabblings in classical, Eastern-tinged sounds and obscure nooks of world music. It takes in specific stories of rock excesses and the foibles of bands, both in the studio and on the road.

* At the 1998 Brit Awards Spinal Tap were called upon to present The Eels with the best newcomer award. The Eels' guitarist and lead singer, E, noted: 'They were bitter about being passed up as Best Newcomer for the past thirty-five years.'

Rock stars not only attest to the astonishing accuracy of the action of *This Is Spinal Tap* but also gladly play along with the joke. In 1992 Gene Simmons, the promiscuous, long-tongued bassist of venerable glam heavy metal outfit Kiss, revealed that he had been having an affair with Nigel Tufnel's girlfriend while Tufnel was out of town on tour. Alice Cooper has described the effect that the Tap's music has on its fans as 'mute-nostril agony'. The film has entered the popular consciousness to such a degree that its scenes are invoked with a word or two. When Björk wanted to explain the hyperactive nature of her time spent living in London in the mid-nineties, all she had to say was that she was living her life 'up to eleven'.

Heavy metal bands are long-lived outfits, and the Tap themselves have been at it on and off for more than two decades (the fictional Tap for more than thirty years). If anyone questions the importance – let alone existence – of the band, they should look no further than the bible of this musical form, *The Virgin Encyclopaedia of Heavy Rock*. Within those pages Spinal Tap have a decent-sized entry which nestles comfortably between pieces on Spider and Split Beaver.

The actors continue to embellish the past of the characters in and around the band. They have discussed the fictional characters who inspired them (sometimes the real ones) and have commented on the film that they feel portrayed them in an unrepresentative and unflattering light. They have provided a detailed patchwork of the history of the group that exists in parallel to the real stories of rock and roll.

This guide presents the story of both Spinal Taps, and so by necessity sometimes moves between reality and the realm of fantasy without making clear the boundaries between the two. It tries to put the extraordinary phenomenon of the Tap into some kind of perspective – too fucking much perspective. Anyway, enough of my yakking, let's boogie . . .

Karl French
May 2000

A

AC/DC

Australian heavy metal band formed in 1973 by Malcolm Young (rhythm guitar), his younger brother, Angus (lead guitar), Larry Van Knedt (bass), Colin Burgess (drums) and Dave Evans (vocals). The group began to make it when Evans was replaced by chauffeur-turned-singer Ronald 'Bon' Scott. On 20 February 1980, Bon Scott passed out in the back of a friend's car after a drinking binge and was later discovered dead, having choked on his own vomit – thus providing one of the chief inspirations for the tragic and mysterious demise of Spinal Tap's drummer Eric 'Stumpy Joe' Childs (Russ Kunkel). In one of the many fake character interviews, David St Hubbins (Michael McKean) discusses his life as a guitarist with F.S. Gotterfunken in the July/August 1984 issue of *Hit Stream*. David's favoured axe is the Gibson SG. The interviewer points out that this trademark is shared with Angus Young, and asks: 'Was there an influence one way or another?'

David: 'I really don't like to say that. They've been around for a number of years as well, since the early seventies. And I can't come out and say, "Yes, Angus was really influenced by me," because our playing is not that similar, really. He's mostly a lead jammer; myself, I'm mostly rhythm guitar. But I think that Angus has definitely carried on the tradition of SG as ultimate rock instrument. I admire his playing very much and, of course, I admire his whole stage outlook – he seems to be not taking himself too seriously and just havin' a good time.'

See eleven.

ACCENTS

One of the uncanny elements of the film is the accuracy of the English accents of the American cast. They were nervous about how the film would be viewed in the UK, but found that not only was it especially well received in Britain but also that in general people couldn't tell that the performers weren't in fact English. Nigel Tufnel (Christopher Guest) and David

St Hubbins, natives of the mythical East London district of Squatney, adopt the indeterminately London tones that place them somewhere between the Leytonstone rockers Iron Maiden and the more genteel, stoned cadences of South Londoners Mick Jagger and Keith Richard. Derek Smalls (Harry Shearer) has an accent that seems to slip between English and American but, as Shearer explains in his commentary on the laser disc version of the film: 'I was more amused by the guys who had this kind of transatlantic sound because they'd been back and forth too long.' So Smalls assumes the mid-atlantic accent of rock stars like Yes's Jon Anderson and David Coverdale of Whitesnake and Deep Purple.

ACOUSTIC

See Thamesmen, The.

ALBUMS

Spinal Tap have released fifteen albums:

Spinal Tap a.k.a. *Spinal Tap Sings '(Listen to the) Flower People' and Other Favorites* (1967)

We Are All Flower People (1968) a.k.a. *The Incredible Flight of Icarus P. Anybody* (1969)

Silent But Deadly (1969) live

Brainhammer (1970)

Nerve Damage (1971)

Blood to Let (1972)

Intravenus de Milo (1974)

The Sun Never Sweats (1975)

Jap Habit (1975) live

Bent for the Rent (1976)

Tap Dancing (1976)

The Gospel According to Spinal Tap a.k.a. *Rock and Roll Creation* (1977)

Shark Sandwich (1980)

Smell the Glove (1982)

Heavy Metal Memories (1983) best of

Flak Packet, *Here's More Tap* and *Lusty Lorry* were recorded but remain unreleased.

The two genuine albums which have actually been released are:
Spinal Tap – The Original Soundtrack Recording from the Motion Picture This Is
   Spinal Tap (1984)
Break like the Wind (1992)

See bootleg.

'ALL THE WAY'

In an out-take a very pissed-off-looking Tommy Pischedda (Bruno Kirby)
delivers pizza to the band's hotel room at three o'clock in the morning.
Nigel engages him in chit-chat about pizza and cookies. This in turn
leads to the scene where Nigel introduces Tommy to the group's stash
of drugs. The band encourage him to get very stoned and he goes on to
sing the Sinatra classic 'All the Way'. He performs the song for an audience
comprising the band members and assorted groupies, using a pizza crust as
a mike, holding a joint in his other hand, and dressed only in his underwear
and one sock. David comes in and bursts into giggles. Tommy ends his
performance with a hummed trumpet solo as the band supply percussion
by slapping their legs. There is much applause, calls for a 'standing o', and
Nigel lights his Zippo. Tommy concludes defiantly, 'That's music,' before
passing out. Nigel announces: 'Mr Pischedda has left the building.' This is
immediately followed by a scene in the limo in which the band take the
piss out of a remorseful Tommy, who seeks reassurance from director Marty
DiBergi (Rob Reiner) that his performance will not make it into the film.
This wish was of course granted. Tommy concludes: 'You know, in my
line of work you spend a lot of time on the outside looking in. And these
guys were nice enough to, you know, let me be on the inside looking out
for a little while, and it was an education.'

See drugs.

'ALL THE WAY HOME'

In a serious, joke-free scene which ended on the cutting-room floor, David
and Nigel sit in a dimly lit rehearsal-room in earnest but inarticulate
discussion of the tension in the band caused by the presence of Jeanine
Pettibone (June Chadwick). With both of them skirting round the issue

of their deep friendship, David pleads with Nigel to express his thoughts. Nigel says: 'I can't say it. I can think it and I can feel it, but I just can't really seem to . . .' The sequence ends with both playing 'All the Way Home' on the same guitar, ending with David strumming the guitar and singing while Nigel imitates a harmonica with his cupped hands.

David and Nigel's recording of the song (which bears a musical similarity to 'Baby Please Don't Go', recorded by Them and a staple of AC/DC's early live set) was made at a studio in their native Squatney, and finally made it on to vinyl on the 1992 album *Break like the Wind*, with the famous opening lines:

> Well, I'm sittin' here beside the railroad track,
> And I'm waitin' for that train to bring her back.
> If she's not on the five-nineteen
> Then I'm gonna know what sorrow means,
> And I'm gonna cry, cry, cry,
> All the way home.

ALL YOU NEED IS CASH

Proto-*This Is Spinal Tap* mock-rockumentary written and directed by Monty Python member and occasional *Saturday Night Live* presenter Eric Idle. This 1978 film traces the history of The Rutles, which proceeds in exact parallel to that of The Beatles. Known as the 'Prefab Four', the band start off by performing in the Cavern, travel to Germany, are managed by an eccentric gay man, play the Royal Variety Performance, receive MBEs, make it big in America where they are championed by Bill Murray the K (other *Saturday Night Live* regulars appear: John Belushi, Dan Aykroyd, Gilda Radner and producer Lorne Michaels), get turned on to tea by Bob Dylan, are taken in by a dodgy guru figure, get married, and finally split up. Neil Innes, who plays the John Lennon-like Ron Nasty, composes the pastiche songs: 'Get Up and Go' ('Get Back'), 'Ouch!' ('Help!'), 'With a Girl Like You' ('If I Fell'), 'Yellow Submarine Sandwich' and 'The Tragical History Tour'. The Yoko Ono equivalent is a Nazi artist who exhibits her work at the 'Pretentious Gallery'. Other guest appearances come from Michael Palin, Roger McGough, Mick and Bianca Jagger, Paul Simon, Ron Wood and, lending his official seal of approval, George Harrison.

See hidden messages.

ALTAMONT

It's nice, it's nice to see your peers, and they come up to you and say, 'Oh, I saw you on Pop, Look and Listen *twenty years ago,' or, 'I went to Altamont in 1969 to hear you, and you didn't show up!'*

– David St Hubbins in 1984

A notorious free music festival held in 1969 which featured performances from the Rolling Stones, Crosby, Stills, Nash and Young, the Flying Burrito Brothers, the Grateful Dead, Santana, and Jefferson Airplane. Hastily relocated from Golden Gate Park in San Francisco to this speedway track, Altamont was anticipated in *Rolling Stone* as '. . . a little Woodstock . . . an instant Woodstock'. It also presented the dark side of Woodstock with the fatal stabbing – by one of the Hell's Angels who were providing security – of a gun-toting fan in front of the stage on which the Rolling Stones were playing. The Tap were due to play but missed a connecting flight.

See *Gimme Shelter.*

'AMERICA'

The track written by Tufnel that was due to feature on the soundtrack to *This Is Spinal Tap* but didn't make it to final cut. It is a mini rock epic of discrete musical episodes in which Tufnel allows himself to express freely a mélange of images and impressions of the country – apple pie, PTA, superhighways, pretty women everywhere. He suggests the notion of the band as innocents abroad by beginning successive verses, 'We came like babies . . .' and then 'We came like children . . .' The song was accompanied by a montage of the band in travelling mode, playing soccer with cops and generally goofing about.

AMNESTY INTERNATIONAL

Spinal Tap performed in the Nottingham celebrations to mark the thirtieth birthday of the human rights group. They played 'Big Bottom', possibly as a tribute to the then boozy TV star Keith Chegwin, who had bared all while guesting with the nudie balloon act 'The Greatest Show on Legs'. Derek Smalls admitted that he had only agreed to play the gig 'because Amnesty is my birthstone'.

128

ANGEL

Heavy rock band formed in Washington, DC in the mid-1970s and famed for their theatrical stage shows which directly inspired the Tap's live presentation of 'Rock and Roll Creation'. Their self-titled début album was released in 1975 and the band finally split up in 1981.

See 'Rock and Roll Creation'.

ANTHEM

Because of a complex series of legal disputes, between 1976 and 1978 the band struggled to perform under the name of Spinal Tap. Anthem was one of the names under which they performed several benefit shows during this period. There is also a Japanese heavy rock group (formed in 1981) of the same name.

See name changes.

APSO, LHASA

A female backing singer who appeared with the band during the mid-1960s when the group experienced a frenzy of name and personnel changes. Little is known of her beyond the fact that she provided the inspiration for the group's classic 'Big Bottom'.

See 'Big Bottom'.

ARMADILLOS

The armadillo, whose place in the story of rock is otherwise confined to an appearance in the video for The Clash's 'Rock the Casbah', rejoices in having been likened to the groins of Spinal Tap. Marty DiBergi confronts David and Nigel with the accusation that their fans are almost exclusively young men. Nigel explains why women avoid the band: 'Really, they're quite fearful. That's my theory. They see us on stage with tight trousers – we've got armadillos in our trousers. I mean, it's really quite frightening – the size. They run screaming.'

ARMPIT FARTING

In an out-take scene, Marty is keen to film the members of the band as they get stoned and amuse themselves making fart noises, using arms and chest. Ian, who in an excised sub-plot expresses his distrust of the director's motives and wants to get some control and money from the project, says to Marty: 'You can't honestly want to pick up three grown men making fart noises.' Marty explains it is part of his attempt to capture their 'character'.

ARRESTED DEVELOPMENT

One of the central themes of the film is the threat posed to the boys'-club atmosphere of the band by Jeanine's arrival on the scene. Marty asks Derek if being in the band for all these years has led to arrested development. Derek explains with characteristically idiosyncratic imagery that it is like going to a National Park and seeing a preserved moose. His childhood is that moose. Marty asks: 'So when you're playing you feel like a preserved moose on stage?'

Derek: 'Yeah.'

ASPARAGUS, FRED

Assumed name of actor playing drummer Joe 'Mama' Besser, the drummer who took over for the Japanese tour after Ric Shrimpton blew up on stage. The name seems to be a rather obscure and not necessarily very good joke, in that Fred Asparagus is in fact the odd name of a green embossing powder. The actor's real name was Fred Reveles. Reveles, born in 1947, made several other notable film appearances, including *The Three Amigos* (1986), *Dragnet* (1987), *Colors* (1988) and *Havana* (1990). In a spooky, life-imitating-art kind of way – although we are not yet talking a curse along the lines of *The Conqueror* (1956), *The Exorcist* (1973) or *Poltergeist* (1982) – Reveles died of a heart attack on 29 June 1998.

See Besser, Joe 'Mama'.

ASTROLOGY

In *This Is Spinal Tap*, Marty asks David about his relationship with Jeanine. David explains that before Jeanine turned up he was, 'cosmically a shambles. I was using bits and pieces of whatever Eastern philosophies happened to drift through my transom.' Cut to the two of them in full, tongues-out meditation. As revealed in the group's background story, Jeanine's affection for all things spiritual and mystical was dampened when she encountered a woman who claimed to be channelling the spirit of the late Louis Armstrong. Jeanine was impressed until she visited a nightclub and discovered that the woman was in fact an impressionist and Armstrong was part of her repertoire, along with James Cagney and Barbra Streisand.

David in interview has discussed his ambivalent feelings towards astrology: 'I'm really fascinated by the way people have been able to discover these, like, orders out of supposed chaos. I've never been so good at it, myself. I mean, I still stare at the sun and I say, "Why?" And then I say, "Ouch," because, you know, I stared at the sun too long. But some people really sit down with a pencil and paper and they say, "I know. We'll say this bunch of stars that looks like a lion – when the sun goes through there, then these people are going to be grouchy, while *these* people are going to be fun-loving and creative." It's, like, they take a stab at order – I think it's admirable, y'know, even if it's, y'know, a complete, y'know . . . fake. Better to stab out in the darkness than to light a single match.'

Derek is altogether more cynical: 'I believe in cosmology, I believe in a philology – it's not a philosophy, it's a study of a philosophy. And I believe in heaven and hell, of course – I would be a hypocrite if I didn't, because we are depicting that so often in our music. I believe in the spirit world, the power of healers to heal, out-of-body experiences. I believe in a civilisation that once flourished on the continent of Atlantis, which had achieved space travel and communication with other planets. I believe that other beings have visited here and made contact with us in previous lifetimes. I believe in reincarnation – I was a Mayan prince. So, those are a few of the beliefs I cherish. But, you know, astrology is such a load of rubbish.'

See Boot, Baba Ram Dass.

AUDIBLE DEATH
A legendary bootleg released on Gaswind records in 1969. Includes the full two-hour version of 'Short and Sweet', as opposed to the truncated 18′ 37″ version on *Silent But Deadly*.

AUSTIN, TEXAS
The setting for the meeting in which Anjelica Huston hands over a Stonehenge model to Ian Faith.

AUTHENTICITY

*As people who played, and who had gotten tired of seeing rock'n'roll movies
where people's hands were in impossible positions when they were supposed
to be playing, we wanted to get it right.*   – Harry Shearer

The band wrote and performed all the music from the film, with collaboration in the composition from Rob Reiner. Shearer has spoken of the
irony that many real bands rely on miming to pre-recorded tracks for their
live performances, while 'the joke band really plays'. Christopher Guest
concludes: 'What we've seen over the years, when we've played live, is
that people want to feel as if they're part of the movie. Because they were
the audience watching this movie, the audience that comes to the show (this
is sort of a circular thing) feel as if they are now in the movie in a funny
way, and they become the audience in the movie and it's very difficult to
separate. It's a very bizarre phenomenon and it's hard to explain but they
know all the songs and . . . we can never tell . . . are they joking? Or do
they know? . . . At what point does this become real or imagined?'

B

BACH, JOHANN SEBASTIAN (1685–1750)

Composer, organist and violinist born into a famed German musical family. Composed church music, chamber and orchestral pieces, and many pieces for organ, harpsichord and clavichord. One of the composers who exerted an influence on the classical excursions of Nigel Tufnel.

See 'Lick My Love Pump'.

BACKSTAGE REQUIREMENTS

Christopher Guest recalls of Spinal Tap's real tours: 'We also suffered many of the ignominies that the band did in the film. Art imitating life that had already imitated art. At one gig there was half a sandwich and a pitcher of water in the dressing room. That was it. At least the sandwich was wrapped in plastic.'

In *This Is Spinal Tap*, Nigel is seen being appeased by Ian as he runs through what is wrong with the backstage catering. He is particularly fazed by the miniature bread: 'I've been working with this for about half an hour and I can't figure it out.' He moves on to the olives. He picks up one: 'Look! Look! Who's in here? No one [picks up a stuffed olive], then in here there's a little guy. Look! So, it's a complete catastrophe.' But after all he vows: 'I'll rise above it. I'm a professional.' The particular inspirations were the peculiar demands made by Jerry Lewis, Yul Brynner and especially Van Halen, who, according to legend, insist on being served bowls of M & Ms with the brown ones taken out.

The exacting and eccentric demands of bands for backstage refreshment have now become part of rock and roll lore. Q magazine has begun a regular monthly feature in which these riders are published, and so we learn that the Chemical Brothers' demands include a crate of Perrier-Joüet champagne, two cases of wine, three bottles of whisky, eight cases of beer and two bottles of rice wine, while, disappointingly, Ozzy Osbourne requires only fresh fruit, water, assorted teas, bagels and steamed fish.

In the original draft of the screenplay, at the opening party Ian is seen talking on the phone to a promoter in Philadelphia, explaining the band's requirements for backstage refreshments, which include: 'a case of Heineken for the band, a case of Coors for the crew, assorted deli platters, a selection of beef sticks, cheese balls and sherried clam puffs in a crystal server, and four dozen Mr Goodbars with the nuts removed'.

BAD NEWS

English satirical heavy metal outfit, synchronous with Spinal Tap, whose film *Bad News Tour* actually appeared in 1982, two years earlier than *This Is Spinal Tap*. The group, created under the Comic Strip umbrella, consisted of Adrian Edmondson, who also wrote the film, as guitarist/vocalist Vim Fuego, Rik Mayall as Colin Grigson (bass), Peter Richardson as Spider Webb (drums) and Nigel Planer as Den Denis (rhythm guitar). The film was made for TV and, following the success of *Spinal Tap*, Edmondson was inspired to revive the band and produce a further film, *More Bad News* (1986). This revival also spawned an album, released by EMI and produced by Brian May of Queen (the LP included a cover version of 'Bohemian Rhapsody' which was also released as a single the following year) and photographs taken by Gered Mankowitz, particularly known for his images of the Rolling Stones.

In 1987 the group went on tour, appearing alongside Iron Maiden at several concerts. Like Spinal Tap, Bad News recorded a novelty Christmas record, theirs being 'Cashing in on Xmas'. Jeff Beck provides a link between the two spoof heavy rock bands, having played with the Tap and provided music for, and appeared in, several of the *Comic Strip Presents . . .* productions from the first series in 1982.

BANISHED

Short-lived US death metal group of the 1990s. Formed in Buffalo, New York, they released only one album under this name, the cover of which seemed to betray a debt to Spinal Tap.

See sexist.

BASS

In an out-take, Derek discusses his pet project, an album consisting entirely of music played on the bass. Marty doubts that there could be much variation, but Derek points out: 'Well, it's not about variation ... It's about the bass as the symbol of the basis of mankind being common humanity ... It's kind of political, it gets into, you know, there wouldn't be unemployment if all the Pakis went back and things like that. But basically it just takes the idea of all bass as our base, is the fact that we are all ...'

Marty: 'Bass.'

Derek: '. . . people. Basses represent us.'

Marty: 'We don't all play the bass.'

Derek: 'No, no, we don't.'

Marty: 'I see what you're saying.'

BECK, JEFF (1944—)
One of the great guitar heroes and occasional Tap-collaborator. He replaced Eric Clapton in The Yardbirds in 1965, and for a short time played alongside Jimmy Page before leaving the group in 1967. He formed the Jeff Beck Group, alongside Rod Stewart, Ron Wood, Mickey Waller, and Nicky Hopkins, who also played with Spinal Tap. Beck has composed music for several *Comic Strip Presents . . .* productions and made his acting début (having appeared with The Yardbirds in *Blow-Up*, 1966) playing a serial killer in *Gregory: Diary of a Nutcase*. Over the past thirty years, Beck has played alongside numerous artists, including Donovan, Jan Hammer, Tina Turner, Robert Plant and (again) Jimmy Page. Beck played in an early line-up of the band, and supplied one of the guitar solos on *Break like the Wind*.

In appreciation of *This Is Spinal Tap*, Beck gave Guest one of his guitars, and in exchange Guest sent Beck the leather jacket that Nigel wears when he comes to his estranged band members in LA with the message from Ian. Beck has achieved many things in a long career that has spanned the entire history of heavy rock, but his greatest contribution to the genre may be serving as the chief inspiration for Nigel Tufnel's peculiarly tall hair. On his commentary for the laser disc version of the film, Christopher Guest talks of the band's inspirations: 'I think it's other people's egos that make them say, "You're doing us." We've had a million people come up and say, "You're doing Black Sabbath," or, "You're doing me." And people have always said to me, "You're doing Beck, you're Jeff Beck." I didn't model this after Jeff Beck, but in people's minds that's what it was.'

BECKER, WALTER (1950—)

Bizarrely the co-founder (with Donald Fagen) of the sophisticated, jazz-tinged masters of irony Steely Dan, bassist and vocalist Walter Becker wrote the parodically opaque technical sleeve notes for the Tap's *Break like the Wind*:

Remarkable as this recording may be on the aesthetic level, it so happens that *Break like the Wind* is equally notable for its breakthroughs in state-of-the-art audio recording techniques. Let me explain.

Firstly, all of the vocals on the current album were recorded and remixed with the astonishing Crosley Phase Linear Ionic Induction Voice Processor System. This device was invented and first used by the late Graehame Crosley and was later perfected for studio use by producer Reg Thorpe, who made the crucial fine adjustments necessary to eliminate background chatter and make the awesome fidelity and signal-to-noise radio of The System stand out, as I believe it does, in the final mixes.

Here's how the Crosley device works when a vocalist sings: a stream of accelerated air particles issue from his vocal cords, out his mouth and out into the room where there is waiting the diaphragm of an expensive vintage tube microphone. This diaphragm does a passable job of imitating the vibration of the air molecules by twitching in its little suspension, which movements are turned into a low level electrical flux in the tiny wires attached to the diaphragm assembly. There are many problems inherent in a system of this sort, including mechanical resonances in the diaphragm itself, variations in the temperature and humidity of the air in the room, and foreign particles issuing from the vocalist himself, all of which result in reduced fidelity for you, the listener. However, the Crosley device does not care one whit about all of these things, for it measures only the flow of ionic muons (small charged particles with an atomic weight of between $1.699669 \times 10{-}19$ Electron Units and roughly twice that much, give or take a teenie bit here and there) past a negatively charged grid. The resulting current is used to modulate a constant voltage which is self-referencing to the known inductance of the system itself and to the body capacitance of The Artist. For in order for the system to work, the vocalist must wear on his person a number of small balance plates which will offset the fields created by the various inanimate objects on his body at the time of the recording; afterwards he may wear what he likes. This seems to do the trick and soon enough a frighteningly realistic and three-dimensional vocal image is suspended in space between the nearfields mounted on the console (Wombat G7s and Holographe 9696, respectively).

The Crosley system has now presented us with a glorious soundstage recreation of Spinal Tap's vocals. This was mixed in with the roar of the band's amps and drums (so loud that mikes were not necessary) and fed to the inputs of the huge BBC 16-channel cassette recorder which the band had carted over from David's home studio. This was then mixed down to acetate and bunged over to the digital mastering format for cassettes and CDs, in which form it is currently gracing your living room or, more likely, your car, as the case may be.

BEGINNING, THE
The film has been taken by many viewers to be a documentary about an inept hard-rock band but, as the actors and director stress, the fakery is apparent from the opening shot, in which DiBergi talks of his devotion to the band, and his aims for his rockumentary. With his camera lens round his neck, he is seen strolling in front of a bizarre array of lights and ladders, there in preparation for an impossibly elaborate set-up. As Michael McKean has pointed out: 'There's a pretentiousness to this opening that smells.'

BEGLEY JR, ED (1949—)
Los Angeles-born Begley, a tall, blond actor playing John 'Stumpy' Pepys, is (as his name suggests) the son of Ed Begley, a reliable character actor and one of the *Twelve Angry Men* (1957). Although most of Begley Jr's recent work has been on TV, he has appeared in a couple of dozen notable films, including *Cockfighter* (1974), *Stay Hungry* (1976), *Blue Collar* (1978), *Goin' South* (1978), *Hardcore* (1978), *Buddy Buddy* (1981), *Eating Raoul* (1982), *Protocol* (1984), *Streets of Fire* (1984), *The Accidental Tourist* (1988), *She Devil* (1989), *Meet the Applegates* (1990) and *Even Cow Girls Get the Blues* (1993). During the making of *Goin' South*, the young Begley hung out with co-star John Belushi, drinking and taking drugs. Within a couple of years he had

forsworn all drugs – unlike his ill-fated chum. He was twice nominated for an Emmy award for his role in TV's *St Elsewhere*, in which Christopher Guest appeared as a guest star in 1982.

BELGIUM

In interviews the band have filled in the details of their history. While The Beatles had crucial formative experiences playing amphetamine-fuelled sets in Hamburg, The Thamesmen learned much of their trade in the Benelux countries. In his interview with *Hit Stream* magazine, Tufnel revealed the important role that the area played in the history of rock: 'And of course the old blues that came from Chicago and Mississippi and all, New Orleans – you trace that back 'cross the Atlantic to Africa. And then from Africa it goes back to, I guess, uh, Belgium.' It was on this early tour that David and Nigel came under the influence of keyboard prodigy Jan van der Kvelk.

BELUSHI, JOHN (1949–82)

Belushi was a comedian, film star, musician and dabbler in drugs who came to prominence as one of the first wave of comedy stars fostered by *Saturday Night Live*. Said to have had a pirate copy of *Spinal Tap – The Final Tour*, the promo reel for *This Is Spinal Tap*, in the Château Marmont when he died.

See Hendra, Tony; Lemmings.

BENT FOR THE RENT

Poor-selling album of mid-1976, which includes 'Heavy Duty'.

BESSER, JOE 'MAMA'

> *He wasn't just a big fat bastard – I mean, he was a lot more than that. He could play almost anything. Unfortunately, he chose to play almost nothing when you wanted him to play everything, or vice versa.*
>
> – Nigel Tufnel on Joe 'Mama' Besser

Drummer, played by Fred Asparagus, who replaced Ric Shrimpton for the band's Japanese tour of 1982, featured at the end of *This Is Spinal Tap*. Besser subsequently 'disappeared under mysterious circumstances', and was declared 'Missing, presumed dead' in 1983.

BEYDA, KENT
One of the film's editors, who began his career as an assistant editor working with John Cassavetes on *Opening Night* (1977). In his commentary for the special laser disc edition of the film, Beyda compared the two experiences: 'People think that his films were improvised, but in fact they weren't – and not nearly as much as *Spinal Tap*, that's for certain. *Spinal Tap* was really much, much more of an improvisational piece than anything Cassavetes ever did, in my experience.' Beyda went on to work as an assistant editor on *Rock 'n' Roll High School* (1979). His post-*Spinal Tap* credits as editor include *Innerspace* (1987), *Alien Nation* (1988), Billy Crystal's *Mr Saturday Night* (1992), *Forget Paris* (1995) and the remake of *The Out-of-Towners* (1999).

'BIG BOTTOM'
Classic Tapular number, taken from the 1970 album *Brainhammer*. Choice lyrics:

> My baby fits me like a flesh tuxedo.
> I like to sink her with my flesh torpedo.★
> Big Bottom,
> Big Bottom,
> Talk about bum cakes,
> My girl's got 'em.

Defending the band from yet another accusation of sexist imagery in this song on *Saturday Night Live* in May 1984, Derek Smalls points out: 'It's about a woman's pair o' cheeks. And it's like sayin', "Oh, because you wrote a song about a woman's nose, then you're not respectin' her as a person." It's about a *nose*.'

The song is both a broader version of Queen's 'Fat-Bottomed Girls' and, more generally, a brilliant pastiche of hard rock's characteristically unsubtle sexual imagery. The repeated use of the leering question 'You know what I mean?' after the blatant lyrics perfectly suggests the way that the thinly codified sexual invitations of many blues lyrics were taken on by rock pioneers and melded to the British Donald McGill/*Carry On* sensibility. Led Zeppelin's Robert Plant and Jimmy Page first bonded by discovering their shared love of early blues performers. A particular favourite, and possibly

★ Hence 'Torpedo Umbrella', Nigel Tufnel's slang term for a condom.

the most seminal of all blues singers for the first generation of rock stars, was Robert Johnson. One of their particular favourites of Johnson's lyrics was his seminal invitation from 'Travelling Riverside Blues':

> Well, you can squeeze my lemon till the juice runs down my,
>   till the juice
> runs down my leg, baby, you know what I'm talking about

Rock is, of course, largely about sex, and the suggestiveness of the blues lyric endures in the words of heavy rock. Anything about cars, trains, planes, food, clothes, tools, guns – especially guns – is about sex. See Deep Purple's 'Highway Star', Kiss's 'Love Gun' (the lyrics to 'Big Bottom' actually include this cryptic expression), AC/DC's 'Sink the Pink', W.A.S.P.'s 'On Your Knees', Saxon's 'Bavarian Beaver', etc.

In the *Hollywood Online* interview, St Hubbins was asked about the inspiration behind 'Big Bottom'. He explained vaguely: 'I was dating a beautiful woman who went by the professional name of Lhasa Apso. Extraordinarily beautiful.'

Derek Smalls interrupts: 'With one great exception.'

St Hubbins: 'But that exception was the inspiration. End of story.'

See Apso, Lhasa; Soundgarden; Tormé, Mel.

BIG IN JAPAN

> *I got the jam but not the bread*
> *But I'm big in Japan.*
>
>   – Tom Waits on 'Big in Japan' from *Mule Variations*

The name of Holly (Frankie Goes to Hollywood) Johnson's first band, and a one-hit-wonder single by Alphaville, 'Big in Japan' is one of rock's great clichés. The idea of being 'big in Japan' suggests exoticism, and is also a sign of the fiscal health of a band – with Japanese records and CDs being more expensive and so generating more royalties. Like so much in the film, the climax to *This Is Spinal Tap* now works as a reference point for rising phoenix-like from the ashes of a disastrous tour and resolving to plod on in the hope of one more shot at the big time. In the final chapter of *Lost in Music*, his reminiscences of life as an almost-was in the music world, Giles Smith writes: 'There's a scene at the end of the movie *This Is Spinal Tap* where the estranged guitarist, Nigel Tufnel, suddenly shows up backstage at some disastrous Spinal Tap show. The band have been spiralling downwards ever since he left and the meeting is a tense one, all bruised pride and wounded ego. But Tufnel brings news. He chews hard and says, "I bumped into Ian. Seems that 'Sex Farm' is in the charts in Japan. It's No. 5 last week, actually, so he asked me to ask you – Tap – if you'd be interested in reforming and doing a tour." Bingo – a reunion back on the road again, the road that never ends.

'So it was hard, at first, to suppress a laugh when Newell phoned the other night. He, too, was chewing hard. And he, too, was talking about Japan. "My solo album is selling quite well over there. They want me to go out and play a few shows. Nothing too strenuous – just for a week or so. But I have to get a band together and . . . Well, do you want to do it?"'

'BITCH SCHOOL'
Opening track on Spinal Tap's 1992 comeback album, *Break like the Wind*. Rather like a mix between 'Sex Farm' and 'Hell Hole'; and in one of several parallels with the career of Australian rockers AC/DC, the song shares a certain canine imagery with their number 'Give a Dog a Bone' from the 1980 album *Back In Black*. 'Bitch School' sees the band exploring the world of the dog-training school, with a certain understated sexual suggestiveness:

I'm gonna chain you.
Make you sleep out of doors.
You're so fetching when you're down on all fours.
And when you hear your master,
You will come a little faster, thanks to
Bitch School.

The band, as ever, denied the common reading of the song's meaning. Tufnel explained that it was intended as a literal song about a 'Bitch School' and that the original version of the number had a line about the petfood Kibble which would have averted all the controversy. In a typically Tapular irony, the sleeve for the single of 'Bitch School' carried a picture of a woman posed on all fours which was banned by MTV. Asked in *Q* magazine how the song represented a growth in maturity from the likes of 'Sex Farm', Smalls explained: 'It's the distance from a farm . . . to a school. Man is born on the farm, and then he goes to school.'

BIZARRE GARDENING ACCIDENT

The manner of original Tap drummer John 'Stumpy' Pepys's death in 1969. The idea of the 'bizarre gardening accident' has entered the language and the popular imagination. Angry Salad, a Boston-based rock band, have released an album by that name and, in a peculiar instance of life imitating art, it is still rumoured that Toto's Jeff Porcaro may in fact have died in this way. Talking of bizarre gardening accidents, Jerry Springer, interviewed by John Sweeney in the *Observer* on 21 February 1999, recalled his personal favourite from all his shows: '"I think they're all stupid." He chuckles. "The wildest show was this guy who was being stalked by a gay guy, and he didn't like that and he cut off his own penis." The choppee had, apparently, come on the show to tell America that, concerned by the gay man's attentions, he had cut off his manhood with an ultra-sharp gardening tool and flushed the remains down the toilet. "That to me was unusual," Jerry observes.'

See Porcaro, Jeff.

BLACK SABBATH

One of the first wave of British heavy metal bands, Sabbath, previously known as Polka Tulk and Earth, were formed in the Midlands in 1969 by Terry 'Geezer' Butler (bass), Tony Iommi (guitar), Bill Ward (drums) and Ozzy Osbourne (vocals). Famous for their continual flirtation with dark mysticism, their seventies life of archetypal rock and roll excess both on the road and in the studio, and Osbourne's unusual appetites, the band have survived to the present day through countless personnel changes, which have included temporary membership by the likes of Rick Wakeman (Yes), Ian Gillan (Deep Purple and Gillan), Ronnie Dio (Elf, Dio, Rainbow) and Rob Halford (Judas Priest).

See 'Stonehenge'.

BLACKWOOD, NINA (1955—)

One of the first MTV VJs, Blackwood had a tiny part in the promo reel

Spinal Tap – The Final Tour as the woman reading Sammy Davis's *Yes, I Can* in a scene in the limo, which inspires Bruno Kirby as the chauffeur to share some of his feelings about Sinatra.

BLOOD TO LET
Tap album, released on the Megaphone label in 1972.

BLUE WORLD CHINA
Obscure skiffle band of the 1950s to whom David sold his first songs.

BOCCHERINI, LUIGI (1743–1805)
Italian composer and cellist. In 'Heavy Duty' Spinal Tap break into a version of his most famous piece, the minuet from the string quartet in E major generally known as the Boccherini minuet.

BOND, PETER 'JAMES'
Drummer who replaced Eric 'Stumpy Joe' Pepys for the album *The Sun Never Sweats*. Bond was himself replaced by Mick Shrimpton after spontaneously combusting on stage at the Isle of Lucy Jazz/Blues Festival. As Nigel recalls in *This Is Spinal Tap*: 'It was tragic, really. He just exploded on stage. He was just like a flash of green light and that was it. Nothing was left. Well there was . . . There was a little green globule on his drum seat.'

David: 'It was a stain, really.'

Nigel: 'It was more of a stain than a globule, really.'

This is perhaps a reference to the tragic death of Keith Relf, a founder member, harmonica player and vocalist with The Yardbirds, which at various times also included Eric Clapton, Jimmy Page and Jeff Beck. In 1976 Relf, aged thirty-three, electrocuted himself playing an electric guitar in his basement.

Nigel says ruefully of Bond: 'For a drummer, he had a very good time. He could actually keep the rhythm pretty much in the ballpark, as you would say, for the whole tune. His death really hit me the hardest, because he owed me money.'

'BONE FARM'
The working title for the controversial single 'Sex Farm'.

BOOT, BABA RAM DASS

The Beatles led the trend for adopting a yogi when they were all briefly in thrall to the teachings of Maharishi Mahesh Yogi. They were with him on a Welsh retreat in 1967 when they received the shattering news that their manager Brian Epstein had died. There were rumours that the yogi had taken advantage of female members of the band's entourage, and the disenchantment felt by Lennon at this is said to have led him to write 'Sexy Sadie'. Naturally the Tap, a band individually and collectively given to serial flirtations with mysticism, had their own guru, as David recalls in his December 1984 interview in *Metalhead*: 'As for religion, well, Nigel was with a guru for many years – Baba Ram Dass Boot. I did attend a few sessions with Dass Boot . . . It was interesting, it was enlightening, even. But Nige was obviously gettin' a lot more out of it than I was because he'd, you know, paid, and I was just sort of like *auditing*.'

BOOTLEGS

There are five declared Tap bootleg albums: *Audible Death*, *Live at Budokkan*, *Got Thamesmen on Tap*, *It's a Dub World* and *Openfaced Mako*.

BOSTON

The band's 1982 date in Boston was the first on the 1982 tour to be cancelled, but Ian Faith memorably reassured the band: 'I wouldn't worry about it. It's not a big college town.'

BRAINHAMMER

Tap album, released on Megaphone in 1970. Includes 'Brainhammer', 'Lie Back and Take It', 'Swallow My Love' and 'Big Bottom'.

BREAK LIKE THE WIND

Spinal Tap's comeback album of 1992. The title song itself is another in the band's flatulence cycle. Tufnel is backed up and squeezed out by fellow axe-meisters Slash, Steve Lukather, Joe Satriani and Jeff Beck. A work of inspired anthemic meaninglessness. Sample lyrics:

> We are the children who grew too fast
> We are the dust of a future past . . .

We are the guests who have stayed too long
We are the end of the endless song . . .

St Hubbins announced it as a concept album: 'And the concept is sales. It sounds crude, but it's part of our new maturity.'

BRYNNER, YUL (1915–85)

Yul Brynner, famous bald film star who provided one of the inspirations for the backstage requirements scene. In his commentary for the laser disc edition of the film, Michael McKean recalls Brynner's contract for backstage provisions demanding: 'Under no circumstances must white eggs be substituted for brown.'

BUCKET

Southampton pub (now called the Bucket and Pail) that has entered rock legend as the place where, in 1964, Nigel and David – then the core of the New Originals – first jammed with John 'Stumpy' Pepys, then a member of the Leslie Cheswick Soul Explosion.

BUDGET

The initial budget for the film was set at around $200,000 to $300,000, but the film ended up costing between $2 million and $3 million, with a figure of $2,400,000 suggested as the likely amount.

BYRON, LORD GEORGE GORDON (1788–1824)

Famed poet and adventurer who, along with Shelley, was likened by Derek to the twin heroes of the Tap, Nigel and David.

See lukewarm water.

C

CARMEN
One of St Hubbins's projects during the fallow period after the aborted tour of Japan in the mid-1980s was an all-scat version of Bizet's *Carmen*, which St Hubbins wrote in collaboration with his father, Ivor, an amateur musician.

CARVEY, DANA (1955—)
Actor/comedian/impressionist, born in Missoula, Montana, who plays Morty's assistant mime caterer at the tour's opening party. Carvey is a veteran of *Saturday Night Live*, a regular on TV's *The Larry Sanders Show* and a co-star of *Wayne's World* (1992) and *Wayne's World II* (1993).

'CASH ON DELIVERY'
A track on the 1992 album *Break like the Wind*. Has a sort of ZZ Toppish rough country-tinged heavy rock feel as the song presents its lyrical blend of financial/sexual imagery:

> Well, you got the eyes, and you got the lips
> With your long blonde hair and your wild young hips;
> You look like a million, including tips . . .

The song features backing vocals from Timothy B. Schmit and Tommy (Krokus) Funderburk. The lyrics see St Hubbins adopting a mood of rare and disarming honesty:

> So if you wanna man who's good and true,
> Who's gonna love you no matter what you do,
> I'd look somewhere else if I were you . . .

CHADWICK, JUNE (1955—)
Chadwick, who plays David's girlfriend Jeanine Pettibone in the film (they

subsequently married), was born in Warwickshire in 1950. Chadwick had several advantages in going for the role – she was English, she was able to improvise and she looked like St Hubbins, which the film makers saw as essential. Before *This Is Spinal Tap*, Chadwick had small roles in films starring pop singers, appearing opposite Jack Jones in *The Comeback* (1978) and David Essex in *Silver Dream Racer* (1980). She went on to feature in *Jumpin' Jack Flash* (1986) and make several appearances in TV shows, including *The A Team* and *Murder, She Wrote*, as well as reprising her role as Jeanine in *The Return of Spinal Tap* (1992). In the laser disc commentary, Karen Murphy commends Chadwick's performance: 'June just took to it like she was a natural. She managed to keep up with the guys, which was really the test.'

CHEAP DATES

The band with which Ronnie Pudding was playing bass until he joined with Nigel, David and John 'Stumpy' Pepys in the New Originals.

CHEEKS, BLIND BUBBA

David St Hubbins' blues idol: 'He wasn't actually blind, though. He was not legally blind, he was myopic.'

CHEESE-ROLLING

A trade promotional film for theatre owners in which Reiner sits at a table discussing the film he has completed. He comes clean that he and his audience, the theatre owners, are there to sell popcorn. 'So forget themes, forget relationships. We've got sex, we've got nudity. There's a naked groupie in this picture with enormous breasts, big nipples. Sensational! We've got rock'n'roll. The kids eat that shit up, they love rock'n'roll, they come back a hundred times. Repeat business – I wish I had a bigger piece of this picture. Stars. You want stars? Forget it. Big stars. I'm in the picture: two-time Emmy winner. *All in the Family*. Monster hit.' Reiner regrets that he has now no clip from the film to show them, but instead has a film about Denmark's Cheese Festival, 'a joyous celebration of cheese'.

This idea was also used in a very similar form as a theatrical trailer.

CHER (1946—)

Born Cherilyn Sarkasian La Pier in California, Cher sang backing vocals on several Phil Spector productions. When she had failed to make it under

Spector's tutelage, she first came to fame as half of the hippie-pop duo Sonny and Cher, who had a string of hits and a successful musical comedy TV show. Having divorced Sonny Bono in 1974, Cher enjoyed a notoriously short marriage to rocker Gregg Allman and later a romance with Gene Simmons of Kiss. Her musical collaborations include work with Meatloaf and Richie (Bon Jovi) Sambora.

Cher was one of the celebrity collaborators on the Tap's comeback project *Break like the Wind*. She sang with St Hubbins on 'Just Begin Again'. The collaboration was hampered by Cher's apparent animosity towards her co-singer, as St Hubbins recalled in a 1992 interview in *The Nose*: 'It was great in one sense that she insisted on me not being anywhere near her when she sings. In fact, the papers said I had to be 100 yards away from Cher when she's actually doing vocals, which would be a house-and-a-half down the road from the studio where we were doing it.'

When asked why Cher didn't join the band in person for their comeback tour, St Hubbins explained: 'We begged, we pleaded, and finally she agreed not to.'

Speaking to Q magazine in April 1992, Nigel Tufnel recalled an awkward amorous moment between him and the famed rock goddess: 'The truth about me and Cher is that I did make a somewhat feeble play for her. It just didn't work out. I said, "Let's have lunch," and she said, "Oh, everyone does that." So I took her to this pet-shop specialising in non-exotic birds. It was called Macaw Blimey! I like to be direct and I said, "If what you are involved right now is not as you would have wished, then please ring me up." It was very English . . . although my trousers were around my ankles at the time.'

CHILDS, ERIC 'STUMPY JOE' (1945-74)

Drummer, formerly with Wool Cave, who replaced John 'Stumpy' Pepys and went on to play on *Brainhammer*, *Nerve Damage*, *Blood to Let* and *Intravenus de Milo*. Died from choking on vomit, although of course it still isn't known whose. Smalls recalls: 'Big hands, big feet, big heart. Small lips. Thin hair. Big ears. That really says it all. I mean, you could use that to make a police sketch of him.'

'CHRISTMAS WITH THE DEVIL'

Track that appears on *Break like the Wind*. It is a novelty record based around the band's interest in Satanism:

The elves are dressed in leather
And the angels are in chains
(Christmas with the Devil)

The sugar plums are rancid
And the stockings are in flames
(Christmas with the Devil) . . .

No bells in Hell
No snow below –
Silent Night, Violent Night

It includes contributions from Timothy B. Schmit and Tommy Funderburk on backing vocals. The band performed this number when they appeared on *Saturday Night Live* in May 1984.

CIVIC ARENA, SEATTLE
The gig was cancelled leading to a hastily rearranged appearance at the air force base's monthly 'at ease' weekend.

'CLAM CARAVAN'
'Kashmir'-style song that features on *Break like the Wind*. Choice lyrics:

The sun's not your friend in the desert
Like he is at home
(Is at home).
The wind has a name in the desert
(Sirocco!)
But it's barely known.
(Rarely known).

It includes Nigel Tufnel coming over all Jimmy Page/George Harrison with a coral sitar solo. It also features Luis Conte (Roger Waters/Phil Collins) on percussion and Steve Lukather on piano. The track was first planned as the title song from Tufnel's solo project, *Nigel Tufnel's Clam Caravan*. The title was originally chosen by the writers as a possible band featuring in the Tap's mythical past, in a similar vein to another of their suggestions, Lobster

Canyon. The title of the project was in fact initially supposed to be 'Calm Caravan' but was rendered in its familiar form by a printing error which Tufnel chose not to correct as he felt it would become another of rock's great mysterious and magical happenings. Asked what the worst moment in his career had been, Tufnel said: 'Well, it's pretty consistently bad, y'know. I think right after I did "Clam Caravan", my solo record, was maybe the very worst.'

CLAYPOOL, LES

In *The Return of Spinal Tap*, Claypool, bassist with Primus, reveals that he has always been a fan of Derek Smalls and shows off the tattoo on his left shoulder that could be Smalls, Lemmy or, indeed, both.

CLEVELAND

The venue where the band are shown totally unable to find their way to the stage. Smalls complained to journalist Jim White in the *Independent* on 24 February 1992 of Marty DiBergi's stitch-up job that resulted in the unflattering portrait of them in *This Is Spinal Tap*: 'Well, for example, he filmed nights when we had no problems finding the stage. Did he use that material? No.'

CLEVER

See Fame, Duke.

'COPULATION'

David, in an out-take, talks to Marty of the rapport he has with his fans when he is on stage: 'If we're doing something extremely lewd then my thoughts are very much of copulating with each female in the audience – of age, I mean I'm not a cruel person.'

COURGETTE

See zucchini.

CREATURES, THE

Skiffle band in which David first played guitar. Not to be confused with the splinter band of Siouxsie and the Banshees of the same name.

CREDIBILITY GAP, THE

A sort of proto-Tap, this satirical rock band featured Shearer and McKean as well as David L. Lander and Richard Beebe. They toured clubs and colleges in the late sixties and early seventies and recorded several albums before grinding to a halt, as Shearer has noted: 'Beebe left the group in 1975 and the group left the group a year later'.

CRICKET BAT

Ian: 'Certainly in the topsy-turvy world of heavy rock, having a good solid piece of wood in your hand is quite often useful.' In a scene almost entirely missing from the finished film, the band sit around a hotel room looking exhausted. David offers: 'Maybe we are dead. Maybe we've passed away in some sort of mishap, and we're just sort of suspended because . . .'

Derek: 'There's no room yet.'

Ian comes in and shows them what they should be doing, and sets about smashing up the room with his cricket bat. Having destroyed everything, including the TV, a mournful Nigel says meekly: 'You know, I was really looking forward to watching that nature show. I can't do that now.' The depressed group decide to cheer themselves up by going to see Elvis's grave.

CRYSTAL, BILLY (1947—)

Actor, comedian, writer and director born in Long Beach, NY. Much of his part as Morty the Mime caterer was cut from the final film. He featured in a sub-plot in which he explained the background to the catering company he ran called 'Shut Up and Eat'. Crystal went on to work with Reiner on the hit romantic comedy *When Harry Met Sally* (1989) alongside Bruno Kirby. Crystal and Kirby also appeared together in *City Slickers* (1991).

CUCUMBER

See zucchini.

'CUPS AND CAKES'

Single recorded by The Thamesmen, dated on the soundtrack album only as *circa* 1965. This is a very brisk, 'Penny Lane'-style ditty with naïve, meaningless lyrics conjuring up a more innocent time:

You've got to take tea, won't you take it with me,
What a gay time it will be.

The mask slips a little in this recording, as McKean's pronunciation of the word 'cups' suggests that St Hubbins started his singing career with a vaguely Midlands/North-West twang. It is this piece of the band's pre-history that is playing on the radio in the Memphis hotel room that ends with the DJ commenting that the band now resides in the 'Where are they now?' file.

CURTIS, JAMIE LEE

See Guest, Christopher.

Derek's on-stage pod fiasco.

Viv destroys planets on-the-road.

On tour, Marty captures the band's character.

'Before I met Jeanine, my life was cosmically a shambles.'

The armadillo in Derek's smalls.

Viv is blessed with one thing other Tap members lack: actual musical ability.

Artie Fufkin, Polymer Records.

Tommy's stoned rendition of Sinatra's 'All the Way'.

D

DAVIS JR, SAMMY

See Pischedda, Tommy; Yes I Can.

'DEATH SELLS'

See _Smell the Glove_.

DE MORNAY, REBECCA (1961—)

LA-born actress who plays a groupie friend of David's in the original promo reel, _Spinal Tap – The Final Tour_. After a début appearance in _One from the Heart_ (1982), De Mornay shot to fame alongside Tom Cruise in _Risky Business_ (1983). After a lull, her fortunes were restored by her chilling performance in _The Hand That Rocks the Cradle_ (1992).

DES MOINES

Another of the tour's cancelled gigs.

DEUTSCH, POLLY

The designer played by Anjelica Huston responsible for constructing the mini Stonehenge stage set.

DiBERGI, JIM

Mysteriously named director of _The Return of Spinal Tap_ (1992).

DiBERGI, MARTY

> _He was all over us like a cheap shoe._   – Derek Smalls on Marty DiBergi

Character chiefly taken from Martin Scorsese in _The Last Waltz_ (1978), though his name is an amalgam of those of several directors: Marty from

Scorsese, Di from Brian De Palma, Berg from Steven Spielberg, and i from various Italians – Fellini and Antonioni, for example. He has protested against the accusations that he stitched up the band in the rockumentary *This Is Spinal Tap*. He insists that the film was the product of his enduring love for the band and cites the two films he turned down in order to work with the Tap: *On Golden Pond – 3D* and *Attack of the Full-Figured Gals*.

In *The Return of Spinal Tap* (1992), we see Marty DiBergi in reduced circumstances in his North Hollywood office, which is situated in a corridor – next to a pay-phone, the men's toilet and a water fountain. Despite appearances, he insists: 'Things have been going pretty well for me.' Of *This Is Spinal Tap*, he claims: 'I just tried to show them in a good light. I thought that showing them not being able to get out of the pod and not being able to find the stage and so on made them more human.' Since his seminal rockumentary, his only known credit has been the obscure *Kramer Vs. Kramer Vs. Godzilla*: 'It didn't work as well as I thought it would. I thought, the juxtapositions of the *sturm und drang*, of which parent is going to get the child, with Godzilla looming over all of them. You know, maybe Godzilla's gonna get the child.

'That, I thought, would be interesting but it turned out the audience didn't take to it as well as I'd thought they would.'

DIBROMA, MARTY
The name of the DiBergi character in early versions of the film's treatment.

'DIVA FEVER'
The track from *Break like the Wind* on which Dweezil Zappa (whose father, Frank, had himself referred to the band in his album *Them Or Us*) performs a guitar solo. Choice lyric, the opening lines:

> Can't go back
> To London,
> Can't go back
> To Swindon,
> Can't go back
> To Waterloo.

> Can't go back
> To Debra . . .
> Can't go back
> To girls like you.

The lines 'Diva Fever/They'll never cure me' suggest it may be a song of groupie love and venereal disease.

DIVORCE
In an out-take, Derek is seen talking to his lawyer on the phone about his wife's divorce demands being printed in a full-page ad in a British music paper. He pleads: 'I mean can't we just have her killed. You know people.'

DOBLY
It is during the Seasons restaurant scene where Nigel and Ian express the contempt they feel for Jeanine as she tries to interfere with the band's presentation. She wants the band to be made-up, Kiss-like, according to their astrological signs. Even worse, before this she talks of how David's vocals have been poorly recorded on *Smell the Glove*: '. . . you don't do heavy metal in dobly.' Kent Beyda recalls: 'Whenever I'm dubbing a picture, invariably someone says, "Let's do it in dobly" or "This goes to eleven." I mean, it comes up really any time I'm in an audio situation.'

DON'T LOOK BACK
D.A. Pennebaker's seminal rockumentary of Bob Dylan's UK tour of 1965. One of the declared inspirations for *This Is Spinal Tap*, the film offers a seemingly candid view of the young, supremely confident Dylan on tour. We see him granting an audience to his nervous acolyte Donovan who sings 'To Sing for You' in a nearly embarrassing homage to his idol. Dylan is shown suffering from the everyday niggles of touring, such as singing 'The Times They Are A-Changing' with an initially dysfunctional mike – it isn't plugged in. He also memorably and mercilessly mocks a journalist from *Time* magazine, criticising him for his hypocrisy and lecturing him on the nature of truth, which Dylan considers would be captured in a photograph of a 'tramp vomiting into the sewer'. The film influences *This Is Spinal Tap* in its *cinéma vérité* look, in the way it captures the backstage atmosphere and

continual tour negotiations. The most obvious reference in the later film is the getting-lost-backstage scene. After the Manchester gig, Dylan and his entourage are seen scurrying around backstage desperately trying to find their way out, and Dylan enquires urgently: 'Where's the door?'

DOSE, THE

At the Atlanta Record Convention, at which the controversy over the band's proposed cover for *Smell the Glove* comes to a head, Nigel and David are seen sporting matching cold sores on their lips. This is a ghostly pointer to a major sub-plot that was dropped in the editing process. It relates to the lead singer of The Dose, the new-wave band that supported Spinal Tap on the early leg of the Tap Into America tour, who gave most of the band herpes.

In an out-take in which the notion of The Dose taking the support slot is proposed, Ian puns: 'Maybe there's just two of them. Maybe it's a Spanish group.' When the Tap finally see their support at a sound-check, they are initially annoyed that their own stage-time is delayed. Then, when they catch sight of the lead singer, Nigel and David are instantly love-struck. After hearing a few seconds of their ordinary-sounding warm-up, David says to a bewildered Ian: 'We might think about hiring them as like a permanent support act.' Because, he explains, they are like a counterpoint to their own style – a genius, black and white, yin and yang twist.

In the scene in which a stoned Tommy starts singing 'All the Way', Viv is seen briefly chatting to the lead singer of The Dose and asking about the sore on her lip. She explains: 'Oh, it's just a sore. I get 'em once a year.'

In a further out-take, which can be seen on the special laser disc edition of the film, Ian brings the band the good news about the upcoming Seattle gig at a 6,000-seat venue. They stand around practising 'America', with the couplet:

> Jumbo jet begins to rise
> A grateful nation waves its bye-byes.

David renders 'grateful' as 'grapefruit'. David, Derek, Nigel and Viv are all sporting their herpes sores and explain to Ian that The Dose are not working out as their support band.

David: 'They're killing us. They're killing us, they really are.'

Ian: 'You mean they're outplaying you?'

Derek: 'If only they were.'

The four of them continue to fudge about how they don't mesh, how it's a mismatch, before Derek attempts to lend the argument some clarity: 'It's like Marxism, there's synthesis, and there's antithesis, and there's, no, I don't know, but I mean there's no the third one, whatever that was.'

Only a conspicuously sore-free Mick protests, but the band democracy sees The Dose kicked off the tour.

The first draft of the screenplay ends with shots of Ian and Jeanine backstage at the Japanese gig, with Jeanine, who may have enjoyed a dalliance with Ricky, Nigel's short-lived replacement, sporting a conspicuous sore on her lower lip.

DOUBLE-NECKED BASS

The monster that Derek plays was bought by Shearer from the music store B.C. Rich in LA. In the laser disc commentary, he recalls spotting it and saying: '"That I have to have. What's the point of it?" They said there really isn't one. I said: "That's perfect."'

DRESCHER, FRAN (1957—)

Born in Flushing, New York, Drescher plays Bobbi Flekman. Like the rest of the performers in the film, Drescher largely improvised her role. She made early appearances in two pivotal music films – *Saturday Night Fever* (1978) and *American Hot Wax* (1978). After *Spinal Tap*, she featured in Guest and McKean's Hollywood satire *The Big Picture* (1989), as well as *Cadillac Man* (1990) and *Jack* (1996). She was nominated as Best Comedy Actress two years running, in both the Emmys and the Golden Globe Awards, for her starring role in the TV sitcom *The Nanny*. In 1996 Drescher was chosen by *People* magazine as one of the fifty most beautiful women in the world.

DRUGS

Drugs are notable for their absence in the film. There is a brief shot of groupies snorting coke or amyl nitrate from a tiny container before the Cleveland gig; and before the 'Jazz Odyssey' gig, Viv sits backstage talking to Derek about the prospect of sampling some 'Mendocino Rocket Fuel'. Christopher Guest explains the lack of drugs on screen in the finished film: 'We had a big discussion about that, and one of the reasons you don't see it happening more is that they wouldn't have allowed that, they would have gone over to the cameras and said, "Go away now. We don't want to see you." It wouldn't have been realistic to show that.' Karen Murphy rather contradicts this idea in her commentary for the laser disc edition of the film, saying: 'Oh, there are so many scenes with drugs and alcohol and groupies in the movie. You would love to see that film.'

In the out-take where a very pissed off Tommy delivers pizza to the band and their groupies in their hotel room at three o'clock in the morning, Tommy is reluctantly encouraged by Nigel to stay and chat. Nigel shows him a Charles and Diana commemorative cookie box that is filled with drugs and drug paraphernalia. Nigel encourages Tommy to hold a joint, and then to smoke it. Tommy splutters, and then grins as his face is stroked by a groupie. This leads directly into the 'All the Way' sequence.

Similarly, in some of the extra material in the 'Troggs Tapes' sequence, Mick, sitting next to the exasperated Derek at the control desk, suggests that David and Nigel's big problem is that they need another joint. In the screenplay, we learn that the tour bus that takes the band around the Midwest has a locked entertainment area containing supplies of drugs, alcohol, helium and nitrous oxide.

In the band profile featured in the April 1992 edition of Q magazine, St Hubbins recalled that he had stuck to natural drugs: psychedelics and mushrooms. Nigel commented: 'I was even more organic. I used to take Bovril. Steam it in a basin and put my head over the basin and waft it, waft it. You'd feel really dizzy and dancey after a while. It's an aphrodisiac and it's legal.'

Speaking of cutting down on his narcotic consumption, Nigel has said: 'My drug days are over, and I've found a new way of approaching my craft without the use of drugs.' Asked what it is, he replies: 'Well, it's drinking, mostly . . . But even that is not really done to a large extent any more. I'm just too fucking old, really. I mean, I have a drink at night, a drink in the morning, and that's it.'

See 'All the Way'.

DRUMMERS

Rock'n'roll keeps ya young – but you die young.   – David St Hubbins

The history of rock and roll is littered with stars who died premature, unnatural, and sometimes bizarre deaths. The story of Spinal Tap reflects the dangerous profession of rock drumming, although, as the cases of Brian Jones, Jim Morrison, Jimi Hendrix, Janis Joplin, John Lennon, Tim Hardin, Tim Buckley, Lowell George, Marc Bolan, Ronnie Van Zant, Elvis Presley, Paul Kossoff, Keith Relf, Steve Marriott, Otis Redding, Eddie Cochran, Duane Allman, Richie Valens, the Big Bopper, and Buddy Holly prove, one way or another it is more dangerous being a guitarist and/or vocalist.

The reputation of rock drummers dying young stems largely from three infamous cases. Keith Moon of The Who was one of rock's most notorious hell-raisers. He was fond of dressing as a Nazi, and boasted of having disposed of countless cars and trashed innumerable hotel rooms, resulting in a lifelong, worldwide ban from Holiday Inns. Moon was also a prodigious drinker, and at various times broke his spine, both ankles, both wrists and his collarbone. He was once advised by a thoughtless accountant that, as he was liable for a large tax bill, it would be in Moon's interests to spend some of his money so that he could claim it as expenses against the tax that he owed. Inevitably, within six weeks, Moon had spent all his money. Oddly, he died of an overdose of Hemineverin, a medication he was taking to alleviate the symptoms of alcohol withdrawal.

In 1974, drummer Robbie McIntosh and bass guitarist/vocalist Alan Gorrie, both of the Average White Band, were at a party hosted by entrepreneur Stuart Moss. Moss produced a quantity of white powder, some of which McIntosh and Gorrie proceeded to snort, believing it to be cocaine. It turned out to be heroin laced with strychnine. Gorrie survived – allegedly having been nursed back to health by Cher – while McIntosh was taken back to his hotel room, where he died a few hours later.

The true inspiration for Eric 'Stumpy Joe' Childs is John Bonham, the wild-man drummer of Led Zeppelin who died by choking on his own vomit in September 1980.

The Tap have gone through six drummers: John 'Stumpy' Pepys, Eric 'Stumpy Joe' Childs, Peter 'James' Bond, Mick Shrimpton, Joe 'Mama' Besser and Richard 'Ric' Shrimpton. Interviewed in *The Nose* prior to the band's comeback tour, Smalls was asked: 'You guys have been auditioning lots of drummers. That's been a big problem, hasn't it?' He answered: 'The auditioning, no. The dying, yes.' For this tour the band held open auditions for the dangerous role of drummer. These were attended by a number of celebrity drummers, including Mickey Dolenz of The Monkees, Debbie Peterson of The Bangles, Stephen Perkins of Jane's Addiction, Gina Schock of The Go-Gos, Rat Scabies of The Damned, and Fleetwood Mac's Mick Fleetwood, who took the precaution of attending in an asbestos suit.

See vomit.

DUNCAN, SANDY (1946—)

American comedy actress. Marty DiBergi has attested to his dedication to the cause of the band by mentioning that, as well as the two enticing film projects, he turned down the opportunity to do a series of Wheat Thins adverts starring Sandy Duncan in order to make the movie.

DUTCHMEN, THE

See name changes.

DWARFS

Smalls and St Hubbins answered questions in a *Hollywood Online* interview in 1996. Smalls was asked about critical hostility to their recent IBM ad. He responded: 'We've never been a critics band, especially now we're making money. They're jealous, they're evil. Most of them are dwarfs.'

Asked by the host of the interview if the band still kept in touch with the 'Stonehenge' dwarfs, Derek said: 'Well, they are a bit hard to find, especially in the dark.'

See 'Stonehenge'.

E

EDITING
The editing process for *This Is Spinal Tap* took nine months. The chief problem, beyond paring down the vast quantity of material, was matching scenes up when, because the film was improvised, the relative positions of the actors altered from take to take. The solution was to ignore this issue, as can be seen markedly in the scenes in which the band meet Duke Fame, and later when Ian shows *Smell the Glove* to the band and the newly arrived Jeanine. The swift camera movements and quick inter-cutting disguise the fact that the characters are constantly shifting their relative positions.

ELECTRIC BANANA, THE
The now defunct venue in Greenwich Village where Marty DiBergi first saw Spinal Tap.

ELEVEN
In one of the great sequences of modern film comedy, Nigel, having shown Marty his beloved guitar collection, introduces him to his Marshall amp: 'This is a top to what we use on stage, but it's very, very special because, if you can see, the numbers all go to eleven. Look, right across the board: eleven, eleven, eleven.'

Marty: 'And most amps go up to ten.'

Nigel: 'Exactly.'

Marty: 'Does that mean it's louder? Is it any louder?'

Nigel: 'Well, it's one louder, isn't it? It's not ten. You see, most blokes will be playing at ten, you're on ten here [*indicating the amp*], all the way up, all the way up, all the way up. You're on ten on your guitar. Where can you go from there? Where?'

Marty: 'I don't know.'

Nigel: 'Nowhere. Exactly. What we do is, if we need that extra push over the cliff, you know what we do?'

Marty: 'Put it up to eleven.'

Nigel: 'Eleven. Exactly. One louder.'

Marty: 'Why don't you just make ten louder and make ten the top number and make that a little louder?'

Nigel [*after a pause*]: 'These go to eleven.'

Motörhead share with Spinal Tap an ineffectual umlaut and the claim to be one of Britain's loudest groups. Lead singer and bassist Lemmy was previously a member of Hawkwind, whose claim to fame beyond their big hit 'Silver Machine' was their proud boast to be Britain's number one loudest band. In Channel 4's 1999 film *Heavy Metal's Top 10*, Lemmy said of Motörhead: 'I would say we're probably the fastest band in the world.' Former lead guitarist Fast Eddie Clarke recalls: 'By the time we got over the top of Lemmy's volume he would always have one notch to go.'

This exchange between Nigel and Marty has become imprinted on the consciousness of every rock star around the world. It has become a shorthand for the obsessive quest among rock bands for that all-important quality of loudness. It has become so embedded in the mythology of rock that the number eleven now has a separate and instantly accessible meaning. On the cover of Martin Huxley's book *AC/DC – The World's Heaviest Rock*, there is a design with the band's trademark thunderbolt cutting through an amp's dial with the knob turned conspicuously to eleven. In BBC TV's *Rock Family Trees: The Prog Rock Years*, keyboardist Keith Emerson talked of where he wanted to go next having split up The Nice, when he was about to form Emerson, Lake and Palmer: 'I loved the trio format. I was happy with that. I didn't want to work with another guitar, because they always cranked their amplifiers to eleven and you couldn't be heard.'

This Is Spinal Tap's supervising editor, Robert Leighton, has recalled: 'One of the oddest things – these switches that go to eleven. The room I cut it in has an air conditioner in it that goes to eleven, and we cut Rob's next eight films in the same room, and we didn't find out until I think somewhere in *Stand by Me* that it went to eleven. It's the only other machine that goes to eleven.' Robert Bauer, head of merchandising on the film, printed T-shirts with the slogan 'Goes to 11'. Karen Murphy recalls: 'Nobody got it. It took like five years for anybody to understand what the T-shirt meant. Now it's a collector's item.'

See Marshall amp; Van Halen.

ETHEREAL FAN

At the beginning of the film, in one of only two scenes (the other being the footage of 'Gimme Some Money') to make it through unchanged from *Spinal Tap – The Final Tour*, a spacy fan says to the camera: 'It's like, you become one with the guys in the band. I mean, there's no division. The music just unites people with the players.' These lines were improvised by the actress Jean Cromie, who was the wife of Timothy B. Schmit of The Eagles and a sometime Tap backing singer.

ETON-HOGG, SIR DENIS
President of Polymer Records played by Patrick MacNee. Sir Denis was knighted for establishing the institution Hogwood, and in an out-take from the film Bobbi Flekman comments waspishly: 'They knight everything over there. I dunno, he founded some sort of summer camp for pale young boys. They call it Hogwood.'

ETON-HOGG, LAUREN
In another playful credit on *The Return of Spinal Tap*, Lauren Eton-Hogg is credited as director of concert footage.

F

FAITH, IAN

*I am the fifth member of Spinal Tap, after all. Their Pete Best, Brian Epstein,
George Martin and Murray the K all wrapped up in one.* — Ian Faith

His description in the film's original treatment reads: 'the band's manager,
who is trying to sign new acts to keep his career afloat while simultaneously
trying to convince Tap that he is still a kick-ass manager operating in their
best interests.'

Faith — his name presumably an unconscious reference to Adam Faith,
the pop star turned manager who played a rock-promoter in *Foxes* (1979)
— is the band's dishonest, sexist and probably anti-Semitic manager. With
his almost genteel accent combined with an apparent relish for violence
and a fondness for dodgy dealings, he is an amalgam of all the colourful
rock managers of the 1960s and 1970s: Led Zeppelin's awesome and violent
300lb former wrestler Peter Grant, Andrew Loog Oldham (The Rolling
Stones), Kit Lambert (The Who) and Brian Epstein. In an out-take Faith
is seen threatening Marty with pulling the plug on the film unless the band
receive a contract for their co-operation.

In the continuing story of Spinal Tap, Ian Faith was reported dead
around 12 November 1990, having indulged in a three-week-long binge
at the Chelsea Hotel in New York which culminated in a seemingly fatal
overdose from a cocktail of drugs. Smalls, St Hubbins and Tufnel were seen
dancing on his grave at his funeral. In case there was any doubt of the band's
reaction to the news of the passing of their erstwhile manager, Nigel Tufnel
has been recorded as saying of the funeral: 'It was really one of the happiest
occasions I can remember in the last half-century.' Yet, in a bizarre parallel
story to the reported sightings of the late Viv Savage, in July/August 1992,
Spy magazine (then edited by Tony Hendra) featured an interview with the
departed manager. He became deeply unpopular with the band because of
what were described as certain 'indiscretions' on his part. He clarified: 'Let's
put it this way: They were collective indiscretions that I had individually

undertaken. I mean, I had individually undertaken the indiscretions, and in some cases committed outright fraud as a representative of the band . . . I actually committed a crime in order to draw attention away from the potentially damaging indiscretions that had been committed by the band collectively, without their knowledge, by me.'

Faith recalls his distress at the reaction of his former charges at his funeral: 'I thought they were just stamping down the dirt. But later, of course, it was reported that they were actually dancing. Dancing, whooping, high-fiving, the works . . . Certainly what I did not expect was the vituperation. I remember, as the first shovelful of dirt hit the coffin, Tufnel yelling, "Bye, Ian. Come back as something I can eat."' Tufnel had had the most problems with the manager, at one stage going so far as to attempt to poison him by placing highly visible blue crystalline rat poison on Faith's salad.

Faith's future plans include a proposed outfit called the Managing Wilburys, a management co-operative that would make touring a thing of the past by travelling around giving career advice to bands who would stay in the same place. He looks forward to collaborating in this enterprise with rock-promoter Bill Graham, and remains unconcerned by the persistent rumour that Graham is in fact dead.

FAME, DUKE
Leader of the band Duke Fame and the Fame Throwers. The band meet him and his manager in the Memphis hotel. The Tap are the victims of their newly selective appeal, while Duke, with whom they once played, is about to play the city's Enormodome. Fame is, by consensus, a wanker. After Fame's departure, David confronts Ian with the complaint that there is essentially no difference between the cover the band wants for *Smell the Glove* and the cover for Fame's latest album – on which he is shown tied down and being taunted by naked and semi-naked women brandishing whips. Ian points out the difference: 'He's the victim.' The band recognise this shrewd twist and David makes his profound observation: 'It's such a fine line between stupid and clever.'

See Ladd, Terry.

FANS
David talking about the extremes of fandom in an interview with *Megahits*

magazine: 'I got a microscopic slide of someone's skin one time. Someone peeled it off some part of her body – I don't know, really – and they made a permanent slide, cemented a little glass pane over it, and mailed it to me. I went round to a chemist's and had a look at it. She had taken such meticulous care with it, I half expected to see in the microscope "Hello, David" or some sort of intricate message. But nothing of that kind really occurred.' In the same issue, Nigel talks of his strangest gift from a fan: 'I got a four-course Italian dinner under foil, and I couldn't quite figure if it was loaded with drugs or what they were doing, but it was just a bowl of spaghetti with meatballs, some steamed zucchini, and garlic bread. Under foil. It was hot, too.'

FAR-EASTERN MUSIC
In an out-take, Nigel sits in his guitar-room explaining to Marty his interest in and experimentation with Indonesian music. As he picks up the acoustic guitar, he offers helpfully: 'I'm writing in the style of an Indonesian folk tune, so this is not one you've heard. So if it sounds familiar, it's not.' He plays two notes.

See Western music.

FIDELITY HALL
Philadelphia venue where the band perform 'Big Bottom'.

FIRST CUT
The first was four and a half hours long without the three hours of interview material that would serve as glue for the finished film. This version of the film is reputedly available as a bootleg video.

FLAK PACKET
Obscure Tap album that was never released.

FLEKMAN, BOBBI
A&R (artists and repertoire) woman for Polymer Records played by Fran Drescher, who is assigned to the band for their comeback Smell the Glove tour. When asked about the inspiration for the character, Christopher Guest explained to me: 'The A&R woman on the road with us during the

Squigtones tour became Bobbi Flekman in *Spinal Tap*. Half way through the tour she disappeared. As in "I'm outta here" – disappeared. We went from flying first-class one day to renting a car ourselves the next and driving to the gigs.'

In the *NME* on 8 September 1984, Guest said of the character who inspired Flekman: 'This woman would show up . . . arriving in her own time with, like, snowballs of coke all over her face. And it was always, "Yer great, yer great, yer great!" then VOOMF! she's gone, we never see her again. Weighed about sixteen pounds, you know, kind of an anorexic addict.'

In the out-take where Nigel announces that his topless groupie friend has lost her contact lens, Flekman asks: 'Does she need her lens to find her clothes?' Then she says to the band: 'Please try and put your hormones in your hip pocket for a while.'

FLOWER PEOPLE PRESS CONFERENCE

In a scene cut from the release version, the band attend a press conference where they are called upon to explain flower power and discuss the Vietnam War, drugs and their own beliefs. They respond to the questions in the flip style patented by The Beatles in their early interviews. David, on how the band feels about its own success: 'It's a feeling within. It's less of a power. If power is compared to light, we are the shadow rather than the power of light.'

Journalist: 'How do you find the women in America?'

David: 'Turn left at the men.'

Journalist: 'What do you think of free love?'

Nigel: 'It's too expensive.'

FOGHAT

British boogie-blues band formed in 1970 by Dave Peverett (guitar/vocals), Tone Stevens (bass), Rod Price (guitar/vocals) and Roger Earl (drums) and who became successful in the US in the mid-1970s. McKean, Shearer and Guest continually insist that the events in the film are *not* based on specific bands or personalities, but acts continue to claim or protest that they are the models for the film. As Michael McKean explained in an interview in the *Guardian* on 15 November 1998: 'We were accused by someone from Foghat of planting a bug in their bus because they swore that we had ripped off the whole idea of the girlfriend taking over and using astrology to plan the tour.'

FRENCHIE'S

A New York restaurant at which Ian books the band a table in a laugh-free out-take.

'FUCK THE NAPKIN'

The punchline to the scene in which Polly Deutsch (Anjelica Huston) shows the Stonehenge model. Considered as a possible title for the finished film.

FUFKIN, ARTIE

> *Do me a favour. Just kick my ass, OK? Kick this ass for a man, that's all. Kick my ass. Enjoy! Come on! I'm not asking, I'm telling with this. Kick my ass!*
>
> – Artie Fufkin

Polymer Records, Midwest Promotion. In an out-take, Artie persuades the band to do a radio appearance at seven the following morning on the show of his old friend J.J. Barnum on W111.

David protests: 'I can't even talk at seven.'

Artie: 'They don't need to hear you talk. It's not so much talking, it's just rapping, really. You go up there, you rap to the people.'

David: 'I can't even open my mouth.'

The band make a compromise offer – to pre-record an appearance. Nigel explains that they go to sleep at 6.15 a.m. Artie gets increasingly desperate: 'But what do I got to do to get you to a radio station at seven in the morning? It's not such a big deal. Do I got to take my whole family and chain them to a radio station to get a record played? Do I have to [*takes an egg from the room-service tray*] take a thing with an egg [*smashes the soft-boiled egg against his forehead*] and smash the thing in my face to get a record played on the air today? You've got to know how important this is. This is important to a man.'

Derek: 'Well we see how important it is to you, Artie, but it's still too early.'

They reluctantly agree to attend the radio show and we see them explain to a fan on the phone why they no longer do 'Stonehenge' on stage. The next call is a rogue one in which the caller asks for clarification about baseball. Just as Barnum is about to get rid of the caller, Mick leaps in with a full and detailed answer to the caller's baseball query.

In *The Return of Spinal Tap*, we catch up with Fufkin in Sydney, Australia.

He talks of having been fired from Polymer: 'I don't know why they let me go. "Sexual harassment" is what they told me. There was no harassment. There was no sexual . . . There was a cute secretary there, Barbara. I was really just trying to give her some insight into what it takes to be in this business what we call "record promotion". It's a tough business.' Now a programmer for Video Magic, Fufkin admits that he wouldn't play 'Bitch School' because it's sexist.

In the *NME* on 8 September 1984, Harry Shearer spoke of how people in the record industry would identify with the spoof: 'A lot of people from record companies bug us now. They take you aside and say: "I'm not like Bobbi Flekman, am I?" If they're more stupid then they brag: "Well, Harry, if I say it myself, I'm the Artie Fufkin of this burgh," not realising it's sort of a damning indictment.'

G

GIMME SHELTER

1970 concert film of The Rolling Stones. *Gimme Shelter* is one of the declared influences on *This Is Spinal Tap*, although the influence is one of helping to shape the general authentic look rather than anything more direct. The film, artfully constructed by co-directors the Maysles brothers and Charlotte Zwerin, documents the activities of the band before, during and after the fateful events at the hastily rearranged free concert at California's Altamont Speedway. The film presents the activities as straight reportage of the urgent negotiations to ensure that the Altamont event took place; and then the performances at the festival and elsewhere of The Stones, Tina Turner, The Flying Burrito Brothers and Jefferson Airplane. We also see the members of the band sitting in an editing suite watching themselves and the actions of the film – most notably Mick Jagger watching and then rewinding the footage of the fatal stabbing of a gun-toting member of the Altamont audience at the hands of one of the Hell's Angels who were hired as security for the event. *Spinal Tap*'s cinematographer, Peter Smokler, served as a cameraman on *Gimme Shelter*.

'GIMME SOME MONEY'

Number featured in the original twenty-minute demo which replaced the proposed first draft of the screenplay. Like The Rutles' 'All You Need is Cash', their parodic version of The Beatles' 'All You Need is Love', this is a rejoinder to The Beatles' 'Can't Buy Me Love'. The track features Ed Begley Jr as John 'Stumpy' Pepys on drums and Danny Kortchmar as Ronnie Pudding on bass. As in the later 'Cash On Delivery', the song subtly explores the crossover between sex and money. Choice lines:

> Don't get me wrong.
> Try getting me right.
> Your face is OK
> But your purse is too tight.

GLIMMER TWINS

The relationship between Nigel and David is like that of countless lead duos of rock bands, but there is a clear similarity to the Jagger/Richard partnership. This is especially strong in the photograph album shots of the two from their childhood in Squatney. These pictures consciously bring to mind the famous shots of the Glimmer twins as childhood friends.

GOLDFINKEL, WENDY

Ian Faith's replacement as Spinal Tap's manager. In Q magazine in April 1992, St Hubbins said of her: 'She used to run our fan-club way back when she was a pudgy Jewish girl.'

Tufnel added: 'Now she's a pudgy Catholic girl.'

GOODBYE POP

The name of the 1975 *National Lampoon* record on which Tufnel, although not named in the credits, made his first appearance.

GOSPEL ACCORDING TO SPINAL TAP, THE

> *This pretentious, ponderous collection of religious rock songs is enough to prompt the question: 'What day did the Lord create Spinal Tap, and couldn't he have rested that day too?'*   – review of *The Gospel According to Spinal Tap*

Tap's 1977 album, released on Megaphone, which was also released under the alternative title *Rock 'n' Roll Creation*. Includes 'Rock and Roll Creation', and 'Young, Gifted and Smug'.

GOT THAMESMEN ON TAP

A little like some of the illicit early live Beatles rarities, this is a bootleg LP of the pre-Tap Thamesmen which is said to have been recorded in an underground club in Rotterdam.

GRACELAND

The sequence was filmed in a park in Altadena. In an out-take we see Tufnel, St Hubbins and Smalls approach the 'King's kingdom'. As they arrive the doors are locked, and the band call out for Mrs Presley before it is pointed out that she doesn't live here any more. In another brief out-take, David is confused by a floral arrangement in the shape of a dog. Nigel spots that it is a hound dog and David is relieved: 'I thought it was an extremely irreverent gesture but now that you've pointed it out, it's very apt.' He wonders: 'Why don't they make gravestones cheerier?' Again, Nigel is there to put him wise: 'I dunno, it's probably because of the whole death thing involved in it.'

See 'Heartbreak Hotel'.

GROUPIES

David said in the 1984 *Metalhead* profile: 'I was surprised at the lack of sex in the film, myself. Because I know that Nigel – Nige has a good time on the road. I, myself, being more like a one-woman man – oh, I enjoy the flirtations and the tease and all that, but when the show's over I'm on to the shower and into the sheets. Alone. But Nige, he's a high roller, he's a basher, and I'm amazed that he didn't get more of that into the film. But I guess even he has some decency. I know that I've never seen him actually perform sexual acts in front of a full camera crew. It's usually only ten or twelve of us in a hotel room.'

Nigel on the science of procuring groupies, describes a common practice in the real world of rock: 'We've got a spotter, y'know . . . It's a bloke who works for us. He stands on stage – by the amplifiers, where you can't see 'im – and he cases the house to see if there are any cute birds. And if there are, he gives 'em a backstage pass and they come and see me, don' 'ey? Call 'im a spotter. I mean, I don't have time while I'm playing to do that work myself, obviously.'

In an out-take, Derek and Nigel interrupt their bitching about Jeanine when David approaches them in a hotel lobby. Nigel and Derek chat up two women at the bar and invite them to their small party upstairs. Nigel has outlined his feelings about women on the road: 'I find that having a lot of women really keeps your bloodstream going. I go after quantity . . . They've got to be under twenty-two, that's my only rule; and not in a hospital bed, that's my only rule.' Nigel's criteria for women were elaborated collectively by the group:

Ric: 'Anything between six and sixty in a skirt is more like it.'
David: 'His rule is anything that casts a shadow.'
Nigel: 'Anything that casts a shadow with tits . . .'
Derek: 'Anything not recently killed.'

GUEST, CHRISTOPHER (1948—)

*It's obviously inherently funnier to have someone who isn't doing something
very well. That is the basis of most comedy. If you're showing people where
it's smooth sailing, where is the joke? If you go back to any movie, even a
conventional movie, with any comedians, they're either not terribly intelligent
or they're not doing something well.*   – Christopher Guest

Born Christopher Haden-Guest on 5 February 1948 in New York City. Son
of Lord Peter Haden-Guest and Jean Hindes, a.k.a. Lady Jean Haden-Guest,
former vice-president of CBS. Guest was educated at the High School of
Music and Art, Bard College in Annadale-on-Hudson, and New York
University, where he befriended fellow student Michael McKean. It was
also at this time that he met Rob Reiner. He started out working in
theatre for several years, before joining *National Lampoon* in its early
days, and was part of a group that performed in the revue *The National
Lampoon Radio Hour*. As well as writing and performing in stage shows, he
took a starring role in the successful parodic musical revue show *Lemmings*.
He also appeared in their revue, *Radio Hour*. After a couple of minor
roles in major films, Guest shared an Emmy award for co-writing the
TV special *Lilly Tomlin* (along with Tomlin herself and *Saturday Night
Live* creator and producer Lorne Michaels). Other notable roles include
Harry Bailey in *It's a Wonderful Christmas*, a TV remake of the classic *It's
a Wonderful Life* (1946), and appearing alongside his brother Nicholas and
three other sets of brothers (Quaid, Keach, Carradine) in Walter Hill's *The
Long Riders* (1980).

   After *Spinal Tap*, Guest, like McKean a decade later, became a regular on
Saturday Night Live, during which time he also directed a number of short
films with co-star Billy Crystal.

   Guest's début as a feature director was the Hollywood satire *The Big
Picture*, co-starring and co-written by Michael McKean. After a made-for-
TV remake of the camp sci-fi classic *Attack of the 50 ft Woman*, Guest
returned to the mockumentary form with *Waiting for Guffman*. With the
tagline 'There's a good reason some talent remains undiscovered', this is
the story of a small town celebrating its 150th anniversary. As part of the
festivities, small-time director Corky St Claire (Guest) stages a show and
invites an eponymous Broadway critic along to see the result. The film,
yet to be released in the UK, co-stars Catherine O'Hara and Fred Willard

(a.k.a. Lt Hookstratten) and employs a similar improvisational approach to *This Is Spinal Tap*.

In 1984 Guest married the actress Jamie Lee Curtis at Rob Reiner's home. Reputedly, Lee Curtis was first attracted to Guest when she saw his picture in *Rolling Stone* magazine, and arranged a date with him through his agent. This meeting was given a slight twist for a fictional meeting between the actress and Nigel Tufnel and has been worked into the ever-evolving mythology of Spinal Tap. In 1996, after the death of his father, Guest was ennobled as the fifth Baron Haden-Guest of Saling. In the *Register of Lords' Interests*, Guest is declared only as: 'Film director'. He is the half-brother of journalist and *bon vivant* Anthony Haden-Guest, who is widely believed to be the model for Peter Fallow, the louche, hard-drinking English journalist in Tom Wolfe's *Bonfire of the Vanities*. Rob Reiner has described his friend Guest as the 'best improviser in the world'.

Credits

As actor in films:
The Hot Rock (1972) – policeman #3
Death Wish (1974) – patrolman Reilly
La Honte De La Jungle (1975) voice – short police operator
The Fortune (1975) – boy lover
It Happened One Christmas (1977) – Harry Bailey
Girlfriends (1978) – Eric
The Last Word (1979) – Roger
The Long Riders (1980) – Charlie Ford
Haywire (1980) – the TV director
Heartbeeps (1981) – Calvin
The Million Dollar Infield (1982) – Bucky Frische
A Piano for Mrs Cimono (1982) – Philip Ryan
This Is Spinal Tap (1984) – Nigel Tufnel
Little Shop of Horrors (1986) – the first customer
Beyond Therapy (1987) – Bob
The Princess Bride (1987) – Count Rugen
Sticky Fingers (1988) – Sam
A Few Good Men (1992) – Dr Stone
A Spinal Tap Reunion: The 25th Anniversary London Sell-Out a.k.a. *The Return of Spinal Tap* (1992) – Nigel Tufnel

Animaniacs (1993) voice – Umlatt of Dunlikus
Waiting for Guffman (1996) – Corky St Claire
Small Soldiers (1998) voice – Slamfist/Scratch It

As actor on TV:
Saturday Night Live with Howard Cosell (1975)
Blind Ambition (1979) – Jeb Stuart Magruder
St Elsewhere (1982)
Saturday Night Live (1984–5) – himself

As director:
The Big Picture (1989)
Morton & Hayes (1991, TV)
Attack of the 50 ft Woman (1993)
Waiting for Guffman (1996)
Almost Heroes (1998)
D.O.A. (1999)

As composer:
This Is Spinal Tap (1984)
Morton & Hayes (1991)
A Spinal Tap Reunion: The 25th Anniversary London Sell-Out a.k.a. *The Return of Spinal Tap* (1992)
Waiting for Guffman (1996)

As writer:
This Is Spinal Tap (1984)
The Big Picture (1989)
A Spinal Tap Reunion: The 25th Anniversary London Sell-Out a.k.a. *The Return of Spinal Tap* (1992)
Waiting for Guffman (1996)

As producer:
Morton & Hayes (1991, TV)

GUITAR SOLOS

> *My guitar solos are my trademark.*   – Nigel Tufnel

The band established themselves as a great live act with their concerts at the Electric Zoo, Wimpton, in the late sixties. The highlight of the show was the two-hour guitar solo from Tufnel and St Hubbins on 'Short 'n' Easy'. This couldn't fit on to their live album of the time, *Silent But Deadly* (1969), and the recorded version was whittled down to a more manageable eighteen minutes and thirty-seven seconds.

The solo we see in *This Is Spinal Tap* was recorded in about half an hour. The idea of playing the guitar with a violin was inspired by Jimmy Page, who used to play his guitar with a bow.

GUITARS

Would you like to meet them?
   – Nigel introducing Marty to his guitars in an alternative take

Rob Reiner has said of Guest: 'Chris is really into all these guitars.' Karen Murphy says of the 'guitar collection' sequence: 'This scene was probably a wet dream.' The items in Tufnel's cherished guitar-room are from Norm's Rare Guitars and Guest's own collection. In the commentary for the laser disc edition Guest can't resist gushing as he raises the guitar: 'This is a '58 Sunburst. These are worth about 60,000 bucks now.' McKean comments: 'This is exactly where Nigel and Chris intersect. This is the overlap point, right here.'

In an extended version of this scene which didn't make it to the final cut, Nigel introduces Marty to his guitars individually. He shows off one of his two 'Flying V's and shows how they would fly if they *were* to fly. Nigel reminds Marty not to touch, and later not to talk while he shows off the reverb on his Brazilian rosewood acoustic.

The band's guitar obsession has been expanded upon in interviews in character. St Hubbins and Tufnel have both appeared in *Guitar Stars*, a regular feature in *Hit-Stream* magazine. St Hubbins talked of his trademark Gibson SG guitar and then listed some others in his collection: a Les Paul Deluxe ('a gift from an American rock star, who for legal reasons I can't mention his name'), a Fender Telecaster, a Gibson J-160, and his first guitar, which was a JimElectro ('Not a DanElectro, which was a fairly famous name; I believe it's his brother or something'). Tufnel's first guitar, which he received when he was seven years old, was a Big Ben, 'actually a very little guitar'. His favourite is his 1955 Gibson gold-top Les Paul.

GUMBY

A sweet if redundant scene which didn't make it to the released version, and which reaffirms Nigel's infantilism. He sits on his hotel bed watching the children's stop-motion animation character Gumby on TV while playing with and talking to a toy of the same character.

H

HAHN, ARCHIE

Accomplished improvisational performer who plays the hotel porter in the Holiday Inn in Chicago. Much of his part ended on the cutting-room floor. In out-takes we learn that he was bringing the band cheeseburgers with fries, bacon with jello, asparagus flambé and stewed prunes with maple syrup.

HAMPTON-CROSS, GLYN

Producer of much of the band's output from their début, *Spinal Tap*, onwards. David has said of him: 'He was a very interesting bloke. He used to work as an office boy, or a sort of runner, at Megaphone, where we first released our, um, first releases. We got to know him around that time, and he was very smart – and big. And when you're big, people think of you as being *not* smart; they don't expect you to be really smarter than them. They treat you like, "Oh, here's a big bloke. I'll be sure not to hurt his feelings or anything or he might kill me." But it turned out that he was busy double-thinkin' them all the time; he was always one step ahead. There was a time there when it looked like he was gonna be head of Megaphone itself, but it didn't work out. He wound up just being head of A&R (artists and repertoire) and he did most of our production as The Thamesmen all the way through Spinal Tap, up until, I guess, the early seventies. I know he did the live album, the *Jap Habit* album, but I'm not really sure. I think he was there for some of *The Sun Never Sweats*, but we did part ways, mostly because he was more interested in a different kind of sound, I think. I think we were going for a more hard sound, like the twin guitar leads and things like that. What he wanted to do was build our audience, make it broader, so he was gonna start bringin' in, like, we were gonna do Broadway show tunes. I thought it was a bum idea, frankly. And it was a bit of a parting of the ways . . . and so that's it. Nice bloke.'

HARD ROCK CAFÉ

This album, subtitled *80s Heavy Metal*, was released on Rhino Records in 1998. Among its sixteen tracks is Spinal Tap's 'Big Bottom'.

'HAVE A GOOD TIME, ALL THE TIME'

See Savage, Viv.

HEAR 'N' AID

The Band Aid of the world of heavy rock. The project was launched by Jimmy Bain and Vivian Campbell of Dio. The resultant *Stars*, a star-studded album, was released in 1986 with contributions from the Tap and many other artists, including Blue Öyster Cult, Iron Maiden, Journey, Judas Priest, Mötley Crüe, Ted Nugent, Twisted Sister, and W.A.S.P.

'HEARTBREAK HOTEL'

The song sung a cappella by Tufnel, Smalls and St Hubbins when they visit Elvis's grave at Graceland. The number was chosen because it was the only Elvis song the production team could secure the performance rights to – Karen Murphy spoke directly to Mae Axton, the song's writer, who is the mother of singer/actor Hoyt Axton. The original plan was for the band to sing 'Love Me Tender'.

'HEAVY DUTY'

> *No light fantastic ever crosses my mind.*
> *That meditation stuff can make you go blind.*
> – the opening lines of 'Heavy Duty'

Not to be confused with the Judas Priest song of the same name from their 1984 album, *Defenders of the Faith*. When asked about the song and if he was contemplating taking legal action against the band, Derek replied: 'Now, if we could afford a solicitor, I'm sure we would.' The Spinal Tap song comes from their 1976 album, *Bent for the Rent*. It was the first song written by the band in real life, and was actually written for and first recorded by McKean's group Lenny and the Squigtones. The track features the extract from *Boccherini's Minuet* and some splendid Tap lines:

> Why waste good music on a brain . . .

> No page in history, baby – that, I don't need.
> I just want to make some eardrums bleed.

HEAVY METAL

The band have been accused in interviews of representing 'false metal' when compared to hardcore acts like Hellhammer, Anthrax, Metallica and Slayer. Nigel has responded angrily, saying that the Tap are 'true to the bone' – and besides, they have never considered themselves 'heavy metal', but rather 'light-to-medium metal'. David has said: 'If we're *false* metal, why do we get so rusty?'

HEAVY METAL MEMORIES

A trailer for the film in the form of an advert for a greatest hits album charting the band's progress from 1965 to 1983, from 'Gimme Some Money' to 'Hell Hole'. Tracks include 'Sex Farm', 'Silent But Deadly', 'The Incredible Flight of Icarus P. Anybody', 'Blood to Let', 'Brainhammer!', 'Bent for the Rent', 'Tonight I'm Gonna Rock You Tonight', 'Break like the Wind', 'Cups and Cakes', 'Rainy Day Sun', '(Listen to the) Flower People', 'Heavy Duty', 'The Sun Never Sweats', '(Again With the) Flower People', 'Nice 'n' Stinky', 'Stonehenge', 'Rock and Roll Creation', 'Gimme Some Money' and 'Big Bottom'.

'HELL HOLE'

Pretty standard heavy rock song of urban misery. Taken from the 1982 *Smell the Glove* album. Choice lines:

> I'm going back to where I started,
> I'm flashing back into my pan.

In *This Is Spinal Tap*, the stage performance features a guitar solo by Nigel during which he reclines backwards and has to be rescued by Moke. It was released as a genuine single accompanied by a genuine video. The video opens with a scantily dressed woman walking along a dirty city street and coming upon the band. Nigel Tufnel sings the verse as the band stand in a grungy flat and hold up dead rats to project the image of the hell hole in which they are trapped. St Hubbins sings the chorus and then we cut to Tufnel sitting at an elegant table in a luxurious room, flanked by a butler and a maid who look a bit like the couple in *American Gothic*. He languishes in his swimming pool with some groupies. To illustrate the lines 'The taxman's coming, the butler quit/This ain't no way to be a man' we see the butler quit and Tufnel being pursued by a dwarf taxman. The song was supposedly not allowed on *American Bandstand* because it contains the word 'hell'. The release failed to establish the Tap as a singles band in the real world.

HENDRA, TONY

Tony Hendra, who plays the band's manager, was founding editor of *National Lampoon* magazine, where he made a series of comedy albums and first collaborated with, Christopher Guest, and editor of *Spy* magazine in 1993–4, when the interview piece that announced Ian Faith's return from the dead came out. He has appeared in *Jumpin' Jack Flash* (1986), *Life with Mikey* (1993), *The Real Blonde* (1997) and *Suits* (1999). He wrote the screenplays for *The Big Bang* (1984) and *The Great White Hype* (1996).

In *Wired*, his biography of John Belushi, Bob Woodward writes of Cambridge-educated Hendra in the early 1970s, then editor of *National Lampoon* magazine, travelling to Chicago to see Belushi to assess whether or not to include him in his upcoming rock parody stage-show *Lemmings*. Belushi shamelessly used the Second City performance as an audition and afterwards invited Hendra, along with the show's cast, back to his place. Woodward writes: 'Hendra told John there were parts of the Second City performance he hadn't liked. In fact, he didn't particularly care for improvisational humour.' It is odd that someone who didn't like improv. should a decade later choose to appear in what is probably Hollywood's most celebrated improvised film. Then again, this may be an example of the Woodward research which led James Belushi to conclude that, having read *Wired*, he was beginning to think that maybe Nixon was innocent after all. Hendra ultimately gave Belushi the job and with it one of his big breaks.

See Faith, Ian.

HERE'S MORE TAP

One of the Tap albums that was recorded but never released.

HESSEMAN, HOWARD (1940—)

Born in Lebanon, Oregon, Hesseman was a member of the improvisational group The Committee. His acting credits include *Cisco Pike* (1972), *Steelyard Blues* (1973), *Shampoo* (1975) and *Silent Movie* (1976). Early experience as a DJ lent authenticity to his co-starring role in the sitcom *WKRP in Cincinnati*, and he enjoyed further success as Billy Connolly's forerunner as star of *Head of the Class.* Hesseman was brought into *Spinal Tap* as an emergency measure, to play Duke Fame's manager, Terry Ladd, at sixteen hours' notice when it became clear that the actor playing Fame looked fine but was too nervous to speak on camera.

See Ladd, Terry.

HIDDEN MESSAGES

In his June 1970 interview in *Rolling Stone*, Charles Manson was asked to explain the prophecies he had found in The Beatles' *White Album*: 'Charlie starts drawing some lines on the back of a sheet of white paper, three vertical lines and one horizontal line. In the bottom area he writes the word "SUB". "OK. Give me the names of four songs on the album." We [David Dalton and David Felton] chose "Piggies", "Helter Skelter" and "Blackbird", and he adds "Rocky Raccoon". Charlie writes down the titles at the top of each vertical section. Under "Helter Skelter" he draws a zigzag line, under "Blackbird" two strokes, somehow indicating bird sounds. Very strange. "This bottom part is the subconscious. At the end of each song, there is a little piece on it, a couple of notes. Or like in 'Piggies', there's 'oink, oink, oink'. Just these couple of sounds. And all these sounds are repeated in 'Revolution 9'. Like in 'Revolution 9' all these pieces are fitted together and they predict the violent overthrow of the white man. Like you'll hear 'oink, oink', and then right after that, machine-gun fire. [He sprays the room with imaginary slugs.] AK-AK-AK-AK-AK-AK!"'

Several rock groups have been accused of hiding cryptic messages in their music, generally by the technique of 'backward masking': having the words recorded and then played backwards in the background of the track. From 1966 onwards there was a persistent rumour that Paul McCartney was dead. If you looked hard enough clues were to be found everywhere – on the cover of Abbey Road and hidden within several of their later songs. In 'I Am the Walrus' there is a sample from a recording of *King Lear* which includes the line 'Bury my body'. In 'Revolution 9' John was believed to say, 'Turn me on, dead man,' and in 'I'm so Tired', 'Paul is dead, man, miss him, miss him'. Fans thought that towards the end of 'Strawberry Fields' they could hear Lennon cry, 'I buried Paul.' In fact, he was saying 'Cranberry sauce'. In *All You Need Is Cash*, Eric Idle, as the show's host, refers to this rumour. He says that it was believed that on The Rutles' 'I Am the Waitress' Nasty can be heard to sing 'I buried Stig'. He reveals that in fact Nasty sang '*I bures tegano*', which is very bad Spanish for 'Have you a water-buffalo?' The other Rutles' rumour is that 'Sergeant Rutter's Only Darts Club Band' spoken backwards sounds like 'Stig has been dead for ages, honestly'. Idle says that in fact it sounds like 'Dnab Bulc Strad Ylno Srettur Tnaegres'.

The allegations of 'backward masking' proved briefly very damaging to Judas Priest. They were accused of inciting two American teenagers to attempt suicide (one successfully) in 1985 through their cover version of Spooky Tooth's 'Better by You, Better than Me'. It was said that hidden in the song was the instruction 'Do it!' The group were finally acquitted in 1993. It has been suggested that Spinal Tap themselves indulged in some homespun backward masking but, not realising that their voices could be electronically reversed, went to the trouble of speaking the words backwards. At times St Hubbins has claimed to be unable to remember if and when the band had included backward masking on any of their tracks. But speaking to *Q*'s Adrian Deevoy about 'Rainy Day Sun' and the accusations of plagiarism, he said: 'We're not pointing the finger, but more disturbing was that we used a lot of backwards sounds and strange spoken word things in a sound collage – and lo and behold just two months later The Beatles do something similar.'

In the July/August 1984 edition of *Hit Stream*, St Hubbins was asked to clarify these rumours, and insisted: 'All our records are carefully screened in that regard. In "Christmas with the Devil" there is a message from the devil, but it's not backward masking – it's there, it's all there . . . It's very clear; it's very simple, as a matter of fact. You've gotta listen carefully, but it's not masked in any way.' The interviewer went on to ask what message the band would insert, if they could. St Hubbins said: 'I s'pose if there *were* any message I'd want, it would be "Turn the fuckin' thing around and play it the right way, schmuck!" It would be interestin' to put that in as a message – you play it backward and it says, "Hey, you're playin' the fuckin' record backward! What's the matter with you! Turn it around and do it right, or don't do it at all. Or trade it in for Huey Lewis and the News."'

See Judas Priest.

HIPPIES
Asked in his 1985 *Mega Hits* interview if he was ever a hippie, Derek

answered: 'Yeah, I guess I was, if you mean did I smoke enormous amounts of hashish and sleep with every girl who had hair longer than her shoulders.'

HOGWOOD
A summer camp for pale young boys, and the project for which Polymer Records boss, Sir Denis Eton-Hogg, was knighted. The band have dismissed this venture as a 'perverts' paradise'.

HOOKSTRATTEN, LIEUTENANT
Character played by Fred Willard. He shows the band around before the concert at Seattle air force base, and tells them how much he enjoys their music – by which he means the whole genre of rock and roll rather than their music in particular. He puts them at ease with a little banter: 'These haircuts wouldn't pass military muster, believe me. Although I shouldn't talk. My hair's getting a little shaggy, too. I better not get too close to you or they'll think I'm part of the band. I'm joking, of course.'

In *The Return of Spinal Tap*, Lt Hookstratten is interviewed from his office in Spokane, Washington. He explains that the incident with 'Sex Farm' haunted him for years afterwards and that any snafu was subsequently referred to as 'pulling a Spinal Tap'. When dummies were required for a test-flight, colleagues suggested that the members of Spinal Tap be used instead: 'They were joking, of course.' Hookstratten admits to having suffered a bout of depression and turning to religion when, having been put in charge of theatrical programming for the camp, he staged an ill-advised, all-white version of *Porgy and Bess*.

See *Return of Spinal Tap, The.*

HOPKINS, NICKY (1944–94)
Classically trained keyboardist who lent his distinctive sound to, among others, The Kinks, The Jeff Beck Group, The Rolling Stones, and Ry Cooder. Plays keyboards on *Break like the Wind*'s 'Rainy Day Sun'.

See 'Rainy Day Sun'.

HOT OIL
It was, in one of those stories of the birth of rock and roll legends, hot oil

that played a key role in the genesis of the band. On their first appearance on *The TV Show*, the oil designed to create smoke to give an appropriately rockular atmosphere to the climax of 'Rock 'n' Roll Nightmare' in fact just created droplets of hot oil which dripped on to the distressed band members. While the prop-man sorted out the problem, the band began to talk to one another in character. The birth of the true spirit of Tap.

HOT WAFFLES
One of the many names that featured in the Tap's mythical past.

HOTEL ROOMS
See cricket bat.

HUSTON, ANJELICA (1952—)
Talking of Anjelica Huston (who played the Stonehenge designer, Polly Deutsch) in the actors' commentary for the laser disc edition of *This Is Spinal Tap*, Christopher Guest says: 'She wasn't a known actress at the time.'

Harry Shearer: 'She was a known daughter.'

Michael McKean: '. . . and girlfriend.'

Daughter of director John Huston, and the long-time girlfriend of Jack Nicholson, Huston emerged from the shadows after *Spinal Tap*, starring in *Prizzi's Honor* (1985), *The Dead* (1987), *Crimes and Misdemeanours* (1989), *The Grifters* (1990) and *The Addams Family* (1991).

Huston had previous post-modern experience of interface with fake cinematic rock stars. In *Annie Hall*, having attended a performance of Annie (Diane Keaton) singing, Tony Lacey (Paul Simon) impresses her with an invitation to his hotel for a quiet drink with 'Jack and Anjelica'.

I

IBM
In 1996 Spinal Tap were approached by IBM to provide a promo campaign to coincide with the Atlanta Olympic Games. The band are shown on stage performing a song called 'Goat Boy' written specially for the advert. The members of the group chat to one another, barely audible above the volume of the track. Nigel says: 'You know, Derek, our third comeback tour could become a logistical nightmare. We've got nutritionists, au pairs, personal trainers . . .'

Derek chimes in: '. . . not to mention the erupting volcano apparatus.'

David: 'Let's bring in IBM. They help plan, manage and run the Olympics, and have been at it since the sixties.'

Derek and Nigel: 'So have we.'★

The band's new sponsors promised to set them up with a new world tour. As Derek Smalls reported it in the *Independent* on 1 June 1996: 'A closer look at the itinerary revealed that this was not to be our third world tour but a Third World tour. So it's your long haul – your Dakka, your Bangladesh. And, really, there's not a lot of logistics involved except "Where's the fucking electricity?" We're bringing loud music to people who don't have food, basically.'

'I'M JOKING, OF COURSE'
See Hookstratten, Lieutenant.

IMPROVISATION
In his commentary for the special laser disc edition of the film, Rob Reiner explains the approach that he, Shearer, McKean and Guest took to the

---

★ Michael McKean in character as David had previously been employed to advertise the American show *SportsCenter* on the ESPN sports network. This advert consisted of David discussing how he composed the station's ten-note audio signature.

improvisatory style of film-making: 'Basically we were, like what they do with documentary films, we were writing with the pieces of film. We were using the pieces of film as a tool to write . . . These are people that all are very proficient in improvisation, I mean, it comes very natural to them. It wasn't a big deal for us. It wasn't like, "Wow, you made this stuff up." I mean, that's what we did . . . Good improvisational actors sometimes have trouble with a script. They have a much more difficult time making pre-written dialogue come out real than they do with coming up with their own . . . It's like doing jazz.'

INCREDIBLE FLIGHT OF ICARUS P. ANYBODY, THE
See *We Are All Flower People*.

INTERVIEWS
The interview extracts quoted in this book, with the actors speaking either as themselves or in character, are genuine except for those from the following publications, which appear in Peter Occhiogrosso's spoof collection *Inside Spinal Tap*: *Teen-o-Rama*, *Mega Hits*, *Screem*, *Hit Stream* and *Metalhead*.

INTRAVENUS DE MILO
Album released in 1974. Marty DiBergi reads the band a review of the album: 'This tasteless cover is a good indication of the lack of musical invention within. The musical growth of this band cannot be charted. They are treading water in a sea of retarded sexuality and bad poetry.' Nigel comments: 'That's nit-pickin', isn't it?' The LP includes the tracks 'Tonight I'm Gonna Rock You Tonight' and 'Saliva of the Fittest'. It is said to be the only album to have achieved gold status in sales and then platinum status in returns.

IRON BUTTERFLY
One of the first heavy-rock bands, Iron Butterfly were formed in San Diego in 1966 by Doug Ingle (organ, vocals), Ron Bushy (drums), Eric Brann (guitar) and Lee Dorman (bass/vocals). It is fitting that there should be strong links between the Tap and Iron Butterfly, for whom the description 'heavy metal' is believed to have been coined. The band plotted a similar

course to the Tap, moving from psychedelia to heavy rock and pushing the envelope of the four-minute pop song to the epic form with their classic 'In-A-Gadda-Da-Vida' (the album of the same name is said to have sold twenty-five million copies). Spinal Tap played their first live gig at Gazzari's on Sunset Strip in a double bill with Iron Butterfly. The groups played two further concerts together, with the Butterfly re-forming for the occasion. Interviewed in the *NME* on 8 September 1984, Shearer notes: 'Yeah, they haven't learned their lesson. Re-formed, not *reformed*.'

ITINERARY
After the New York opening party and opening gig, the tour moves to:
Philadelphia – with The Dose as support band.
Washington, D.C.
Cleveland Ohio – the band get lost backstage.
North Carolina – The Dose kicked off the tour.
Record marketing convention in Atlanta, Georgia.
Memphis – gig cancelled, visit to Graceland.
Little Rock, Arkansas.
Milwaukee, Wisconsin – Jeanine arrives.
Austin, Texas – Ian leaves.
Denver, Colorado – band recording at Rainbow Trout Recording Studios.
Seattle – Nigel leaves at air force base gig.
San Francisco – amusement park Jazz Odyssey gig.
Los Angeles – tour ends.

IT'S A DUB WORLD
See *It's a Smalls World*.

IT'S A SMALLS WORLD
In 1976, during the lull after the disappointing sales of *Bent for the Rent*, the band decamped to Scotland to explore various solo projects. Smalls' album, *It's a Smalls World*, exists now only as an eight-track demo, under the title *It's a Dub World*.

J

JAMBOREEBOP
The fake American sixties pop show on which '(Listen to the) Flower People' is performed.

JAP HABIT
The Tap's second live album, after *Silent But Deadly, Jap Habit* was released in 1975 on Megaphone as a triple album – except in the US, where it was just a double album. Includes 'Nice 'n' Stinky', 'Devil Take the Hindmost' and the instrumental number 'Nocturnal Mission'.

'JAZZ ODYSSEY'

> Fifth, *released the following year (1972), offers too many 'pieces' that could well have been the inspiration for Spinal Tap's* Jazz Odyssey.
> — Tom Doyle reviewing Soft Machine's *Fifth* in Q

Smalls' free-form jazz composition that the band play in desperation at the San Francisco amusement park, in the absence of Tufnel. This is presumably a nod to Led Zeppelin's bassist and – like Smalls – musical thinker, John Paul Jones, who declared himself to have been inspired to pick up the bass by the examples of jazz greats Charles Mingus and Scott LaFaro. There are bass-playing jazz aficionados throughout the rock world, from Steely Dan's Walter Becker (sometime Tap sleeve-note writer) to Tap fan Sting.

Smalls was asked if any of his free-form music was available to the public. He answered: 'Yes, "Jazz Odyssey", like all sound waves, circulates endlessly in the ether. Your problem is finding the proper reception apparatus.'

Tufnel is dismissive of the musical form, saying: 'Jazz is just a series of mistakes without the "oops".'

JERDEN, DAVE
Produced 'Diva Fever', 'Cash On Delivery', 'Stinkin' Up the Great Outdoors' and 'Christmas with the Devil' on *Break like the Wind*. Jerden served

as engineer on Brian Eno and David Byrne's *My Life in the Bush of Ghosts* and has worked as a producer for many artists, including The Rolling Stones, Frank Zappa, Rod Stewart, Talking Heads, Jane's Addiction, Alice in Chains and The Red Hot Chilli Peppers.

JIM

The pet name given to the large skull which is a feature of the band's stage-set. Interviewed in 1984 and asked for his opinions about the wave of New Romantic bands, Derek dismissed them as all looking the same, unlike in heavy metal: 'A metal band or a hard rock band – there's always a distinctive cast to the image, y'know? You can always go, "Oh, yes, that's the one with the skull", or "That's the one with the angry skull", or "That's the one with the skull with the horns", or something like that.'

JUDAS PRIEST

One of the bands to which the Tap have consistently been likened. The group (whose name was taken from the Bob Dylan song 'The Ballad of Frankie Lee and Judas Priest') was formed in Birmingham in 1969 by K.K. Downing and Ian Hill. After various shifts of personnel, the band really took off with the recruitment in 1973 of vocalist Rob Halford. The group went against the grain of emphatically heterosexual heavy rock, with Halford being obviously and openly gay (though he did not come out until the nineties). The members of Spinal Tap have, when interviewed in character, vigorously defended themselves against accusations that they have borrowed elements of Judas Priest's style and presentation, and had the opportunity to return the accusation in the case of their song 'Heavy Duty'.

In one interview Derek was asked how he reacted to Rob Halford's explanation of the reason for the title of the Judas Priest album *Defenders of the Faith*, on which their song 'Heavy Duty' appeared. Halford had talked of the album as a statement of the band's insistence on adhering to the principles of heavy metal and defending them from all adversaries. Derek commented: 'Well, see, this is what I find deficient about them, is their insistence on over-coherence. It's like they've got to explain everything, you know? I mean, if you have to explain it, why do it? That's my, I wouldn't call it a philosophy, but my philately, I guess I would call it.' Reacting to Halford's label as 'heavy metal's intelligent defender', David said: 'Who? Rob Halford? Yeah, well, there you go. What's he doin' playin' heavy metal music, then?

He's slummin', that's what he's doin'.' Both the Tap and the Priest have been at the centre of storms of controversy over subliminal messages hidden within their songs, although this proved rather more grave for Halford and his band-mates.

As part of his research for *This Is Spinal Tap*, Rob Reiner went to see Judas Priest: 'It physically hurt my chest. The reverberation in the hall was so strong that it was, like, resonating in my chest and I couldn't stay there any longer.'

JUMBO PRAWNS
One of the names considered for the band.

'JUST BEGIN AGAIN'
The track from *Break like the Wind* on which Cher sings lead vocals with David. Choice lyrics:

> Life is just a wheel, if it's even real . . .
>
> Just begin again.
> Like bumblebees and hummingbirds.
> Life is just a dream, an unconscious stream,
> A picture worth five hundred words.

These lyrics are not markedly worse than those which have featured on several genuine Cher hits.

K

KAFFANETTI (KAFF), DAVID
Plays Viv Savage. His only other acting experience has come in the TV movie *The Leaving of Liverpool* (1992) and in the features *El Beso del Sueño* (1992) and *No Worries* (1993).

'KICK THIS ASS, FOR A MAN'
See Fufkin, Artie.

THE KIDS ARE ALRIGHT
A 1979 documentary directed by Jeff Stein about The Who, famed for being Britain's loudest, wildest and most destructive band. It was Pete Townshend who first indulged in on-stage guitar-smashing as practised by Nigel in disgust at the Seattle air force base gig. Keith Moon was the ultimate wild-man drummer of rock and roll, who patented the destruction of hotel rooms, imitated by bored rock stars ever since (although in an out-take from *This Is Spinal Tap* the band are too apathetic to smash up the room and Ian has to do it for them). Moon is also prominent in The Who's notorious appearance on the *Russell Harty* chat show featured in this documentary. The footage in *The Kids Are Alright* is gathered together from archive material of the band's fifteen-year history, and the film constitutes one of the key influences on the look and feel of *This Is Spinal Tap*.

See drummers.

KILT
In an out-take, Nigel reveals that even when wearing a kilt he wears spandex underneath.

KIRBY, BRUNO
The actor who plays Tommy Pischedda in the film and also the preceding promo reel. Kirby made his first major impact playing the young Clemenza

opposite Robert De Niro in *The Godfather – Part II* (1974). After appearing with Bill Murray in *Where the Buffalo Roam* (1980) and *This Is Spinal Tap*, Kirby found himself established as a reliable supporting player in mainstream Hollywood films, notably *Birdy* (1984), *Tin Men* (1987), *Good Morning Vietnam* (1987), *When Harry Met Sally* (1989), directed by Rob Reiner and co-starring Billy Crystal, and *Donny Brasco* (1997).

See 'All the Way'; Pischedda, Tommy.

KOBE HALL
The venue for the band's triumphant Japanese gig. The people in charge of recruiting extras had in fact got hold of Chinese, Filipino and other Asian Americans. The producers had to go to LA's Little Tokyo with money to pay Japanese Americans to appear in the scene.

KORTCHMAR, DANNY
Bassist who played Ronnie Pudding and performed on 'Gimme Some Money'. He served as overall producer on *Break like the Wind*. In 1967 Kortchmar, who had played with Peter and Gordon, formed the Flying Machine with his friend James Taylor, which resulted in one album, *James Taylor and the Flying Machine*, which was released in 1971. He has played with Linda Ronstadt, among others, and his production credits include his work for Bon Jovi.

KUNKEL, RUSS
The famed session drummer who appeared as the drummer in the band's first appearance on *The TV Show* and played Eric 'Stumpy' Joe in the band's *Jamboreebop* appearance, during which they performed '(Listen to the) Flower People'. Kunkel, married since 1989 to country singer Nicolette Larsen, has served as producer for Clannad and played with Emmylou Harris, B.B. King and Bob Seger.

L

LADD, TERRY
Duke Fame's manager, played by Howard Hesseman. The band and Ian Faith come across Ladd and Fame near the reception area of the hotel in Memphis. They speak for a couple of seconds before Ladd excuses himself and Fame with one of the film's best lines, improvised by Hesseman: 'Listen, we'd love to stay around and chat but we've got to sit down in the lobby and wait for the limo.'

LAMBSBLOOD
The Christian rock band with which Derek Smalls played before rejoining the Tap for their '92 comeback tour. Their songs include 'Job: What a Bloke'. While with the group, in a rash act of faith and solidarity, Smalls had a fish tattooed on his arm. When he rejoined Spinal Tap he realised the tattoo would be inappropriate in this context, so he had a friend superimpose a tattoo of the devil appearing to be eating the fish.

LAMÉ
The glam-rock band managed by David during the period between the Tap's collapse in Japan and their rebirth in the early nineties. The band had called themselves Diaperload until re-named by their new manager. Unfortunately, punters ignored the accent when pronouncing the band's name. They changed their name again, this time to Bumdummy.

LAST WALTZ, THE
Directed by Martin Scorsese, one of the inspirations for Martin DiBergi, this proto-rockumentary records the last performance by The Band, which Robbie Robertson describes as 'the beginning of the end of the beginning'. The concert features performances from a host of rock, pop and blues stars including Bob Dylan, Eric Clapton, Joni Mitchell, Van Morrison, Ringo Starr, Muddy Waters and Ron Wood. Scorsese had also served as editor on *Woodstock* (1971). Reiner has admitted that he is a big fan of the film. The interview technique of *This Is Spinal Tap* is lifted straight from *The Last*

Waltz, where Scorsese placed himself in front of the camera for some of his chats with the band, of which he was a declared fan. In the interviews the band explain that they got together having been assured that they would get 'more pussy than Frank Sinatra'. Among the film's *Tap*-like moments: the band members discuss the pleasures and pains of sixteen years on the road, and the tensions and joys created by mixing music and women; a very obviously and chronically goofed keyboardist, Richard Manuel, recalls the band's problems with settling on a name: 'It was right in the middle of the whole psychedelia, Chocolate Strawberries and Marshmallow Overcoat – those kind of names.' They were The Hawks and toyed with becoming The Crackers or The Honkies before eventually settling on The Band. In a very Derek-like observation, Robbie Robertson acknowledges what rock and roll had done for them: 'It took us everywhere. It took us to some strange places . . . physically, spiritually and psychotically.'

LEE, ALBERT (1943–)
English-born Lee is a noted country rock guitarist who has played with Chris Farlowe, Emmylou Harris, Eric Clapton and Jerry Lee Lewis. He has the honour of having taken part in two remarkable reunion concerts at London's Albert Hall: he played with the Everly Brothers in 1983 and with Spinal Tap in 1992, when he performed the guitar solo in 'Break like the Wind'.

LEIGHTON, ROBERT
Editor of *This Is Spinal Tap*, the film which marked the turning point of his career after a couple of minor early credits. His work since has been dominated by collaboration with Rob Reiner: he has served as editor on all his films. Other credits include *Bull Durham* (1988) and *Blaze* (1989).

LEMMINGS
Satirical rock stage show of 1973 produced by the *National Lampoon* stable of comics. Tony Hendra, then editor of the magazine, got the project together and produced the show. He chose the title having read a *New York Times* report of the Woodstock festival which likened the rush of hippie music fans to the fabled suicidal rush of the tiny rodents. (Similar imagery is used in *Gimme Shelter* [1970] to describe the fans converging on Altamont.)

Hendra had heard of John Belushi's famed Joe Cocker impersonation and recruited him, and Belushi not only did his show piece but also provided the stage announcements and the crowd's rain-chant. Other contributors included Chevy Chase and Christopher Guest, who co-wrote and arranged much of the music, played guitar and also supplied vocal impressions of Richie Havens, Bob Dylan and James Taylor.

It was during the show's run that Belushi first got a real taste for cocaine and Quaaludes, and Hendra, in learning how to cope with the fluctuating moods of temperamental, drugged-out, ersatz rock stars, did what turned out to be invaluable research for his role as Ian Faith. The *National Lampoon* scene, which also fed into *Saturday Night Live*, both directly and indirectly produced many of the notable comedy/rock/pop hybrids: *Lemmings*, *The Rutles: All You Need Is Cash* (1978), *The Blues Brothers* (1980), *This Is Spinal Tap*, *Wayne's World* (1992). Comedians want to be rock stars, and rock stars want to be film stars. The seriousness with which Dan Aykroyd has talked about the musical philosophy of the Blues Brothers Band, which has toured more extensively than Spinal Tap, betrays the ambition to be taken absolutely seriously as a musician. The blurring between parody and reality that Guest, McKean and Shearer have mentioned elsewhere is captured by Bob Woodward in *Wired* while discussing *Lemmings*: 'Hendra was aware that there was a fantasy growing among the cast that the show was more than parody, that in fact they had potential as musicians and were on the way to becoming a successful rock group – and that drugs were part of that fantasy.'

LENNY AND THE SQUIGTONES
Album released by Michael McKean and David Lander on which Christopher Guest made his first appearance under the name of Nigel Tufnel.

'LET HIM GO'
Although mentioned on neither the sleeve nor the record itself, this is the penultimate track on the Tap's 1992 album, *Break like the Wind*. This uncharacteristically sensitive mournful number with subtle hints of Bowie has Derek, David and Nigel taking turns on lead vocals in a call for compassionate euthanasia as the song tells its sad story of a chronically ill man lying in his hospital bed:

> The nurse hovered near
> And so did the Reaper
> But which had the number

To his private beeper?

Shall he lie there for ever
With a tube up his nose
And his pee-pee and poo-poo
Slipping out through a hose?

The song is punningly referred to as 'Now Leaving on Track 13'.

'LICK MY LOVE PUMP'

This scene was recorded at the Record Plant in LA. Nigel sits at the piano, gently playing a sweet melody.

Marty: 'It's very pretty.'

Nigel: 'You know, just simple lines intertwining, you know, very much like – I'm really influenced by Mozart and Bach, and it's sort of in between those, really. It's like a Mach piece, really. It's sort of . . .'

Marty: 'What do you call this?'

Nigel: 'Well, this piece is called "Lick My Love Pump".'

Tufnel intended the piece – which is recorded in D minor, the saddest of all the keys – to be just the first movement of a four- or five-hour classical work based on the theme of evolution. In his 1985 interview with *Hit Stream* magazine, Nigel spoke of his empathy with the great classical composers: 'Well, Beethoven was deaf, which is the direction *I'm* going in, so I can relate to *that*. Mozart, they just made a movie about him, and he was thirty-five when he died – and I'm older than that, so I feel lucky about that. And Bach, y'know, he just had all these children, so he must've been, y'know, dippin' the oil stick quite a bit. So I can really sort of relate to all of 'em, really.'

LINDBERGH AIR FORCE BASE

The Seattle venue where the band's performance of 'Sex Farm' was interrupted by radio signals. The incident prompted Nigel's furious departure.

'(LISTEN TO THE) FLOWER PEOPLE'

The single taken from the 1967 'summer of love' album *Spinal Tap Sings '(Listen to the) Flower People' and Other Favorites*. Choice lyrics:

Flower people walk on by
Flower people don't you cry . . .

Final Beach Boys-style harmony moves into dissonance before fading out. The band's appearance on *Jamboreebop* singing this song was the first sequence of film to be shot. Harry Shearer recalls: 'Shot it on tape and transformed it to film to give it that horribly over-saturated but under-focused look.' Russ Kunkel, famous studio session performer, appears on drums.

David St Hubbins has recalled of the time: 'Yes, that "Flower People" bit was real, we certainly did go through a psychedelic period. At least, I guess we did – it's all a bit unclear to me now . . . You'll have to understand that when I picture the year 1967 in my head, the "7" is sort of smeared and it just winds up . . . I kind of come out of the smear at '71. So it's, like, a bit of a blur to me.'

LIVE AT BUDOKKAN
The second live Japanese set, this was also the name of a bootleg album released on Japtap in 1975.

LIVE SCENES
All the scenes of the band performing live were recorded over a five-day period. The production had use of 600 extras for one day only, during which three numbers were recorded. For the remainder they had to make do with around forty to sixty people.

LOST BACKSTAGE
In an out-take from the sequence in which the band are lost backstage at the Cleveland gig, we see Nigel reason: 'Logically, we should say, "Have we tried all the ways possible to get where we're going?"'

Derek says: 'Yes, yes, we have.'

Nigel: 'So, we should be there.'

Derek: 'We're there now.'

Nigel: 'Logically, we're playing.'

Derek: 'Logically, we're on stage now. So fuck logic, let's go.'

Nigel encourages everyone to fan out, while he plans to stay there constantly shouting 'Hello'.

LOVELY LADS, THE
The first band in which Nigel played. While David's first musical experience was in a skiffle group, Nigel recalls The Lovely Lads as a 'scuffle' band: 'Well,

skiffle was so snotty, y'know, so we called it scuffle. And once in a while, we'd bash a few heads.'

LUKATHER, STEVE
Lead guitarist with US soft-rock band Toto, famous for late seventies–early eighties hits 'Hold the Line', 'Africa' and 'Rosanna'. Lukather played on *Break like the Wind*'s title song, and also served as producer on that track as well as 'Just Begin Again', 'Springtime' and 'Clam Caravan', on the last of which he played piano. Lukather has been a trouper as a session guitarist and producer, collaborating with Cher, Steve Stevens (Billy Idol's sometime axeman) and Eddie Van Halen, among many others.

LUKEWARM WATER
Derek talks to Marty of the group's delicate balance: 'We're very lucky in the sense that we've got two visionaries in the band. You know, David and Nigel are both like, like poets, you know – like Shelley or Byron and people like that. They're two totally distinct types of visionaries. It's like fire and ice, basically, you see, and I feel my role in the band is to be kind of in the middle of that – kind of like lukewarm water, in a sense.'

LUMBAR PUNCTURE
Pedants have pointed out that a bunch of English musicians would not call themselves Spinal Tap as this is the American name for the medical procedure known in Britain as lumbar puncture. In this procedure, carried out in order either to extract fluid for diagnosis or to inject drugs directly into the cerebro-spinal fluid, a needle is inserted into the spine in the lumbar region, through the ligaments, between the bones, through the dura mater and into the spinal canal.

LUSTY LORRY
One of the three lost Spinal Tap albums.

LOVE BISQUITS, THE
The name the band briefly assumed after The Hot Biscuits and before finally settling on Spinal Tap.

M

MACH

See 'Lick My Love Pump'.

MacLOCHNESS, ROSS

Keyboard player, formerly with Kilt Kids, who replaced Denny Upham for the Tap concept album *The Sun Never Sweats*. MacLochness was in turn replaced by Viv Savage. He recorded one solo album, *Doesn't Anyone Here Speak English?*, and then left to become a missionary in Namibia.

MacNEE, PATRICK (1922—)

Actor born in London, who plays Polymer Records' boss Sir Denis Eton-Hogg. MacNee declared himself uncomfortable with the film's improvised approach and requested that his very brief contributions be scripted. MacNee served in the navy in World War II, made his film début in *The Life and Death of Colonel Blimp* (1943), and appeared in Olivier's *Hamlet* (1948). He found fame as Steed in the 1960s cult TV series *The Avengers* and its 1970s successor, *The New Avengers*. His later films include *The Howling* (1981) and *A View to a Kill* (1985).

'MAJESTY OF ROCK, THE'

Song from *Break like the Wind* which the band used to open their comeback shows and performed at the Freddie Mercury memorial concert. Superior, celebratory pomp-rock with profoundly meaningless lyrics:

> And it feels so real you can feel the feeling! . . .
>
> We're in this together, and ever . . .
>
> And I'm sure each of you quite agrees:
> The more it stays the same, the less it changes!

St Hubbins was asked in *The Nose* about the lyrical significance of the lines:

> And that's The Majesty of Rock!
> The Mystery of Roll!
> The darning of the sock,
> The scoring of the goal!
> The farmer takes a wife,
> The barber takes a pole . . .

He explains: 'We were scraping for one more rhyme for "roll". It's always the last thing. I mean, really, it's the last thing we could come up with. We'd already used "hole".'

MANAGING WILBURYS, THE

See Faith, Ian.

MARBLE ARCH

The production company owned by Lew Grade which gave Reiner, Guest, McKean and Shearer $60,000 to write a script. Instead they used the money and their own personal finances to make the twenty-minute demo reel, *Spinal Tap – The Final Tour*. Marble Arch eventually passed on the project, which was produced by the now-defunct production company Embassy Pictures.

MARSHALL AMP

Christopher Guest speaks in his commentary for the special laser disc edition of the film of how he has worked with the hi-fi company since the time of the film's production: 'Marshall made a special plate for me that went up to eleven. Subsequently they have done some ads with me, and now the new amp that they made for me actually goes up to infinity on the dial. They made a real amp that goes up to twenty. That's the one that people can buy in the stores now for real. But mine goes up to infinity. This has been ripped off just big time. Almost every amp company now sells nobs that go up to eleven.'

Tufnel has become so closely associated with the Marshall brand name that when Jim Marshall, the creator of the company, was inducted into

Hollywood's Rock Walk hall of fame, he was accompanied on his auspicious day by Christopher Guest in the guise of Tap's axeman.

McKEAN, MICHAEL

Actor playing David St Hubbins. McKean was born on 17 October 1947. The second of three children, he grew up in Manhattan before attending the Carnegie Mellon Institute and then New York University, where he befriended fellow student Christopher Guest. The two started writing songs together in 1967. McKean moved to Los Angeles in 1970, where he formed the comedy ensemble 'The Credibility Gap' with Harry Shearer, David L. Lander and Richard Beebe. McKean, Shearer and Lander were hired as writers for the new sitcom *Laverne & Shirley*, which co-starred Penny Marshall who was then married to Rob Reiner. McKean and Lander had evolved two characters, 'Lenny' and 'Ant'ny', who were worked into the show as Lenny and Squiggy. The two were originally scheduled to make occasional appearances but soon became popular favourites, and were regulars on the show for seven years. McKean built a spoof music act around the character of Lenny, and this band, Lenny and the Squigtones, was the first to perform what became a Tap favourite, 'Heavy Duty'.

Having appeared a couple of times as a guest on *Saturday Night Live*, McKean joined the regular cast in 1984, at a time when the show was in decline. Among his other TV appearances was his role as Gibe in the cult adult sitcom *Dream On*, for which he occasionally wrote and directed. He also co-wrote with Guest *The Big Picture* (1989), a loosely Tap-like satire on the film biz in which the ubiquitous Kevin Bacon is the film-graduate-Candide who is seduced and corrupted by Hollywood. It features several decent cameos from the likes of John Cleese, Roddy McDowall, Jennifer Jason Leigh and Martin Short.

Besides his moment of glory as St Hubbins, McKean has made a name for himself, like Shearer, as a voice artist, and in supporting – often faintly sinister – corporate/nerdy roles.

Selected credits

As actor in film:
Cracking Up (1977)
More Than Friends (1979)

1941 (1979) – Willy
Used Cars (1980) – Eddie Winslow
Young Doctors in Love (1982) – Dr Simon August
This Is Spinal Tap (1984) – David St Hubbins
Clue (1985) – Mr Green
D.A.R.Y.L. (1985) – Andy Richardson
Classified Love (1986)
Jumpin' Jack Flash (1986) – British party guest
Double Agent (1987) – Warren Starbinder
Light of Day (1987) – Bu Montgomery
Planes, Trains & Automobiles (1987) – state trooper
A Father's Homecoming (1988) – Michael
Short Circuit 2 (1988) – Fred Ritter
Hider in the House (1989) – Phil Dreyer
Earth Girls are Easy (1989) – Woody
The Big Picture (1989) – Emmet Sumner
Flashback (1990) – Hal
Book of Love (1990) – adult Jack Twiller
True Identity (1991) – Harvey Cooper
Murder in High Places (1991) – Pettibone
A Spinal Tap Reunion: The 25th Anniversary London Sell-Out a.k.a. *The Return of Spinal Tap* (1992) – David St Hubbins
Memoirs of an Invisible Man (1992) – George Talbot
Man Trouble (1992) – Eddy Revere
Coneheads (1993) – Gorman Seedling
Across the Moon (1994) – Frank
Airheads (1994) – Milo
The Radioland Murders (1994) – Ric Rochester
MacShayne: Final Roll of the Dice (1994)
The Brady Bunch Movie (1995) – Mr Dittmeyer
Edie & Pen (1996) – Ric
The Pompatus of Love (1996) – sitcom star
Jack (1996) – Paulie
That Darn Cat (1997) – Peter Randall
Nothing to Lose (1997) – Phillip Barrow
Still Breathing (1998) – New Mark
With Friends Like These (1998) – Dr Maxwell Hersh

The Pass (1998) – Willie
Small Soldiers (1998) voice – Insaniac/Freakenstein
Killing Mrs Tingle (1998)
Final Justice (1998) – Merle
Archibald the Rainbow Painter (1998) – J.P.

As actor on TV:
Laverne & Shirley (1976) – Leonard Kosnowski
Grand (1990) – Tom Smithson
Dream On (1990) – Gibby Friske
Sessions (1991) – Dan Carver
Dinosaurs (1991) voice – Ansel/guy in lab
Animaniacs (1993) voice – various roles
Saturday Night Live (1994) – host
Lois and Clark (1994) – Dr Fabian Leek
Saturday Night Live (1994–5) – himself
Nanny (1995) – Ph.D. Noel Babcock
Friends (1995) – Mr Rastatter
Star Trek: Voyager (1996) – Fear the Clown/computer character
Caroline in the City (1996) – Father Damian
Space Ghost Coast to Coast (1997) – himself
The Weird Al Show (1997) – miner
Murphy Brown (1998) – Denis Page
LateLine (1998) – President of MFNSN
The Closer (1998)
The X Files (1998) – Morris Fletcher
Veronica's Closet (1998)

As composer:
This Is Spinal Tap (1984)
Morton & Hayes (1991)
A Spinal Tap Reunion: The 25th Anniversary London Sell-out a.k.a. *The Return of Spinal Tap* (1992)
Waiting for Guffman (1996)

As writer:
This Is Spinal Tap (1984)

The Big Picture (1989)
A Spinal Tap Reunion: The 25th Anniversary London Sell-Out a.k.a. *The Return of Spinal Tap* (1992)

As Director:
Laverne & Shirley (1982)
Rich Hall Show (1988)
Dream On (1990)
Morton & Hayes (1991)
Tracey Takes On (1996–97)

MEGAPHONE
The Parlophone-like label on which the band appeared before signing to Polymer. Releases for Megaphone include the triple live album *Jap Habit*. The relationship between band and label turned very nasty towards the end as David has recalled: 'They got an injunction against us ever setting foot on any professional stage or recording-studio floor. So if we could've found a way to hang from the ceiling and work, we would've done that.'

MELODY MAKER
In the music paper's 'Films of the Year' chart *This Is Spinal Tap* came a respectable fifth, with esteemed critic Brian Case noting: 'Far and away the funniest film of the year was *This Is Spinal Tap*. For pop music fans who dimly suspect that they're wasting their pocket money on musically incompetent, pea-brained greed-heads, this could be the clincher.'

MENDOCINO ROCKET FUEL
See drugs; Savage, Viv.

MERCURY, FREDDIE (1946–91)
At the Freddie Mercury Tribute Concert at Wembley Stadium on 20 April 1992, Spinal Tap appeared on the same bill as Guns 'n' Roses, Def Leppard, U2, Metallica, George Michael, Tony Iommi, Roger Daltrey, Ian Hunter, Mick Ronson, David Bowie, Annie Lennox, Elton John, Brian

May, Roger Taylor and John Deacon. The Tap performed 'The Majesty of Rock'.

METAL DETECTOR
See zucchini.

MILAGE
The group with which Smalls played immediately before joining the Tap. They recorded just one album, *Milage 1*. A 'pre-Traffic Traffic', they had, as Smalls has recalled, 'a flute player *and* a piccolo player, which was a bit much, I think, in the reed department'.

'MIME IS MONEY'
See Crystal, Billy.

MOBY DISK
The real record shop where the disastrous signing session takes place. The scene was based on an experience Shearer and McKean had when they were appearing in Tucson, Arizona with the Credibility Gap. Their sound and light requests were all ignored; Lou Denis of Warner Bros Records begged them to kick his ass. As Shearer recalls: 'He wouldn't give us the satisfaction of getting mad at him.' Shearer says that Denis now proudly boasts: 'I'm the "Kick my ass" guy.'

MOOSE
See arrested development.

MOZART, WOLFGANG AMADEUS (1756–91)
Prodigious composer of operas, orchestral symphonies, concertos, chamber music, piano sonatas and church music.

See 'Lick My Love Pump'.

MULLAHS OF INVENTION, THE
After his fake death, one of Ian Faith's schemes was to manufacture and manage an Iranian band of this name.

MURPHY, KAREN

*I mean, if I heard that idea myself today I wouldn't want to touch it with a
ten-foot pole.*   – Karen Murphy on *This Is Spinal Tap*

Producer Karen Murphy's post-*Spinal Tap* credits include co-producing *True
Stories* (1986) and producing *Drugstore Cowboy* (1989), *The Cutting Edge*
(1992), *Twenty Bucks* (1993), Christopher Guest's *Waiting for Guffman* (1996),
and *D.O.A.* (1999). She has said: 'The role of producer in *Spinal Tap* I've
always described to other people as the role of a rodeo queen . . . I felt that
my job as much as anything else was to make sure that I helped Rob and the
guys keep the focus on what the movie was supposed to be about, because a
lot of the scenes were so much fun it was really important we got what we
came to get.'

MUSIC MEMBRANE, THE

The London venue in which the band performed their first concert as
Spinal Tap, in December 1966, with the line-up Tufnel, St Hubbins,
Ronnie Pudding (bass), Joe 'Stumpy' Pepys (drums) and Denny Upham
(keyboards).

N

NAME CHANGES

In their early days playing together, Nigel and David and their band-mates appeared under various names: The Originals, The New Originals, The Thamesmen and The Dutchmen. In the eighteen months after the group's first taste of chart success as The Thamesmen, with 'Gimme Some Money', they made numerous further name changes: Chuckles, Rave Breakers, Hell Cats, Flamin' Demons, Shiners, Mondos, The Doppel Gang, The Peoples, Loose Lips, Waffles, Hot Waffles, The Mud Below, The Tufnel-St Hubbins Group and Silver Service. During a period of contractual problems in the mid-1970s they were forced to perform under a variety of different names, including Anthem and The Cadburys. Among the other names considered for the group was Jumbo Prawns, which, in an obscure in-joke, in fact features as one of the acts promised by Rob Reiner as Wolfman Jack in the band's first broadcast appearance on *The TV Show* in 1978.

NASH, GRAHAM (1942–)

Rock star, born in Manchester, who was a founder member of the Hollies before forming Crosby, Stills, Nash & Young in 1967. He appears in *The Return of Spinal Tap* as the man who goes into Jeanine's shop, The Drippery, complaining of trouble with his chakra ball.

NERVE DAMAGE

Album released on Megaphone in 1971.

NEW ORIGINALS, THE

See name changes; Originals, The.

'NICE 'N' STINKY'

Track from the Tap's live album *Jap Habit* that became a big US hit in 1977.

NIGEL TUFNEL'S 'CLAM CARAVAN'

See 'Clam Caravan'.

NILFORD-ON-NULL

The Midlands birthplace of Derek Smalls.

NONE MORE BLACK

See *Smell the Glove*.

O

OPENFACED MAKO
A Spinal Tap bootleg, released by Hammerhead records in 1980, consisting of out-takes from the *Shark Sandwich* sessions.

ORIGINALS, THE
The first band in which Nigel and David played together. They were forced to change their name because there was another band in the East End of London at the same time with the same name – so David and Nigel's The Originals became The New Originals. Then The Originals changed their name to The Regulars, so David considered changing his band back to The Originals, but decided: 'What's the point?'

OTIUM CUM DIGNITATUM
The Tufnel family motto, meaning 'Leisure with Dignity'.

OTTO SHOW, THE
The episode of *The Simpsons*, for which Shearer is a regular voice-artist, in which Bart goes to his first heavy metal concert when Spinal Tap play Springfield. Marge is heard saying optimistically: 'I hope the Spinal Tap don't play too loud.' We see that Bart is wearing a T-shirt bearing the words:

Spinal Tap
World Tour

London
Paris
Munich
Springfield

Another T-shirt on sale outside the concert venue shows the band kicking Gadaffi's ass. In a backstage interview with Bill and Marty of KBBL, the band are asked: 'Fellas, I'm going to hit you with a phrase that has dogged you throughout your career – washed-up? Here you are among the top 105 concert acts today. What's your secret, guys?'

The band responds with: 'We're very big in Bulgaria, and whatsisname, the other garia?'

During the concert, where the Tap perform 'Break like the Wind', their giant inflatable devil hovering over the stage develops a slow puncture ('We salute you, our half-inflated Dark Lord'). Then the concert descends into chaos after a laser-beam is directed into the band's eyes. On his *Two Cents* personal opinion show, Kent Brockman reports from the scene: 'Tonight, the city weeps as, for the first time ever, a hockey arena becomes the scene of violence. Of course, it would be wrong to suggest this sort of mayhem began with rock and roll. After all, there were riots at the première of Mozart's *The Magic Flute*. So, what's the answer? Ban all music? In this reporter's opinion, the answer, sadly, is "yes".' Inevitably, Bart is inspired to become a rock star.

The episode is not among the great cartoon series' finest, but has some moderately amusing Tap moments and, most importantly, points to the group's unique high-profile ironic status.

P

PARNELL, RIC (R.J.) (1951—)

Plays with drummers Mick Shrimpton and twin brother Ric. Born in London on 13 August 1951, Parnell is the eldest son of Jack Parnell, the famous British jazz drummer who played for many years with the Ted Heath Band. Ric's younger brother Marc is also a drummer, whose credits include playing with Joan Armatrading. Ric followed in the footsteps of Carl Palmer when he played alongside Chris Farlowe in Atomic Rooster in the early 1970s. He has also played for Horse and Nova.

PEPYS, JOHN 'STUMPY' (1943–69)

The Tap's first drummer, played by Ed Begley Jr. Described by David in *This Is Spinal Tap* as 'A great, tall, blond geek with glasses . . . good drummer'. Pepys sadly died in a bizarre gardening accident. His other claim to fame is that he is the only rock star to get busted at his own funeral. Reflecting some years later on the tragically early passing of his colleague, Nigel said: 'I mean, it hits you quite hard to have a member of your group that you've been creatively involved with, y'know, die. It's quite a traumatic thing . . . But it's also amusing. Sure. You've got to look at death on the light side once in a while, and think: "Well sure, he's dead, innit sad? But it's sort of funny, innit?" That's the way I look at it.'

See bizarre gardening accident.

PERSONNEL

After Tufnel's sudden departure from the band towards the end of their American tour, a heavily sedated St Hubbins confides in Marty, saying that soon Nigel will be of no more significance to him than any other of the thirty-seven people who have at one time or another been members of the band.

In the eighteen months following The Thamesmen's first chart success and the numerous changes of band name, the fast turnover of members included: Nick Wax, Tony Brixton, Dicky Laine, Denny Upham (all keyboards), Jimmy Adams, Geoff Clovington (horns), Julie Scrubbs-Martin, Lhasa Apso (backing vocals) and Little Danny Schindler (vocals, harmonica). Ronnie Pudding was the original bassist, replaced by Derek Smalls. Ross MacLochness was Viv's predecessor on keyboards. Then there are the six known drummers (Pepys, Childs, Bond, Shrimpton, Besser, Shrimpton) although only the first four had thus far appeared. Add to that David, Nigel, Derek and Viv. This makes a total of twenty-one, leaving eighteen mystery members lurking somewhere in the band's convoluted history.

PERSPECTIVE

See Graceland.

PETS

In fanzine interviews during the early eighties, Nigel and David talked about their love of their pets. Nigel (since famous for his love of animals, as shown by his pet-travel charity) had a conure, a South American parrot, while David and Jeanine had two Shar-Peis, called Mr Pip and Dragon Princess. Of the latter, known to David as 'Drag', he said: 'Strange lookin' dog. You know what it looks like? It looks like it was a larger dog with tighter skin, and then someone grabbed him by the anus and pulled as hard as he could and the face has sort of collapsed inward. And that's the best I can describe it.'

Derek has a fondness for boa constrictors.

PETTIBONE, JEANINE

One of the things I objected to in the documentary, though, was the treatment of Jeanine. I really don't think she came off that well; she certainly didn't come off as the Jeanine I know. It was shocking to both of us, really, because that's not her at all.   – David St Hubbins on *This Is Spinal Tap*

After his initial sighting of The Dose and their lead singer, David is seen in an out-take discouraging Jeanine from coming along on the tour, speaking to her on the phone as Derek calls out: 'This one's for the lads.'

The presence of Jeanine (whose surname is in ironic counterpoint to the well-endowed David) supplies what McKean, Guest and Shearer

This is scenery?

Stonehenge.

Marti talks with Nigel in his guitar shrine.

Tap's support band, The Dose.

'We've got a bigger dressing room than the puppets? Oh, that's refreshing...'

Jeanine and journalist.

David St Hubbins...and why not?

Viv and the lead singer of The Dose. 'Oh, it's just a sore. I get 'em once a year.'

The Rainbow Trout Recording Studio.

Tap's two visionaries: 'like fire and ice, basically'.

Stinkin' up the great outdoors.

call 'The Yoko plot'. She represents the threat posed to the central duo by the appearance of a woman. Nigel and David are the core of the band, with obvious reference to Jagger/Richard, Lennon/McCartney and Page/Plant. Women are meant to be entertainment on tour and steady girlfriends or wives are anathema to the whole experience. In one of their many interviews in character Derek, David and Nigel flesh out the character of Jeanine with some more of the band's abundant back-story. Nigel says: 'Jeanine's very user-friendly.' David says she is: 'Perhaps not a great businesswoman, but a great *woman* woman, if you know what I mean . . . And that's something they [Nigel and Derek] can never know, except sporadically. When she has a few too many.' Derek adds: 'In brief spurts, as it were.' In scenes dropped from the final film, Jeanine was shown to have had a fling with Nigel's replacement guitarist, Ricky. The idea of the woman somehow working her way selectively through the band, and also the joke of the lead singer of The Dose, is presumably supposed to evoke Anita Pallenberg, who had an affair with Brian Jones before settling down with Keith Richard, whose jealousy she provoked through her explicit sex scenes with Mick Jagger in *Performance* (1969).

Jeanine is a woman threatening the childish gang that the band represents. Nigel is instantly disturbed when he finds out that Jeanine is planning to join the tour. As soon as she arrives she sows seeds of division. Nigel and Ian feel pathetically threatened by her as she comes up with her plans for a new look and direction for the band.

In *Rotten: No Irish, No Blacks, No Dogs*, John Lydon writes of his experiences in the Sex Pistols with his mate Sid Vicious and Sid's girlfriend, Nancy Spungen. After the break-up of the band, Rotten wanted to work again with Sid, who assured him that he had given up drugs: 'I told him to meet me at Gunter Grove so we could talk – provided he didn't bring Nancy, which he did. Nancy was getting at Sid and wanted to be his manager. The ego games were so appalling, it resembled something out of that rock'n'roll satire movie, *Spinal Tap*.' Like so many other ingredients and characters in the film, Jeanine has come to be a kind of shorthand for a woman who threatens band stability. Jeanine is part Yoko, part Linda, especially for her sudden appearance onstage with a tambourine during 'Jazz Odyssey'.

Jeanine has written of her first meeting with her 'Shogun', her 'Dream

Warrior'. She was throwing the *I Ching* for a recently deceased friend at a party when David walked in: 'And so it came to pass: the 700-year-old dead Japanese warrior and the 645-year-old dead Japanese princess (me) became as One.' After the disastrous end to the band's 1982 tour of Japan, Jeanine became Jeanine Pettibone-St Hubbins when she and David got married. The reason for tying the knot was so that they could get American citizenship and thus stay together in California. Unfortunately, they had failed to appreciate that in order to acquire a Green Card one person in the marriage had actually to be American.

See Foghat.

PISCHEDDA, TOMMY

Chauffeur played by Bruno Kirby. The special resentment between chauffeurs and rock stars reached its crisis point in 1976 when The Who's Keith Moon accidentally ran over and killed his own chauffeur, Cornelius Boland.

Kirby developed a detailed character for the chauffeur, based on a friend of his, which he and Reiner subsequently captured in *Tommy Rispoli – A Man and His Music*. In this thirteen-minute film, Rispoli drives Reiner from the airport and talks of his problems with his girlfriend. In an extensive out-take from *This Is Spinal Tap* Pischedda fleshes out his fixation on Sinatra, which turns out mainly to be about Tommy's mother. After his father's death, Tommy bought tickets for himself, his mother and brother for a Sinatra concert at Carnegie Hall.

Tommy says suddenly: 'Frank and my mom go back a long way.'

Marty: 'They know each other?'

Kirby: 'Well, they don't know each other but Jilly's father used to deliver ice to my mother's house in the Village.'

There follows a rather inconsequential story about Sinatra's effect on Tommy's mother which ends with: 'I'll tell you another great story.' This leads to a further wilfully aimless, punchline-free story in which he rambles semi-coherently about Sinatra's popularity and his extensive charity work.

See 'All the Way'.

PLASTERCASTER

Legendary rock chick Nancy Godfrey, who appears in action in the political cult film *W.R. – Mysteries of the Organism* (1971). She was also immortalised in song by Kiss. Godfrey was famed for her collection of plaster casts of rock stars' dicks. Apparently Jimi Hendrix is the star exhibit. In a sequence featured in the original script for *This Is Spinal Tap*, Derek and Viv are seen in their Memphis hotel room with their bums immersed in plaster as a favour to two groupies who collect casts of rock stars' bottoms. After a chat about the other famous arse-casts they have, the groupies strip the plaster off Derek and Viv – but too soon, and the casts are shapeless messes.

PODS
See 'Rock and Roll Creation'.

POLYMER RECORDS
The Polydor-soundalike label, run by Sir Denis Eton-Hogg, to which Spinal Tap signed after leaving Megaphone in 1980. Polymer released two Tap albums, *Shark Sandwich* and *Smell the Glove*.

PORCARO, JEFF
Drummer of Toto, who may have died in a bizarre gardening accident. In 1992 Porcaro died after suffering a heart attack. The causes of the coronary remain unclear. One story is that it was brought on by excessive cocaine-ingestion. There is another, rather more interesting, theory that Porcaro was spraying insecticide in his garden and inhaled too much. Ironically enough, if that weren't already enough irony, Toto's lead guitarist, Steve Lukather, served as a producer and guitarist on Spinal Tap's *Break like the Wind* in the same year.
See **bizarre gardening accident.**

PRIMUS
Oddball heavy rock outfit formed in San Francisco in 1984. Founder member and bassist Les Claypool has a tattoo of Derek Smalls on his left arm.

PRODUCER
See **Murphy, Karen.**

PROTEST MUSIC
Asked in the 1970 *Teen-o-Rama* interview why the band never did political

or protest songs, Derek, ever the thinker, answered: 'If you mean "Eve of Destruction", that kind of thing, I don't know. That isn't the vibe that I want to send out. We want to send out a positive vibe, which is why we did "Flower People". To me, a protest song is . . . How can you dance or rock or shake your fist or your fanny when you're going, "Oh, right, the politician's being bad"? That's "head" music – and I don't mean psychedelic – not rock'n'roll. That's not what we're about. Rock'n'roll is sex music, body music. Head music is, like, for Frank Sinatra. Frank Sinatra should be singin' protest songs, logically. When you figure it out, it makes sense.' Asked what kind of protest songs Frank Sinatra would sing, Derek eleborates: '"Get off the Backs of the Mafia, Bobby Kennedy", or whatever. But I mean, it makes sense. "Let's Put Hoffa Together", y'know? I dunno what's on his mind, but somethin' like that.'

PUDDING, RONNIE
Early bassist, played by Danny Kortchmar, who left Spinal Tap after '(Listen to the) Flower People' (which he wrote) to form his own band, Pudding People. A prodigy who performed at the Albert Hall when he was two, Pudding is recalled by Tufnel as musically gifted relative to his band mates: 'Very inventive sort of chap, y'know – he'd write music! He knew how to make those little dots, he'd make these little sort of balloon things on this lined paper and everything, and link 'em together with little strings and all that, the whole bit.'

Pudding People released the single 'I Am the Music', on the B-side of which was a live version of 'Rubber Biscuit' recorded in Playton Hall, Moulting. Ronnie also recorded one solo album, *I Am More Music*. Asked if there was any animosity surrounding Pudding's sudden departure, Nigel said: 'Oh, yeah. There was quite a bit of animosity, actually – *huge* animosity. I'd say *screaming hatred* was more to the point.'

PUPPET SHOW
When the depleted band arrive at the park in San Francisco, they are dismayed to find that they are second on the bill to a puppet show, although Jeanine points out that she had repeatedly asked the promoters to have the band's name appear first. She reassures David: 'We got a big dressing room.'

David snarls: 'Oh, we got a bigger dressing room than the puppets, well that's refreshing.'

The art/life interchange of *This Is Spinal Tap* is such that – without having to acknowledge the resonance of the story or the source of the joke – Stephen 'Tin Tin' Duffy, while recalling his early days with Duran Duran, said to Stuart Jeffries in the *Guardian* on 14 April 1999: 'Our second gig was at the puppet theatre in Cannon Hill Park in Birmingham. It was 50p to get in that night. The puppets had bigger dressing rooms.'

Q

QUEEN

See Mercury, Freddie.

R

RACISM

See bass.

RADIOHEAD

Interviewed by Michael Collins in the *Independent* on 18 July 1988, Radiohead's lead singer, Thom Yorke, spoke about the idea of having a documentary made about him and the band: 'We're the post-Spinal Tap generation. Everything we do and have done has been taken the piss of.'

RAINBOW TROUT RECORDING STUDIO

The venue for the recording sessions captured in *This Is Spinal Tap*. These sessions were marked by the tensions that broke out into verbal altercations between Tufnel and St Hubbins, reminiscent of those on the notorious *Troggs Tapes*.

'RAINY DAY SUN'

Track from *Break like the Wind* that in Spinal Tap legend originally appeared as the B-side to '(Listen to the) Flower People'. This is a brilliant pastiche of late 1960s pop and rock psychedelia, with particularly obvious borrowings from The Kinks, The Small Faces, The Rolling Stones' 'Ruby Tuesday', various Beatles tracks, including 'I Am the Walrus' and 'A Day in the Life', and The Doors' 'Light My Fire'. Responding to the plagiarism charges in Q magazine in April 1992, St Hubbins said: 'You're talking about "Sunny Afternoon", right? Firstly, it was written before The Kinks' song. Months before. And that tape, strangely enough, disappeared.' The track features the London Panharmonic Orchestra, Eric 'Stumpy Joe' Childs on drums and Nicky Hopkins on keyboards. Hopkins, a prolific session keyboardist, played with The Who, Dusty Springfield and The Kinks in the sixties. He also played with The Jeff Beck Group, with John Lennon on 'Imagine', and with Ron Wood. The track is produced by T-Bone Burnett, who has enjoyed notable collaborations with Bob Dylan, Elvis Costello and Richard Thompson.

REGULARS, THE

See name changes; Originals, The.

REINER, ROB (1945—)

Born in New York City on March 6 1945, Reiner is the son of esteemed veteran comedian and director Carl and jazz singer and actress Estelle, who appears memorably as the woman who will have what Meg Ryan is having at the end of the orgasm scene in *When Harry Met Sally* (1989). Like Shearer, Reiner made an early TV appearance on *Alfred Hitchcock Presents*. He attended UCLA and honed his improvisation skills in various groups: he formed 'The Session', whose other members included Richard Dreyfuss, and later 'The Committee' alongside his future wife, Penny Marshall. Reiner made his big-screen acting début in his father's *Enter Laughing* (1967) and he later took small roles in *Where's Poppa?* (1970) and *The Jerk* (1979). He cut his teeth as a writer when he joined Steve Martin, who would enjoy his greatest success as a film comedian in the 1970s and early 1980s under the direction of Carl, in the writing team for the popular TV show *The Smothers Brothers Comedy Hour*. Reiner got his big break in 1971 when he was cast as Mike Stivic in the long-running comedy series *All in the Family*, itself based on Johnny Speight's *Till Death Us Do Part*. Stivic was Archie Bunker's son-in-law, the equivalent of the Tony Booth character. Reiner won Emmy awards as the Best Supporting Actor in a comedy role in 1974 and 1978, and was nominated in 1972, 1973 and 1975.

Of his directorial début Reiner has said: 'It was very, very hard for me to get this picture off the ground.' This is an understatement for a project with a gestation period of around four years. Reiner and the three principal actors developed the idea, and with some seed money from Lew Grade's Marble Arch films enhanced by their own contributions, they came up with the twenty-minute promo reel *Spinal Tap – The Final Tour* in 1982. Reiner is a proficient keyboard player and vocalist and collaborated with McKean, Guest and Shearer on the songs. The original plan had been for Reiner to be one of the band members himself but, as Shearer quips: 'He ended up directing this because he didn't look good in spandex so he couldn't be in the band.'

What shouldn't be overlooked in the success of *This Is Spinal Tap* is Reiner's contribution, first in his role as Marty DiBergi as a foil for the band's gags, and also for supplying several of the film's sharpest lines – especially the album reviews, which he wrote and delivered to the band for the first time when the cameras were rolling.

But it is his intuitive skill as a director, having absorbed the required look of genuine rockumentaries, that gives the film its crucially authentic look. He also had to address the problem of coverage and retakes on an almost entirely improvised shoot where it was difficult to get people to do and say the same thing twice. As he recalls in his commentary for the special laser disc edition of the film: 'Basically, generally you remember what you said – except for Chris Guest, who never remembered anything that he said.'

During the shoot, when not in front of the camera himself, Reiner would stand next to cameraman Peter Smokler, who usually knew where to point the camera anyway, and either whisper in his ear where Smokler should turn or, at times, physically turn him round. Similarly, in the editing process Reiner led and contributed to the team which consisted of the three editors – Robert Leighton, Kent Beyda and Kim Secrist – Reiner himself and the three stars. The film's structure evolved with what is essentially a succession of gags built around the band, developing into a narrative of the near dissolution and final, if temporary, redemption. As can be seen in the out-takes (and reputedly in the bootleg of the original four-and-a-half-hour cut), there was plenty of material to play with. It was ruthlessly honed to a taut eighty-two minutes.

After *Spinal Tap*, Reiner gradually established himself as a reliable and versatile director. He has twice filmed works by Stephen King, both times with adapted screenplays by William Goldman, the creator of *Butch Cassidy and the Sundance Kid* (1979) and *Marathon Man* (1976). *Stand By Me* (1986), based on Stephen King's short story *The Body* and set in King's fictional town of Castle Rock (which gave its name to Reiner's production company), is a sweet and effective piece of nostalgia featuring an early appearance from River Phoenix and narration from Reiner's old improv. buddy Richard Dreyfuss. *The Princess Bride* (1987), adapted by Goldman from his own book, is a brilliantly sophisticated and witty post-modern children's adventure with notable appearances from Billy Crystal and Christopher Guest.

When Harry Met Sally (1989), a wonderfully Woody Allen-like romantic comedy with a neat Nora Ephron script, established Billy Crystal as a bankable film star and featured a likeable performance from Bruno Kirby. Reiner would play the Kirby-type sidekick role in Ephron's equally charming *Sleepless in Seattle* (1993), which co-starred *When Harry Met Sally*'s Meg Ryan. After a successful return to Stephen King in the sharp and sinister *Misery* (1990), which re-launched James Caan's career, Reiner went on to the unconvincing *A Few Good Men* (1992) and the whimsical *North* (1994), before returning to form with the underrated *The American President* (1995).

Having divorced Marshall in 1979, Reiner married Michelle Singer in 1989. In recent years the couple have devoted much of their time to supporting research into early childhood development. This work included Reiner directing *I Am Your Child*, a 1997 TV-special starring, among others, Rosie O'Donnell, Billy Crystal, Robin Williams, General Colin Powell, and Bill and Hillary Clinton. In the Golden Globes he has been nominated four times in the Best Director category and was nominated five times in the Best Supporting Actor category for *All in the Family*.

Speaking of the easy collaborative improvised process on *This Is Spinal Tap*, Reiner has said: '*The Sure Thing* was more like a first film than this for me, because it was more of a traditional film and I was completely inexperienced doing that kind of thing. This was easy for me, this was like falling off a log.'

Credits

As actor in film:
Enter Laughing (1967) – Clark Baxter
Halls of Anger (1970)
Where's Poppa? (1970) – Roger the defendant
Summertree (1971) – Don
Thursday's Game (1974) – Joel Forrest
How Come Nobody's on Our Side? (1975) – Miguelito
Fire Sale (1977) – Russe
The Jerk (1979) – truck driver who picked up Navin
This Is Spinal Tap (1984) – Marty DiBergi
Throw Momma from the Train (1987) – Joel
The Spirit of '76 (1990) – Doctor Cash

Postcards from the Edge (1990) – Joe Pierce
Misery (1990) – helicopter pilot
A Spinal Tap Reunion: The 25th Anniversary London Sell-Out a.k.a. *The Return of Spinal Tap* (1992) – Marty DiBergi
Sleepless in Seattle (1993) – Jay
Mixed Nuts (1994) – Dr Kinsky
Bullets over Broadway (1994) – Sheldon Flender
Bye Bye Love (1995) – Dr Townsend
For Better or Worse (1996) – Dr Plosner
The First Wives Club (1996) – Dr Morris Packman
Mad Dog Time (1996) – Albert the chauffeur
I Am Your Child (1997)
Primary Colors (1998) – Izzy Rosenblatt
The Story of Us (1999)
Ed TV (1999) – Dr Witaker
The Muse (1999) – himself

As actor on TV:
All in the Family (1971) – Mike Stivic
Free Country (1978) – Joseph Bresner
More Than Friends (1979) – Alan Corkus
Million Dollar Infield (1982) Monte Millar
Morton & Hayes (1991) – himself (show also created by Reiner)

As director:
This Is Spinal Tap (1984)
The Sure Thing (1985)
Stand By Me (1986)
The Princess Bride (1987)
When Harry Met Sally (1989)
Misery (1990)
A Few Good Men (1992)
North (1994)
The American President (1995)
Ghosts of Mississippi (1996)
I am Your Child (1997)
The Story of Us (1999)

As producer:
Free Country (1978)
More Than Friends (1979)
The Princess Bride (1987)
When Harry Met Sally (1989)
Misery (1990)
Morton & Hayes (1991)
A Few Good Men (1992)
North (1994)
The American President (1995)
Ghosts of Mississippi (1996)
The Story of Us (1999)

As writer:
More Than Friends (1979)
This Is Spinal Tap (1984)

As composer:
This Is Spinal Tap (1984)

TV guest appearances:
Hey, Landlord (1966) – teenager
Hey, Landlord (1967) – big guy
The Andy Griffith Show (1967) – Joe the printer's apprentice
The Partridge Family (1970) – Snake
The Odd Couple (1974) – Sheldon (alongside Penny Marshall)
Saturday Night Live (1975) – host
The Rockford Files (1976) – Larry Sturtevan
Denis Miller (1994) – himself
The Larry Sanders Show (1994) – himself
Frasier (1998) voice – Bill

RETURN OF SPINAL TAP, THE
In February 1992, the re-formed Spinal Tap – St Hubbins, Tufnel and Smalls with Mick Shrimpton's twin brother Ric on drums and C.J. (Caucasian Jeffrey) Vanston (Toto, Richie Havens) on keyboards – embarked on a genuine

world tour. The group played dates in the UK, Sweden, Norway, Germany, Australia, America and Canada before the tour's final date at London's Albert Hall on 7 July. The film *A Spinal Tap Reunion: The 25th Anniversary London Sell-Out* a.k.a. *The Return of Spinal Tap* is a record of the concert.

The stage show opens with the disembodied heads of Tufnel, St Hubbins and Smalls appearing on screen looking a lot like an odd cross between Queen on the video for 'Bohemian Rhapsody', Beckett's *Not I*, Astrid Kirchherr's photos of The Beatles and the credit sequence to *The Brady Bunch*.

> Nigel Tufnel: '. . . The knock of bonewhite knuckle on the dreamdoor . . . The hellhowl from the well of the forgotten . . . The spinning coin – headtail, headtail, headtail . . . The sudden shout, the misremembered voice . . .'
>
> All: '. . . We have returned . . .'
>
> Smalls: '. . . The darkyears set ablaze with soundfire . . . The deathpony tosses its bloody mane. Shattered sleep and fantasy made flesh . . . The crows . . . the crows!'
>
> All: '. . . We have returned . . .'
>
> St Hubbins: '. . . When the daemon dances . . . when the Kraken wakes . . . When hill and glen swarm with doomlocusts and all else is emptiness . . .'
>
> All: '. . . We have returned. . .'

We cut to the support band, The Folksmen (Guest, Shearer and McKean as a group of cheery, ageing folkies dressed like The Beach Boys in the early days), warming up. They play an extract from one of their numbers and are interrupted by an assistant advising them not to take the stage.

The band are introduced by Bob Geldof, who declares: 'Usually if I show up at an evening like this it is because there is some greater, more profound meaning. Unfortunately, tonight is totally devoid of any meaning whatsoever. So will you please welcome home at last, live from hell, Spinal Tap.'

The set consists of:

'Tonight I'm Gonna Rock You Tonight'. The band could hardly begin with any other number. As the first chords strike up, Tufnel, St Hubbins and Smalls appear – flying on to the cage, suspended by cables. Tufnel can't get down to the stage and tries to cut his cables.

After this opening number St Hubbins screams: 'Good evening, Greater London.'

Smalls adds: 'How are you all feeling tonight? Do your balls hurt, too?'

'Cash On Delivery', for which Smalls introduces his designer 'dollar-sign double-necked bass'.

'America' – during the drum solo Tufnel kisses the bra of the bra-and-panties set that adorns his amp.

'Hell Hole'. Tufnel plays his souped-up Marshall amp guitar with special added section to make it even louder.

'The Majesty of Rock', for which the band appear in regal garb.

'Just Begin Again', which David introduces by reading out a note the band received from an unnamed female collaborator: 'You should know that I would be with you on tour, I would be travelling with you and singing at your side every step of the way, were it not for the fact that I do not choose to do so. But please be aware that my heart and at least one other organ travels with you wherever you go.' The performance includes the supporting vocal from Cher which emanates from the mouth superimposed on several huge portraits of her projected on to a screen hanging above the stage.

'Sex Farm' – including a new rap verse.

'Stonehenge'. The stage performance is intercut with pictures of roadies struggling to squeeze the oversized stage set through the venue's stage doors. The set doesn't make it but there are a couple of dancing dwarfs for Nigel's solo, which he plays on his double-necked mandolin.

'Rock and Roll Creation' features new egg pods from which St Hubbins and Tufnel emerge effortlessly. After a short struggle a man dressed as a chicken gets out of the third. Derek then appears from off-stage, to Nigel's bewilderment.

'Bitch School' and '(Listen to the) Flower People' are followed by the group's acoustic set which is, according to Derek 'often duplicated, never imitated'.

'Rainy Day Sun', which David introduces: 'Once upon a time you know there was a beautiful country called the sixties, where all the children always wore smiling faces regardless of the state of their other organs.'

'Celtic Blues'.

'Clam Caravan' featuring an exotic dance by a dwarf in a veil, 'The Amazing Shasbah'.

'All the Way Home' concludes the acoustic set.

'Break like the Wind' features a guitar solo from Albert Lee, and is accompanied by a cut-out of a mythical wind-god and a gale blowing across the stage to prove that the song is indeed about the awesome power of the wind.

'Diva Fever'. During Tufnel's epic, woo-wooing guitar solo in which he bites a guitar, throws horseshoes at another before firing a toy gun at it and then playing it with his feet while juggling three tennis balls, Smalls leaves the venue and goes to a restaurant, while St Hubbins gets a full facial, a leg-wax and a pedicure. Smalls concludes: 'We hope you enjoyed his solo twice as much as we did.'

'Stinkin' Up the Great Outdoors' and 'Christmas with the Devil', with miserable Santa and mean-looking elves, lead to the climax.

'Big Bottom', during which Jim the skull is joined by Jill, a vast bum. Tufnel, St Hubbins and Smalls all play bass, and are joined by cavorting groupies.

'Let Him Go'. St Hubbins says of their encore piece: 'We do have one final word for you. Well, actually, it's about 110 final words strung together in a final lyric.' The doves of peace are released but fall, dead, to the stage, and Derek screams: 'Fuck the doves.'

The live sections are inter-cut with pre-recorded pieces where we catch up with what the band and other figures from *This Is Spinal Tap* have been up to for the previous decade. From Martin Short we also learn of Spinal Tap's role in bringing together Liz Taylor and Larry Fortensky.

The film, partly a sequel to *This Is Spinal Tap*, is an essential for every Taphead.

Christopher Guest recalls of his personal return to the Albert Hall: 'I hadn't been inside the Hall since I was a child. My great-aunt Lady Swaythling had a box there.'

See DiBergi, Marty; Fufkin, Artie; Hookstratten, Lieutenant; Squatney.

REVIEWS

The album reviews that Marty reads out were all written by Reiner. He hadn't told the other actors what they would be, hence their reactions of genuine surprise and amusement.

See *Gospel According to Spinal Tap, The*; *Intravenus de Milo*; *Shark Sandwich.*

RICKY

After Nigel's sudden departure from the band during the débâcle at the Seattle air force base, Jeanine arranges for a replacement in the shape of a leading young San Franciscan guitarist by the name of Ricky. He becomes an instant threat to the other band members in terms of looks, charisma and talent. He also has a fling with Jeanine. All of the Ricky material was removed from the release version of the film, and none of it even makes it to the out-takes as featured in Criterion's laser disc version.

'ROCK AND ROLL CREATION'

Track featured on the soundtrack, and soundtrack album, taken from the 1977 concept album of the same name, which also goes under the title 'The Gospel According to Spinal Tap'. Choice lyrics:

> 'Twas the rock and roll creation,
> 'Twas a terrible big bang,
> 'Twas the ultimate mutation,
> Yin was searching for his yang . . .

The song seems – conceptually, at least – to be a hybrid of AC/DC's 'Let There Be Rock' and 'Rock 'n' Roll Damnation', both of which feature on their album *If You Want It You've Got It*. The track has entered musical legend because of the trouble Derek Smalls had emerging from his pod during the performance of the song, as captured on *This Is Spinal Tap*. The original idea for the band to be born on stage out of large pods was borrowed from seventies heavy-rock band Angel.

For U2's Popmart tour, the show's designer, Willie Williams, and the band themed the show around the notion of a 'giant, sci-fi disco supermarket'. One of the innovative ideas they came up with was to have the group emerge from a giant lemon. Asked what inspired the idea, Williams replied: 'Spinal Tap, actually. We needed a pod-like object for the band to come out of like they did in the movie. The thing about the lemon gag is that we felt that the more smoke there was the better, because it was the pure Spinal Tap moment. So we really poured the smoke on. Of course, at that moment, Las Vegas decided to have the stillest wind ever. So The Edge comes down from the stairs, and he knows to start his guitar he has to kick a switch on his foot-pedal. Well, he can't see his hand in front of his face and he ended up on his hands and knees, feeling around for the pedal. Later he said to me, "There I was at the début, the première opening night, and this voice came into my head: 'I am Derek Smalls.'"' Music-press headlines everywhere trumpet U2's simultaneous discovery of humour, irony and the joys of all things Tapular.

The big problem for Shearer during the shooting of the 'Rock and Roll Creation' scene was that it was in fact very easy for him to open the pod which was being held closed by a man below the stage. Similarly, there was a dispute during the editing of the film between Reiner, who insisted on the sound of the banging being heard above the music, and McKean, who pointed out that this was rather unrealistic.

Citing it as another example of Marti DiBergi's negative slant on the band in *This Is Spinal Tap*, St Hubbins said to Jim White in the *Independent* on 24 February 1992: 'I'd say eighty per cent of the time, well, seventy-five, well, OK, sixty per cent of the time Derek got out of that pod during "Rock and Roll Creation" perfectly OK. Couple of times it doesn't open, and DiBergi puts that in the film. Why does he use that bit? Exactly.'

'ROCK 'N' ROLL NIGHTMARE'

The song performed by the Tap on their first TV appearance on *The TV Show* in 1978, in which they parodied the late-night rock show *Midnight Special*. The band, who had not as yet developed their distinctive logo, are introduced by Rob Reiner impersonating Wolfman Jack, the famous DJ who played himself in George Lucas's seminal coming-of-age, rock and roll film *American Graffiti* (1973). The band – Tufnel, St Hubbins and Smalls – are augmented by Loudon Wainwright III on keyboards and Russ Kunkel on drums. The song does not yet bear the hallmark of classic Tap:

> I've been a rocker since I don't know when,
> I've been a roller since way back then,
> Oh yeah.
> But late at night when the boogie's through,
> I go to bed just the same as you,
> Oh yeah.

> But when the rock 'n' roll nightmare comes,
> The devil's gonna make me eat my drums!

(David) Eat my drums?
(Eric) Not me.

ROCKLOPEDIA BRITTANICUS

The entry on Spinal Tap is on page 743 of this esteemed music bible, and is as featured on the inner sleeve of *This Is Spinal Tap*'s soundtrack album:

SPINAL TAP (1964–?): Veteran hard-rock unit noted for their high volume assault and dogged persistence. David St. Hubbins (g) and Nigel Tufnel (lead g) formed nucleus of band, THE ORIGINALS, Squatney, East London, 1964. Late 1964 founded THAMESMEN with Ronnie Pudding (bs, ex-CHEAP DATES), and John (Stumpy) Pepys (drms, ex-LESLIE CHESWICK SOUL EXPLOSION, see Cheswick, Les & Mary). Released 'Gimme Some Money' b/w 'Cups and Cakes' (Abbey, 1965). Toured extensively in Benelux nations, with Jan van der Kvelk (kybds). Returned in UK as DUTCHMEN.

Period of intense personnel turnover followed, accompanied by wholesale name-changes, including: RAVEBREAKERS, DOPPEL GANG, SILVER SERVICE, BISQUITS, LOVE BISQUITS, TUFNEL–ST HUBBINS GROUP. A-side of first Spinal Tap single '(Listen to the) Flower People' b/w 'Rainy Day Sun' (Megaphone 1965) penned by Pudding, who left the band to form PUDDING PEOPLE, releasing single 'I Am The Music' and album *I Am More Music* (Megaphone 1967). With replacement Derek Smalls (ex-pioneer all-white Jamaican band SKAFACE), band recorded first album, *Spinal Tap* (released in US as *Spinal Tap Sings '(Listen to the) Flower People' and Other Favorites*), went gold in UK. Sales of follow-up album *We Are All Flower People* were disappointing. Tap toured Europe in support of then-hot *Matchstick Men*, developing harder twin-guitar style. Live recording of landmark appearance at Electric Zoo, Wimpton, UK produced third album, *Silent But Deadly*.

Pepys, suddenly dead in tragedy, replaced by Eric 'Stumpy Joe' Childs (ex-WOOLCAVE). Albums recorded by this line-up included: *Brainhammer*, *Blood to Let*, *Nerve Damage*, and *Intravenus de Milo*. For ambitiously flawed concept LP *The Sun Never Sweats*, Tap hired Ross MacLochness (kybds, ex-KILT KIDS) and replaced 'Stumpy Joe', dead in sudden tragedy, with session drummer Peter 'James' Bond. This line-up toured Far East in 1975, released second live album, *Jap Habit*. MacLochness, retired to missionary work in Namibia, later released solo LP, *Doesn't Anybody Here Speak English?* On *Bent for the Rent*, band's late-arriving glitter attempt, Viv Savage (kybds, ex-AFTERTASTE) came aboard. Press attention was momentarily attracted when band sued Megaphone for back-royalties, and label threatened to countersue, charging 'lack of talent'. After 'Nice 'n' Stinky' from two-year-old *Habit* became surprise American hit in 1977, Tap signed with Polymer Records, replaced Bond, who had died with tragic suddenness, with Mick Shrimpton (ex-Eurovision Song Contest house-band), released *Shark Sandwich* (1980) and *Smell the Glove* (1982).

Though neither a critics' nor a public favorite, Spinal Tap continues to fill a much needed void.

ROMA '79

Film released in 1976, directed by Marco Zamboni, in which Derek plays a doomed heavy. It was inspired by the opening fantasy sequence from Led Zeppelin's *The Song Remains the Same*. In a scene of heavy-handed symbolism, Peter Grant is dressed as a thirties-style gangster being driven around in a vintage car. As the car pulls up at a country pile, a Tommy gun is fired by a henchman. Two of Grant's men enter a room and open fire on a rival gang, in the process offing a man with no face and a wolfman who seems to bleed milk. Grant looks in at the mayhem and then leaves again enigmatically. We cut to doves flying and the credit sequence, a scene of the New York skyline with speeded-up film – like *Koyaanisqatsi*, only cheap-looking.

See zucchini.

RUTLES, THE

Spoof Beatles band led by Eric Idle and Neil Innes, who made their first appearance in *Rutland Weekend Television*.

See 'All You Need Is Cash'.

S

SAINT HUBBINS
Over the closing credits of *This Is Spinal Tap*, David reveals that Hubbins was a real saint and is indeed the patron saint of quality footwear.

ST HUBBINS, DAVID (1943—)

A shallow genius is better than a smart fool.   – David St Hubbins

The character outline in the film's original treatment reads: 'DAVID ST HUBINS [*sic*] – also lead guitar in the band, also a co-founder as well as lead singer. Works hard at patching up his image as the band's sex symbol, and writes the much-needed bridges for Nigel's cumbersome musical efforts.'

St Hubbins was born at the Squatney Women's Hospital on 13 August 1943. Attended the Sulfur Hill Academy for Boys, a public school he remembers as being marked by 'a rougher breed of gentility'. St Hubbins is generally overshadowed in guitar virtuosity by Tufnel and, as seen in the Rainbow Trout Recording Studio sequence, is prone to occasional lapses in competence. He started to play the guitar at the age of about twelve or thirteen. Asked why he chose the guitar, he explained: 'Well, it was the most portable of all the instruments, I think, with the exception of vocals, which are extremely portable.'

In *The Return of Spinal Tap*, we see David in his new life in Pomona, California. He is shown inflating a football – since 1988 he has been employed as a coach at a soccer clinic, mostly working with four- and five-year-old girls, for which he receives a stipend: 'A stipend is like money, but it's such a small amount that they don't really call it money. They call it a stipend. I also get a discount whenever I need to have anything inflated.' St Hubbins also works on his golf game, receiving coaching from country music great Kenny Rogers.

His other ventures include managing small local garage bands, such as Meconium, and working with Jeanine in her two shops. One, 'Potato

Republic', specialises in 'itchy Irish clothing'. Next door is the New Age shop, the Drippery.

In an out-take from the *Troggs Tapes* scene at Rainbow Trout Recording Studio, Derek recalls Ronnie Pudding's assessment of David: 'Lazier than a dead budgie.'

SATRIANI, JOE (1957—)

Guest guitarist on the title track of the album *Break like the Wind*. Satriani, born on 15 July 1957, taught Metallica's Steve Hammett and Steve Vai, with whom he collaborated, along with Eric Johnson, on the album *G3 Live in Concert*. Generally a solo and session performer, he has played with Mick Jagger and also Deep Purple, replacing Ritchie Blackmore in 1994.

SAUCY JACK

Derek and David were asked in their *Hollywood Online* interview about their long-cherished musical project. St Hubbins: '*Saucy Jack* has been workshopped within an inch of its life.'

Smalls: 'Its destiny is to be a work in progress. If it's ever finished it'll die.'

St Hubbins: 'Actually, we performed some tunes at a surprise party for Stephen Sondheim.'

Smalls: 'He left before making any comment, although he was heard to mutter "Taxi" enigmatically.'

In the way of Spinal Tap, there is now a sci-fi fantasy musical called *Saucy Jack and the Space Vixens*, 'a story full of murder, mayhem and outrageous comedy' written by Charlotte Mann and David Schofield, with music by Jonathan Croose and Robin Forrest. The show has appeared at the Edinburgh Festival, on tour in the UK and America, and was staged in early 1999 at the Queen's Theatre in London's Shaftesbury Avenue.

Speaking to Jim White in the *Independent* on 24 February 1992, St Hubbins said of the ongoing project: 'We have nine songs we're workshopping at the moment, but I think we're caught in the vacuum between Sweeney Todd and Jeffrey Dahmer. I suppose we could do it as *Saucy Jeffrey* now, or even *Jeffrey Sauce*.'

SAVAGE, VIV

The film's treatment reads: 'the keyboard player and blessed with the one thing the other Tap members lack: actual musical ability. Were it not for a wife and kids, he could actually front a band of his own, something the other band members can only fantasise about.'

Formerly with Aftertaste. Beyond his musical abilities, Savage is known for his fondness for the mysterious 'Mendocino Rocket Fuel', and Derek has hinted at Viv's major role within the band as a 'great procurer of certain road necessities'. Savage died in a freak gas explosion while visiting the grave of Ric Shrimpton. It turned out that he had secretly been a drummer as a child, as Smalls explained to *The Nose* in 1992: 'The curse, somehow, if there is a curse, knew that he was hiding the fact that he played drums.' There is a rumour that a Viv Savage-lookalike is going around trading on his looks and performing as 'The Viv Savage Experience'. Savage's simple philosophy of life was: 'Have a good time, all the time.'

SAXON
Saxon, one of the leading bands in the New Wave of British heavy metal, were formed in Yorkshire in 1977 by Peter 'Byll' Byford (vocals), Paul Quinn (guitar), Graham Oliver (guitar), Steve Dawson (bass) and Pete Gill (drums), who was later in Motörhead. Harry Shearer went on the road with the band for a British tour to pick up some bass-playing hints in preparation for his big-screen role as Derek Smalls.

SCHLECK SMORBROD
The Norwegian for Shit Sandwich, as discovered by Harry Shearer when he opened the film in Norway at a midnight screening.

SCHMIT, TIMOTHY B. (1947—)
Born 30 October 1947 in Sacramento, California, Schmit sings backing vocals for 'Cash On Delivery' and 'Christmas with the Devil' on *Break like the Wind*. A bass guitarist and vocalist who joined The Eagles in 1979, Schmit has also played with countless artists, including Poco, Linda Ronstadt, Steely Dan, Elton John, Toto, Bob Seger and Don Henley.

See ethereal fan.

SCREENPLAY
The original screenplay, dated 10 September 1982, begins with roughly the same intro by DiBergi (then still called Marty DiBroma) as that included

in the film. He promises: 'The documentary you are about to see is a microcosm, a macrocosm, even – if you will, a bit of a minicosm of a world most of us can only fantasise about.' The story proper opens with the road crew unloading and testing equipment at a venue, and moves on to a selection of interviews with fans. The band are collected by a limo driver called Arnie Katkavicz who will annoy the members with his repetitive rant about Michael Douglas leaving Philadelphia.

There are a number of notable differences between the screenplay and the finished film. There is an interview with Nigel and David filmed at Nigel's sixteenth-century Scottish castle (the scene is headed EXT. ENGLISH CASTLE); extracts from which were to be peppered through the film.

The screenplay describes a sequence in which the band play the Maraville Star Theatre in Chicago. The audience is in a fever of anticipation when the band hit the stage and strike one enormously loud power-chord – which is followed by an instant power-cut, making it a very short, anti-climactic concert.

It also includes the press conference from the time of the Flower People tour which was filmed but failed to make it to the final cut. It can be seen on the Criterion laser disc version of the film.

Backstage at a concert in South Bend, David's fourteen-year-old spikey-purple-haired son Jordan shows up.

After the blow-up in the cafe, Ian decides to stay on and ends up having a fling with Jeanine while the band are stuck in their fractious recording sessions.

Ian is seen to be spreading himself too thin by representing other bands, including The Dead Geezers.

Marty DiBroma proves himself to be a pretentious wannabe auteur with his cinematic meditation on America to accompany Nigel's conceptual track (then known as 'King of America'). The film features travelogue shots of Washington's iconic clichéd landmarks, such as the Lincoln Memorial, the White House and the Washington Monument. Again, this sequence was filmed in a recognisable form but failed to make it to the final cut.

A teenage Taphead shows up. He is a hanger-on and obsessive fan of the band.

When Nigel leaves the tour and the band, he is replaced by Ricky, an unprepossessing nineteen-year-old who is transformed into an Adonis by the time of his first stage appearance.

SELLERS, PETER (1925–80)

One of the chief inspirations for the film was *Trumpet Volunteer*, a classic comedy record produced by the fifth Beatle, George Martin, in the late 1950s. In it Peter Sellers plays an inarticulate East End rock'n'roll star, Twit Conway (loosely based on Tommy Steele), who is being interviewed by a plummy BBC reporter, also played by Sellers.

'SEX FARM'

> It happened by complete accident the first night. We were just kicking around in a club that we played every Tuesday, and I was playing the guitar and it hit the ceiling. It broke, and it kind of shocked me 'cause I wasn't ready for it to go. I was expecting everybody to go, "Wow, he's broken his guitar," but nobody did anything, which made me kind of angry and determined to get this precious event noticed by the audience. I proceeded to make a big thing of breaking the guitar. I pounced all over the stage with it, and I threw the bits on the stage, and I picked up my spare guitar and carried on as though I really meant to do it.
>
> – Pete Townshend in *Rolling Stone*, September 1968

A.k.a. 'Sex Farm Woman' and with a working title of 'Bone Farm', this is the song played at Lindbergh air force base in Seattle. The band is on top form lyrically, with subtly suggestive rural imagery:

> Getting out my pitchfork
> Poking your hay . . .
>
> . . . Slipping out your back door
> Leaving my spray . . .
>
> . . . Planting my seed

Talking of the relative lyrical crudeness of the band's back catalogue, Derek cites 'Sex Farm' as being part of their new mature direction: 'We're taking a sophisticated view of the idea of sex and . . .'

Marty helps him out: 'putting it on a farm.'

When the song was performed at the Lindbergh air force base the guitar Tufnel smashed was a cheap fake Stratocaster. The pay-off of the sequence (set up in the scene where Nigel shows off his radio pick-up to Marty) with the interference on the PA was based on Christopher Guest's experience of seeing a production of *A Midsummer Night's Dream* in Central Park which was interrupted by the radio signals from a local cab company.

SEXIST

When the Tap are met with accusations of being sexist on the provocative cover of *Smell the Glove*, Tufnel asks plaintively: 'What's wrong with being sexy?' Around the time of the film's release, the enigmatic Peter Occhiogrosso asked Nigel: 'Do you have any sympathy for the German heavy metal band Scorpions who have had their latest LP rejected by some American stores for being too sexy?'

Nigel: 'Too sexist?'

Occhiogrosso: 'No, theirs was sexy.'

Infantile sexism is at the heart of heavy metal, and this aspect of the film is another of its many elements that have fed back into the music world. This is shown in the entry for the death metal outfit Banished in *The Virgin Encyclopaedia of Heavy Rock*: 'Several commentators were struck by the sleeve artwork of their 1993 album [*Deliver Me Unto Pain* (Death – as opposed to their first album, *The Dead Shall Inherit*, which was released on Deaf)], designed by Tim Vigil from Faust Comic Books – unconsciously echoing a sentiment in the spoof "rockumentary" *This Is Spinal Tap*, their guitarist Tom Frost justified the cover thus: "It's not like a sexist thing in the sense that it's real. The picture has all women in it – even the demon in the middle is a woman, with a huge strap-on horn . . ."'

SEXY

See sexist.

SHAFFER, PAUL

David Letterman's band leader who plays Artie Fufkin in the movie and its sequel of sorts, *The Return of Spinal Tap*. He did a whole scene in which he desperately tried to get the band to do an early morning radio appearance, the climax of which is the slightly deranged record promoter smashing an egg on his own head. Sadly, when the radio sequence itself fell a bit flat and failed to make the final cut, this scene also had to be sacrificed.

See Fufkin, Artie.

SHANK HALL

Venue in Milwaukee, Wisconsin at which the band perform 'Gimme Some Money' in a sound check shortly before the arrival of Jeanine. The entire film was shot in LA, but now there is a real venue in Milwaukee called the Shank Hall, the logo for which includes a mini Stonehenge.

SHARK SANDWICH

Album released on Polymer in 1980 which includes the tracks 'No Place Like Nowhere', 'Throb Detector' and 'Sex Farm'. Presumably the title is an arcane reference to the shark's most celebrated contribution to the dark history of rock and roll. On one of several tours of America in 1969 Led Zeppelin stayed at the Edgewater Inn in Seattle, an establishment famed and favoured because in certain rooms patrons could fish directly from their balcony. Legend has it that with the help and encouragement of Richard Cole – the band's notorious, hedonistic roadie – Robert Plant, John Bonham and unspecified members of the group's entourage took advantage of this feature. Having landed several sharks, the boys cut up the fish and inserted the pieces into the vagina of a (reputedly) willing – and, unbelievably, very grateful – groupie who, according to Cole, proceeded to enjoy multiple orgasms. In his account of Led Zeppelin, *Hammer of the Gods*, Stephen Davis reports Cole's alternative version of the story, which has the boys catching not shark but red snapper. It was this that was then inserted into the red-headed groupie's vagina, affording Cole the opportunity to make the bizarre and unsavoury pun: 'Let's see how *your* red snapper likes *this* red snapper.'

Little is known of the album itself, beyond the review quoted by Marty: 'Shit Sandwich.' This fits into the tradition of famously dismissive short reviews. Charles Shaar Murray's review of Lee Hazlewood's LP *Poet, Fool or Bum* was the succinct: 'Bum.' Shaar Murray also once succumbed to the obvious temptation and wrote of a Yes album: 'Maybe.' Goodman Ace said of the film *I Am a Camera* (1955): 'No Leica.' C.A. Lejeune said of *Millions Like Us* (1943): '. . . and millions don't.'

SHEARER, HARRY (1943—)

Harry Shearer, the Tap's own Derek Smalls, was born on 23 December 1943. He was a child actor, appearing on TV in *The Jack Benny Show* and *Alfred Hitchcock Presents*, and playing Eddie Haskell in the pilot of the long-running hit *Leave It To Beaver*. Shearer made his début in *Abbot and Costello Go to Mars* (1953) and had a small role in that year's *The Robe* – the first film made in CinemaScope – starring Richard Burton and Jean Simmons. So Shearer may in fact be the missing link between Jean Simmons and Gene Simmons. Shearer studied political science at UCLA, and after college did various jobs, including covering LA's Watts riots for *Newsweek*. He was a member of The Credibility Gap, along with Michael McKean, touring and making records with this satirical group who also produced one film together, *Cracking Up* (1977). Shearer worked as a writer on *Saturday Night Live* from its beginning in 1975 and was a cast member for two seasons – 1979–80 and 1984–85. He has guested on many top TV shows, including *Ellen*, *Murphy Brown*, *LA Law*, *Chicago Hope*, *Dream On* and *Friends*, as well as directing and appearing in *The History of White People in America Vols I and II* alongside McKean and Fred Willard a.k.a. Lt Hookstratten.

It is as a vocal performer that Shearer has really made his mark, having lent his skills to countless radio shows and humorous records. He has his own satirical radio programme, *Le Show*, and provides voice-overs for many adverts. Over the past decade he has been a prominent member of the cast of *The Simpsons*. His many characters include: Montgomery Burns, Waylon Smithers, Ned Flanders, Seymour Skinner, Kent Brockman, Lenny, Dr Julius, Hibbert, Dr Marvin Monroe, Jasper, McBain, Otto, Rev. Timothy Lovejoy, Herman the military antique store owner, Scratchy, Dr Pryor and Jebadiah Springfield as well as God, the Devil and Hitler.

His vocal skills have tended to pigeon-hole him in films – he has several times played DJs, anchor men and TV execs. Beyond *This Is Spinal Tap*, Shearer's only film-writing credit is as co-author with Albert Brooks of the screenplay for Brooks's début feature, *Real Life* (1979). Brooks was an occasional guest performer with The Credibility Gap.

Shearer has released a comedy record, *OJ on Trial: The Early Years*. So, spookily, he also supplies an unusual link between Bart and O.J. Simpson.

Credits

As actor:
Abbot and Costello Go to Mars (1953)
The Robe (1953) – David

Cracking Up (1977)
Real Life (1979) – Pete
The Fish That Saved Pittsburgh (1979) – television news reporter
Animalympics (1979) – voice
One Trick Pony (1980) – Bernie Wepner
American Raspberry (1980) – trucker's friend
Loose Shoes (1980) – narrator
The Right Stuff (1983) – recruiter
This Is Spinal Tap (1984) – Derek Smalls
Flicks (1987) voice – narrator
Plain Clothes (1988) – Simon Feck
My Stepmother's an Alien (1988) voice – Carl Sagan
Hometown Boy Makes Good (1989)
Pure Luck (1991) – Monosoff
Blood and Concrete (1991) – Sammy
Oscar (1991) – Guido Finucci
The Fisher King (1991) – sitcom actor Ben Starr
A Spinal Tap Reunion: The 25th Anniversary Sell-Out a.k.a. *The Return of Spinal Tap* (1992) – Derek Smalls
A League of Their Own (1992) – newsreel announcer
Wayne's World 2 (1993) – Handsome Dan
Speechless (1994) – Chuck
I'll Do Anything (1994) – audience research captain
Little Giants (1994) – announcer
Thrill Ride: The Science of Fun (1997) – narrator
My Best Friend's Wedding (1997) – poetry reader
Godzilla (1998) – Charles Caiman
The Truman Show (1998) – Mike Michaelson
Small Soldiers (1998) voice – Punch-It
Dick (1999) – G. Gordon Liddy
Chicanery Moon (2000) – Tom Lewis

As composer:
This Is Spinal Tap (1984)
A Spinal Tap Reunion: The 25th Anniversary London Sell-Out a.k.a. *The Return of Spinal Tap* (1992)
Waiting for Guffman (1996)

As writer:
Real Life (1979)
This Is Spinal Tap (1984)
A Spinal Tap Reunion: The 25th Anniversary Sell-Out a.k.a. *The Return of Spinal Tap* (1992)

As director:
The History of White People in America: Vol I (1985)
The History of White People in America: Vol II (1986)

TV guest appearances:
Murphy Brown (1990) – Chris Bishop
Dream On (1993) – Steve the producer
LA Law (1993)
Animaniacs (1993) voice – Ned Flat
Ellen (1994) – Ted
Frontline (1995) – Larry Hadges
Friends (1995) – Dr Baldharar
Chicago Hope (1996) – 'Nowhere Man'
ER (1997) – John Smythe
The Visitor (1997) – Louis Faraday
The Panel (1998) – himself
Style and Substance (1998) – himself
The Simpsons (1990—)

SHELLEY, PERCY BYSSHE (1792–1822)

Romantic poet ('Prometheus Unbound' and 'To a Skylark') and translator (Plato's *The Republic*).

See lukewarm water.

SHIT SANDWICH

See *Shark Sandwich*.

'SHORT AND SWEET'

Song mentioned in early draft of screenplay, in the midst of which the band leave the stage as Ric performs an epic drum solo. The number was in fact a feature of the band when they developed their twin-lead-guitar style in the late 1960s. It features as a pared-down 18.37 twin guitar solo from Tufnel and St Hubbins on 'Silent But Deadly'.

SHRIMPTON, MICK (1948–82)

Characterised in the film's treatment as: 'the band's latest drummer. The three previous ones having met with bizarre deaths. His drug habits indicate that such an end is mightily possible for him as well.'

Before playing with the Tap, Shrimpton's previous claim to fame had been as drummer with the Eurovision Song Contest house band. Suffered a similar fate to his predecessor, Peter 'James' Bond, when he exploded on stage at the LA show at the end of the band's comeback tour documented in *This Is Spinal Tap*.

See Parnell, Ric (R.J.).

SHRIMPTON, RIC

Drummer and twin-brother (younger by twenty minutes) of Mick who played with the band on the 1992 comeback tour. David has said of Ric: 'He still runs twenty to thirty minutes late for rehearsal, but for a drummer that's very conscientious. Counting all the session men and temporaries, he is our thirteenth drummer. But don't tell *him* – he'll be worried sick. I think that thirteen is a lucky number in his case. As long as he keeps from urinating on the third rail, or something, he should last a long time.'

See Parnell, Ric (R.J.).

SHUT UP AND EAT

The name of Morty the Mime's mime catering company. In out-takes of the sequence at the tour's launch party (filmed at the Hollywood Athletic Club) Morty explains the concept of the food/mime hybrid to Marty: 'I used to be an actor. But I could never remember my lines, so I figured "Shut up, don't say nothing." My father sort of started this 'cos at home, every day, he used to say the same thing to me: "Shut up and eat." So that's what we do. It's the name of the company.'

The waiters use guilt as a means to get their customers to eat. When people see a mime waiter expending all that effort walking against the wind across the room or mourning a dead bird, people feel obliged to eat: ''Cos the food is not that good.'

SIGNINGS
In out-takes from the Disc 'n' Dat record-shop signing sequence, the band get just two fans approaching their stand. The first hands over the record for the band to sign, but as David points out: 'This is not our album, it's train sounds.'

The young man explains: 'I listen to a lot of that too . . . I already have all of yours and I intend to play this at the same time – listen to them both at once. I do that when my parents go out of town. My parents have a stereo and I have one and when they go out of town for a transfusion I put both on at once.'

Derek asks: 'Is something wrong? Are they ill?'

The fan explains: 'No, they just, every six months or so . . .'

Derek: 'Like, get the blood washed.'

Fan: 'My father's a mechanic, and he says it's the same for an automobile.'

This is based on the myth about Keith Richards that began in the early seventies when his problems with heroin were well publicised. It was said that he would regularly travel to a private hospital in Switzerland where he would enjoy a complete blood transfusion.

A second fan arrives with a copy of the album for them to sign, black on black. He asks them the name of the album and the band point out the signs saying: *Smell the Glove*. The kid says: 'Oh, man, I thought that was, like, a contest or something.' He can't read the signatures, and there follows an elaborate scene in which he has to tilt the album in the light to see that it is in fact signed.

SILENT BUT DEADLY
The band's live album released on Megaphone in 1969, taken from the recordings of their Electric Zoo concerts in Wimpton. Includes tracks 'Silent But Deadly', 'Breakfast of Evil' and 'Short 'n' Easy'.

SILVER SERVICE

One of the band-names the Tap used in the past.

See name changes.

SIMPSONS, THE

American cartoon series.

See Otto Show, The; Shearer, Harry.

SINATRA, FRANK (1915–98)

See 'All the Way'; protest music.

SINCLAIR, JOHN

See Uriah Heep.

SKAFACE

All-white Jamaican-influence band with whom Derek Smalls played before attending the London School of Design.

SKULL

See Jim.

SLASH

Stoke-on-Trent-born lead guitarist with Guns 'n' Roses. Played with Spinal Tap on their 1992 comeback album, *Smell the Glove*. Confided to Andy Gill in an interview in the *Independent* on 23 May 1992: '*Spinal Tap* is the epitome of what Guns 'n' Roses are as a rock'n'roll band. If anything had ever hit close to home, *Spinal Tap* was it.'

SLIME-MOULDS

In an out-take David discourses on the slime-mould: 'Slime-moulds are so close to being both plant and animal that it's like they can't make up their minds. And they're thinking now that maybe this is who's been running the earth all this time. It's been the layabouts who can't commit – the slime-moulds – 'cos there's more slime-mould than any other protoplasm on the planet. And, if they wanted to, if they finally made up their minds to commit to being either plant or animal, they could take us over like that.' [*clicks fingers*] He explains that slime-mould is responsible for many slips, and that these slips are not accidents – they are attacks.

SMALL SOLDIERS

Joe Dante's 1998 near re-make of his own *Gremlins* (1984) in which a renegade kid hopes to revive the fortunes of his father's toy-shop by selling a new line of advanced military toys, not realising that the figures have been fitted with super-powerful computer chips. The Commando Elite declare war on the kid, who has taken in Archer, the leader of the Elite's sworn enemies, the Gorgonites. This bunch of pacific freaks include Punch-It (voiced by Harry Shearer), Insaniac/Freakenstein (Michael McKean) and Slam Fist and Scratch It (both Christopher Guest). In a move typical of supreme film-buff Dante, the credits read:

> The Commando Elite
> > Voices by original cast members of *The Dirty Dozen*
> > Ernest Borgnine
> > Jim Brown
> > George Kennedy
> > Clint Walker
>
> The Gorgonites
> > Voices by the members of Spinal Tap

So Hollywood anoints Spinal Tap as a force of righteousness in the universe. The film is dedicated to its late co-star, *Saturday Night Live* alumnus and Shearer's fellow *Simpsons* star, Phil Hartman.

SMALLS, DEREK ALBION

> *God made more off-road than road. So be it!*   – Derek Smalls

Character outline from original treatment: 'DEREK SMALLS – bass guitar. One-time art student who's in the throes of a particularly ugly marital dissolution.'

Smalls, the senior member of the band, who has described himself as being in 'the higher echelons of youth', was born in 1941 in Nilford-on-Null in the West Midlands – the cradle of heavy rock, producing Robert Plant and John Bonham of Led Zeppelin, Black Sabbath as well as Slade. At the age of seventeen he enrolled at the London School of Design (although elsewhere it has been said that he joined the school in 1965), having, he has said, been attracted largely by the institution's initials. So he brings to the band's elaborate back-story the art-school element that is a feature of many British bands (The Beatles, Roxy Music, Queen, etc.). His plan was to break into the world of advertising, heeding the words of advice given to him by his father, Donald 'Duff' Smalls: 'Der, advertising will always be there, there will always be advertising until the Russians take over – and maybe even *they'll* do advertising.'

In the period when the band split up in the mid-1970s, Smalls recorded his solo LP, *It's a Smalls World*, an album which carefully avoided melody: 'I really tried that, I really tried to just do rhythm and harmony, and no melody at all. Because I felt at the time that that was the way to go; and I was wrong.'

In *The Return of Spinal Tap*, we see what Smalls was up to in the lull between 1982 and the band's reunion tour in 1992. We travel with him and his father around Nilford. They are in the van used for his father's telephone sanitising business, known as 'SaniFone'. We see him at work cleaning a phone, and, having done so, he remarks: 'After a summer of sanitising people's telephones you really do appreciate rock'n'roll more than ever.'

His other major project was a lucrative contract writing jingles for the Belgian Milk Board. Sample: 'Milk – if it was any richer it'd be cream.' He invested the money he earned unwisely in London's Docklands. He also toured for a while in the late eighties with a Christian rock band, Lambsblood, with whom he played the Monsters of Jesus Festival.

When asked what his motto would be, Derek couldn't choose between 'Not a woolly-head' and 'Fuck my ex-wife's lawyer'.

SMALLS, PAMELA

The unseen wife of the band's bassist, Derek, who is divorcing him in one of the story-lines dropped from the final version of the film. On the phone to Simon, his London-based lawyer, Smalls refuses to grant her the Lamborghini or the Earth Station, but finally concedes: 'Give her the Mini.'

SMELL THE GLOVE

It's like, how much more black could this be? And the answer is none.
None more black. – Nigel Tufnel describing the cover of *Smell the Glove*

The album, the band's fourteenth, was originally to have been released with the cover-design favoured by the band. Bobbi Flekman voices her objections to Ian Faith: 'Ian, you put a greased, naked woman on all fours with a dog-collar round her neck and a leash and a man's arm extended out up to here [*she indicates her forearm*] holding on to the leash and pushing a black glove into her face, to sniff it. You don't find that offensive?! You don't find that sexist?!'

Ian replies: 'No, I don't. This is 1982.'

Bobbi: 'That's right, it's 1982. Get out of the sixties. We don't have this mentality any more.'

Ian: 'Well, you should have seen the cover they *wanted* to do. It wasn't a glove, believe me.'

When copies of the finished album are delivered to the band, they turn out to be entirely black. Bobbi had already suggested that the cover should be blank by citing the example of The Beatles' *The Beatles*, universally known as *The White Album* for obvious reasons. There is an established history of rock bands forced by their labels to ditch tasteless album covers. The Beatles themselves were forced to replace the original artwork for their American compilation release *Yesterday and Today*. The original design featured John, Paul, George and Ringo gathered for a portrait with their familiar carefree, cheeky scouse grins. Only they are all wearing white coats and covered in the dismembered body parts of dolls, and hunks of raw meat. The entire pressing of 750,000 copies was withdrawn and the picture replaced with a more conventional shot of the group posed in and around a large suitcase. John Lennon had also wanted to have a cut-out of Adolf Hitler on the cover of *Sgt Pepper's Lonely Hearts Club Band*, but it was removed shortly before the final photograph was taken.

Many artists have created a stir with controversial cover-art for their albums, notably David Bowie, whose canine genitals were airbrushed from

Guy Peelaert's painting of him as a man-dog for the cover of *Diamond Dogs*. Bowie had previously been forced to replace the image of himself wearing a dress (designed by the mother of Tap collaborator Slash), with an innocuous cartoon for the cover of *The Man Who Sold the World*. The British version of Jimi Hendrix's *Electric Ladyland* boasted on the cover a slightly distorted photograph of a group of naked women. This image didn't make it to the US release. The self-titled album of short-lived supergroup Blind Faith (Ginger Baker, Eric Clapton, Ric Grech and Steve Winwood) had on its cover a photograph of a naked pubescent girl clutching a shiny silver phallic model plane. After protests the image was replaced with a band photograph, and then finally, for a third pressing, the original picture was restored with a 'Collectors Edition' label placed coyly over the girl's nude chest. Controversies about record-sleeves have continued to crop up. For their album *Appetite for Destruction*, Guns 'n' Roses reluctantly agreed to move from the cover to the inside sleeve their preferred image of a woman having been raped by a robot.

The chief source for the *Smell the Glove* story was presumably the advertising campaign for the Rolling Stones' 1976 album *Black and Blue*. The giant billboard poster featured a semi-naked woman, battered and bruised (with a prominent bruise on her inner thigh), with her legs spread wide apart and resting on a copy of the gate-fold album open, revealing a portrait of the group. Were the imagery not already blatant enough, she is shown to say: 'I'm black and blue from the Rolling Stones and I love it.' This poster inspired fury and was defaced by representatives of Women Against Violence Against Women, and, with calls to boycott all products of the record company Warner, the campaign was eventually abandoned. Mick Jagger concluded: 'Fuck them, if they can't take a joke.'

The idea of an all-black album cover has subsequently been adopted by both Prince and Metallica, either in homage to the Tap or in response to The Beatles.

SMITH, WONDERFUL
Actor playing the janitor in 'Hello Cleveland' lost-backstage sequence.

SMOKLER, PETER

> *People wrote notices saying, 'Bad camera work, really shaky.' They didn't get that. They didn't get that all these things were studied comments on other types of documentaries.*   – Robert Leighton, editor

Documentary film maker whose film on the EST founder, Warner Erhardt, racing Formula One cars (*Today Is for the Championship*) got him the job as *This Is Spinal Tap*'s cinematographer. Also served as a camera operator for some of the LA footage in *The Return of Spinal Tap*. A veteran of similar rockumentaries, including working as a cameraman on *Gimme Shelter*, Smokler was given to asking his director between takes: 'What's funny about this? This is no different from what I do.' Reiner would reassure him: 'Trust me, this is funny.' Since *This Is Spinal Tap*, Smokler's feature credits include *Problem Child 2* (1991). On television he has worked on the *Larry Sanders Show* since 1992 and has been nominated for Emmys in 1997 and 1998.

SONG REMAINS THE SAME, THE

One of the key inspirations for *This Is Spinal Tap*, this 1976 film of Led Zeppelin, directed by Peter Clifton and Joe Massot, won the *Films and Filming* magazine award for best documentary of the year. This accolade is surprising for two reasons. First, the film is only partly a documentary, mixing as it does fantasy sequences of the band and their manager Peter Grant at play with footage of their stage show at Madison Square Gardens. Second, it is, as the band themselves conceded, pretty dreadful. It is not without interest, as we see the group perform some of their best numbers ('Since I've Been Loving You', 'Whole Lotta Love' 'Stairway to Heaven', 'Dazed and Confused'). There is plenty of John Bonham's drumming (more than enough on 'Moby Dick' alone, which proves that drum solos were invented only to make guitar solos seem exciting), Plant in reasonable but not sparkling form, and some decent noodling from Page, including some of his trademark Nigel Tufnel-style bowing of the guitar.

The fantasy sequences are pretty risible, with Plant's Excalibur fantasy actually rather less embarrassing than John Paul Jones's foppish sketch, and John Bonham's tedious drag-racing wet-dream. In his vanity playlet, Jimmy Page is a mountaineer climbing towards a strange, bearded old man at the mountain's summit who begins to grow younger, becoming Page before travelling back in time still further, returning to the foetus, and then ageing again. The symbolism of the sketch is not entirely clear, but it may mean that in the course of one of Page's solos we all mysteriously grow a little older. Like the other rockumentaries cited as influences on *This Is Spinal Tap*, *The Song Remains the Same* is echoed in the atmosphere rather than in any specific details.

SOUNDGARDEN
US grunge band formed in 1984 by Chris Cornell (vocals), Kim Thayill (guitar), Hiro Yamamoto (bass) and Matt Cameron (drums). Having supported Guns 'n' Roses on tour and become a best-selling act in their own right, they finally split up in 1997. In June 1992, the CD version of their single 'Rusty Cage' included a live cover-version of Spinal Tap's 'Big Bottom'.

SOUNDTRACK
Running order:
'Hell-Hole' (3.06)
(From the LP *Smell the Glove*)

'Tonight I'm Gonna Rock You Tonight' (2.35)
(From the LP *Intravenus de Milo*)

'Heavy Duty' (4.26)
(From the LP *Bent for the Rent*)

'Rock and Roll Creation' (4.06)
(From the LP *Rock and Roll Creation*)

'America' (3.29)
(Previously unavailable)

'Cups and Cakes' (1.31)
(Single, *circa* 1965)

'Big Bottom' (3.31)
(From the LP *Brainhammer*)

'Sex Farm' (3.19)
(From the LP *Shark Sandwich*)

'Stonehenge' (4.36)
(From the LP *The Sun Never Sweats*)

'Gimme Some Money' (2.24)
(Single, 1965)

'(Listen to the) Flower People' (2:33)
(From the LP *Spinal Tap Sings '(Listen to the) Flower People' and Other Favorites*, 1967)

SPINAL PAP
Sign held up by chauffeur Tommy Pischedda when waiting to meet the band in *This Is Spinal Tap*.

SPINAL TAP
Eponymous début album released in 1967 on Megaphone. Released in the US as *Spinal Tap Sings '(Listen to the) Flower People' and Other Favorites*.

SPINAL TAP SINGS '(LISTEN TO THE) FLOWER PEOPLE' AND OTHER FAVORITES
The US title of the band's début album released in 1967 on Megaphone. The album includes '(Listen to the) Flower People' and 'Have a Nice Death'.

SPINAL TAP – THE FINAL TOUR
The name of the treatment completed on 6 July 1981, and of subsequent promotional film that stood in for a screenplay. The twenty-minute film opens with a blurred picture of a man taking the stage at an apparently otherwise empty auditorium and sitting at a piano. We cut to a picture of a plane landing and then several images of the band, Ian and various groupies going through airports. Derek Smalls has longer hair, St Hubbins' hair is straight. Then we cut to interviews with fans, including the 'Ethereal Fan' who appears in the completed film, while in the background we hear 'Tonight I'm Gonna Rock You Tonight', which we then see the band perform live.

The members are introduced as in *This Is Spinal Tap* but Viv is played by a tall, curly-haired blond man. In the first interview with the band they discuss their roots and early days, and we see the familiar black and white film of 'Gimme Some Money'. The group discuss the now familiar tragic history, with the death of 'Stumpy' Pepys and Peter 'James' Bond exploding on stage. But in this early version we learn that Stumpy Joe died from an overdose of Sudafed (a nasal decongestant).

At a hotel in St Louis, there is a version of the hassles with hotel suites, again with a receptionist that Ian dismisses as a 'twisted fruit', but here he is appeased by the offer of complimentary prawn cocktails. We cut to a scene in which Marty, the band and some groupies are relaxing in a jacuzzi. DiBergi mentions that their music has been dismissed in *Rolling Stone* as 'simple and brainless'. Tufnel protests: 'How can you call music "simple and brainless" if there are 10,000 young kids standing on their chairs, wiggling their fists?'

St Hubbins: 'Each one of them with a perfectly good brain. I've seen a number of brains out there.'

The band perform 'Heavy Duty' and then there is the sequence of Derek being stopped at the X-ray machine. In this version, when he has to reveal the surplus contents of his pants it turns out to be a bunch of metal rings wrapped in a hanky. The controversy of the cover of *Smell the Glove* is revealed as Ian is on the phone talking to a record company while Marty and the band sit in his office and discuss the significance of this hitch. After a live performance of 'Big Bottom', the scene shifts to New Jersey, where the band are picked up by the chauffeur (Bruno Kirby), who talks of his love for Sinatra and dismisses the band as 'fucking limeys'. The scene in which Nigel plays 'Lick My Love Pump' is pretty much fully formed, although we learn that the piece was written for the bass clarinet.

The prelim to 'Stonehenge' and the performance is also much as in *This Is Spinal Tap*. We cut back to the jacuzzi, where a chat about the harmony and mutual love that exists in the band leads directly into the scene of the furious row in the studio, during the course of which Derek is seen clearly to be the group's producer. There is then a quick scene in which Marty and Ian talk about the increasingly selective appeal of the band. The band members are convinced that they are getting better with the passing of time. Tufnel talks of how their music is 'not just like garbage any more'. St Hubbins: 'Yeah but it was great garbage.'

Tufnel: 'It was fun garbage, anyway.'

Smalls: 'It was popular garbage, too.'

The group perform 'Sex Farm', which is inter-cut with pictures of their groupies smashing up the hotel room on behalf of the band members who are too tired to trash their own room.

The promo ends with St Hubbins philosophising in the jacuzzi: 'Every time it's been the end of the rainbow, there's been one more colour.'

SPINAL TARP
The name by which Lieutenant Hookstratten addresses the band when he shows them around the Lindbergh air force base.

SPINE TAPE
The sign held up by the chauffeur in *Spinal Tap – The Final Tour*, the twenty-minute promotional film.

'SPRINGTIME'
Nigel Tufnel's song that wishes for homogeneous seasons, from *Break like the Wind*. Features some Page/Plant-style lead vocal versus lead guitar noodling. Choice lyrics:

> Smell the roses
> Smell the grass
> Old man winter can kiss my arse

Also features a rare moment of the Tap treating sex directly:

> Time for loving in the park
> Wear a jumper when it gets dark
> Mind the prickles
> Mind the dew
> Wash your willie when you're through

Probably the only anti-spring record in the heavy rock canon.

SPYNAL TAP
When the band was choosing a name for the fictional group, this was the spelling originally intended. Spinal Tap themselves were initially going to

call themselves Spynal Tap. They changed their minds and spelled it the way it has become known because they wanted to fit in with the trend for band-names being misspelt, as Derek has explained: 'We found out later we spelled it right by mistake.'

SQUATNEY

The East London borough where St Hubbins and Tufnel grew up. In *The Return of Spinal Tap* we see David and Nigel revisiting their old Squatney haunts. They stop to marvel at the adjoining houses where they lived – numbers forty-five and forty-seven – and Tufnel says wistfully: 'In the old days these were like mansions to us. Well, not really, more like hovels – but they were large.' The pair reminisce about the poverty they experienced, when they were forced by circumstances to eat cotton-wool balls dipped in water and then deep-fried.

Later we see the duo passing their old neighbourhood pub, The Gun, formerly The Bun, before that The Bun and Puffin, before that The Queen's Lips, before that The Restless Cheese. They move on to Squatney Road and the now-derelict site of the recording studio where there used to be a plaque commemorating 14 December 1961, the date Tufnel and St Hubbins recorded the Squatney anthem 'All the Way Home'.

Asked exactly where Squatney is, David replied: 'At sort of an obtuse angle to the right of the Embankment and straight on till morning.' When asked why it is sometimes hard to find the area on maps of London, Nigel explained: 'Yeah, well, you know, for a while they took it *off* the map. 'Cause they were so ashamed – it was not a great tourist area and they figured, y'know, people who *lived* there knew where it was, so why put it on the map?'

STATUS QUO

Long-running heavy rock band, formed in 1962 by Mike 'Francis' Rossi, John Lancaster, Alan Key and Jess Jaworski (later enhanced by the arrival of John Coughlan, Roy Lynes and Ric Parfitt), which influenced the creators of Spinal Tap. Famed for their lack of inventiveness and their immutability, the band's early years were marked by a Tapular flirting with various musical forms and names (The Spectres and Traffic Jam). The Quo, like the Tap, enjoyed a short-lived psychedelic phase during which, like the Tap, they scored their first hit in 1967, with 'Pictures of Matchstick Men'. The song inspired part of the Tap's complex back-story. After the success of their début album, *We Are All Flower People*, the band sacked keyboard player Denny Upham who went on to join the Matchstick Men. By the early seventies Status Quo had developed the style which would remain unchanged over nearly three decades, skirting close to self-parody but eventually emerging as a reliable, perennially unfashionable good-time band.

STEVENS, BRINKE

Actress who appears as the woman on Derek Smalls' right at the Recording Industry Convention in Atlanta. Stevens went on to appear as a scream queen in several horror movies, including *Psycho III* (1986) and *Scream Queen Hot Tub Parties* (1991).

STING

Sting was up for a part in Reiner's *The Princess Bride*. As the director recalls: 'He told me that he had seen it [*Spinal Tap*], you know, like, fifty times and when he watched it he didn't know whether to laugh or cry because it was so close to his experiences.'

'STINKIN' UP THE GREAT OUTDOORS'

Track from *Break like the Wind*. A jaunty, country-tinged, environmentally concerned number featuring Waddy Wachtel (Melissa Etheridge, Bob Seger, The Everly Brothers, Rolling Stones) on slide guitar and Jimmie Wood on harmonica. The song is both a celebration of the outdoor rock festival ('Ain't nothing like a festival crowd/There's too many people so we play too loud') and an exploration of the practical problems of drinking too much:

We had a drink going up in the plane,
We had another coming down again.
We got more at the airport bar,
And then some home-brewed stuff in the promoter's car.
Here we go, on with the show,
We're bubblin' under and we're ready to flow,
Wound up! Turned loose!
Ain't got the power but we sure got the juice and now we're . . .

'STONEHENGE'

In ancient times, hundreds of years before the dawn of history, lived a strange race of people – the druids. No one knows who they were, or what they were doing, but their legacy remains, hewn into the living rock – of Stonehenge.

So begins one of the Tap's finest moments, Tufnel giving full artistic vent to his Jimmy Page-like take on the most mystical of English monuments. The song is taken from the 1975 album, *The Sun Never Sweats*. Tufnel's fascination with mysticism led him to try to read *The Book of Kells* but he admitted to having no more success with reading that than he had subsequently with *The Book of Lists*.

In a *Teen-o-Rama* interview in August 1970 Tufnel is asked about how he is inspired to write songs. Nigel: 'They come as dreams. I wake up, usually about three or four in the morning, having had a dream, and that's the beginning of the song.'

Interviewer: 'Like, for instance?'

Nigel: 'Well, "Stonehenge" happened like that. I woke up, and I woke up knowing some of the words. I was sleeping with a young lady I had seen the night before – she was a Eurasian lass – and I woke up sort of suddenly and I just said, "Stonehenge, where the demons dwell, the banshees live, and they do live well." And I wrote it down – I keep a little notepad by my bed – and I got up and went over to my piano-room and started working on it. Then I ring up David in the morning, he comes by and we finish it off.'

It has been widely claimed that the Stonehenge idea was taken from a notorious Black Sabbath live extravaganza. For their 1984 Born Again tour Black Sabbath planned a theme for their stage set. In BBC TV's *Rock Family Trees – Sabbath Bloody Sabbath*, Ian Gillan, then briefly the band's vocalist, recalls the meeting with the designers, LSD: 'We were all going "Something earthy, maybe." And Geezer said: "Stonehenge." The bloke says: "That's a brilliant idea. How do you visualise it?" He said: "Life-size of course."'

Butler takes over the story: 'Stonehenge came down and it was three times bigger than the original Stonehenge. We had to hire the NEC [Birmingham's National Exhibition Centre] for the rehearsals because that was the only place it would fit – and that was without the stage. Everybody was going: "No, it'll be all right in America, all the places are bigger over

there. We'll still take it with us.' So we took it there and the first gig was
this place in Canada. We couldn't even get it in the doors in this place,
never mind put it on the stage.'

Ian Gillan continues the story in an interview in the December 1994 issue
of *Mojo* magazine: 'On the last day of rehearsal we're wondering what this
dwarf is doing hanging around backstage. When we do the dress rehearsal
the dwarf emerges in a red leotard, long yellow finger-nails and little yellow
horns. He's going to be the baby [a diabolical baby is featured on the cover
of the *Born Again* album].

'Then we hear this horrendous screaming sound – they've recorded a
baby's scream and flanged it – and suddenly we see this dwarf crawling
across the top of Stonehenge, then he stands up as the baby's scream fades
away and falls backwards off this thirty-foot fibreglass replica of Stonehenge
on to a big pile of mattresses. Then dong, dong – bells start tolling and all
the roadies come across the front of the stage in monks' cowls, at which
point "War Pigs" starts up. By now we can see the kids are either in stitches
or wincing in horror.

'After spending forty grand a day to achieve all this, someone had econo-
mised by not actually trying out the dry ice in the afternoon run-through. So,
as I stride confidently towards my prompt book [Gillan, whose relationship
with the rest of the group was uneasy, had, he boasted, never managed
fully to commit the lyrics to memory], not even knowing the first word
of the song, I'm suddenly shocked to see a chest-high cloud of dry ice is
beating me to the front of the stage. So there I am after this big opening,
kneeling down, swatting the air and trying to read my line, popping my
head above this cloud every now and then. Someone shouted, "It's Ronnie
Dio!" [diminutive sometime lead vocalist with the Sabs].'

At first this may seem like a case of the events in the film being inspired
by real incidents, but this is already improbable as the tour happened the
same year *This Is Spinal Tap* was released. Shearer, Guest and McKean have
often talked about the eagerness of bands and people in the music business
to associate themselves with the film, to claim that they are the source for
characters and events.

Christopher Guest reiterated this central point to me: 'The fact is, it's not
based on any specific group but some of those bands refuse to believe it.'

In the post-Tap world, the pomposity and seriousness of much rock
requires the addition of humour and irony, retroactively if necessary. The

simple fact is that the 'Stonehenge' sequence features in the twenty-minute demo *Spinal Tap – The Final Tour*, which was made in 1982. Nevertheless, the Tap themselves certainly borrowed the idea of a Stonehenge set being too big for the venue for their 1992 reunion appearance at the Albert Hall, when there are shots of roadies struggling and failing to fit the huge monoliths in through the stage door. This points to a practical advantage of the film's Stonehenge set. With the heavy skull and unwieldy pods difficult to transport and expensive to store in between shows, as Karen Murphy says: 'That's why the Stonehenge actually became a good symbol of the band because it was foam and light and easy to carry around.'

The synchronicity of the Black Sabbath/Spinal Tap débâcle is indicative of the fact that the film and the band, even at their most outlandish, capture an essence of truth about the music world. Andy Kershaw, writing his Rock Diary in the *Independent* on 17 November 1989, remarks: 'An incident involving Soul II Soul at the Big World Studios would not have been out of place in *Spinal Tap*. A grand stage set was planned, involving polystyrene letters, six feet tall, in red, yellow, blue and green spelling "Soul II Soul". A number of children were to augment the usual line-up, and they intended to perform on top of the lettering. When the designers delivered the letters they were a full six inches.'

STUPID

See Fame, Duke.

SUB-PLOTS

The chief sub-plots dropped from the final film are: the recording of the radio jingles to support the tour; The Dose and herpes story; Artie Fufkin's scene persuading the group to get up early for a radio appearance in Chicago and their appearance on the show; Derek's divorce proceedings; the friction between Marty and Ian concerning the contract for the film; Nigel discussing at length his devotion to the kids' TV show *Gumby*; Nigel's replacement Ricky (not featured on the special edition); and Derek showing off to Marty his acting experience in *Roma '79*. The other extra material included in the special edition are extensions to scenes existing in the film: the preamble to Derek's penile enlargement; more scenes with Tommy and the mime caterers; a longer scene at Elvis's grave, including the band's problems in getting into Graceland; extended scenes of Marty being shown Nigel's guitars; more bits with Derek, Nigel and their tour groupies; much more stuff at the Rainbow Trout Recording Studio.

SUN NEVER SWEATS, THE

Concept album released in 1974. Features 'The Sun Never Sweats', 'Daze of Knights of Old', 'The Princess and the Unicorn', 'The Obelisk' and the classic 'Stonehenge'. As the cover, which features the band walking along a massive Union Jack towards the setting sun, suggests, this is a concept album themed around the idea of Britannia. The title came from a mishearing by Smalls of the saying, 'The sun never sets on the British Empire.' The title track features on *Break like the Wind*. It has a pomp rock feel. In the lyrics Smalls, the band's great thinker, reveals himself as someone who has read widely and deeply on England's history:

> Empire. It was here and now it's gone.

The idea of Empire is explored using Smalls' characteristic playfulness with philosophical conceits:

> Even the biggest elephant never forgets . . .
>
> . . . Even the hardest concrete never quite sets . . .
>
> . . . We may be gods or just big marionettes . . .

The atmosphere of Empire is also evoked in the number's sound, as the track includes a musical quotation from 'The British Grenadiers'.

SWISS ARMY

After the collapse of the band's 1982 Japanese tour, the members went their different ways, Nigel travelling across Europe and, in a bizarre, Elvis-like move, managing to enlist in the Swiss army. He recalls: 'The Swiss army is very lovely, as armies go. Somewhere between a scout troop and a school for waiters. They don't have any bullets in their guns. Don't print that, because they like to *think* they're frightening people – but they're water guns.'

T

TV SHOW, THE
The scene of the band's first public appearance as Spinal Tap in 1978. **See 'Rock 'n' Roll Nightmare'.**

TAPHEAD
In the strange world of the Tap, the notion of the Taphead was introduced in the original script, in which a devoted fan inveigled himself into the world of the band and started hanging out with them towards the second half of the tour. The character, although an irritant to the members of the group, stays with them and ends up as the only one having a good time as the band disintegrates.

TEDDY NOISE
Group for which Derek played bass during the time he attended the London School of Design. As he remembers: 'It was during the Mods and Rockers era and we were Rods.'

TEN COMMANDMENTS OF ROCK AND ROLL
Six of the ten commandments of rock and roll, as outlined in the band's *Hollywood Online* interview:

St Hubbins: 'Number one – rock and roll keeps you young, but you die young.'
Smalls: 'Number two – don't covet thy neighbour's guitar.'
St Hubbins: 'Number three – if it's too loud, you're too close.'
Smalls: 'Number four – if you can read this, you're too close.'
St Hubbins: 'Number five – there are no more commandments.'
Smalls: 'Number six – memorise previous commandments.'

TENNANT, VICTORIA (1950—)
Actress born in London who was married to Steve Martin and was twice his co-star (*All of Me*, 1982 and *LA Story*, 1991). Tennant was seriously considered to play Jeanine Pettibone, but lost out to June Chadwick.

TENNIS

In a cutting-room-floor scene, Marty tracks Nigel down to the LA apartment in which he is staying, having left the tour. Nigel's host is a TV actor who is teaching Tufnel the fundamentals of tennis. Nigel shows off his ability to balance a ball on the racket face. An unimpressed Marty asks: 'That's what you've been doing since you left the band?' Nigel reveals that he has also been thinking. Of his future, he says that he has been writing a new song. Marty lets him know that he senses that David is missing him. Nigel says he misses him too but mainly as a writing partner: 'Something happens when we write a song together . . . We sort of become the same writer when we're writing together, I suppose.' He says he is considering a solo career, and has given up smoking for three days: 'Y'see, I'm sort of getting back to the way the Japanese look at it. They say: "A flat ocean is an ocean of trouble, and an ocean [*long pause*] of waves can also be trouble." So it's like that balance. You know it's that great oriental way of thinking, where they think they've tricked you and then they have.'

THAMESMEN, THE

One of the early incarnations of the band.

As part of the warm-up for the European leg of their 1992 comeback tour, the Tap played a secret acoustic gig at the Borderline in central London on 8 April 1992 billed as 'The Thamesmen – Acoustic Matinee Performance'. The gig was an unlikely matinee appearance for the notorious late-risers. But the acoustic side of the event was even more controversial, with the band using what looked like their normal instruments. According to Mark Wareham in his review from the *Independent*, Tufnel clarified the confusion: 'It's acoustic, but we're electronically boosting it.'

See name changes.

THEMELAND AMUSEMENT PARK

In Stockton, California. Venue for post-Nigel gig where the newly four-piece band are billed below the puppet show and are forced to essay Derek's free-form composition, 'Jazz Odyssey'.

See puppet show.

THIS IS SPINAL TAP

Shortly after the film's release, David was asked how the film had changed the band's fortunes. He replied: 'I do know that critics who used to pass us off as sort of a nobody band are beginning to re-emerge and, uh, say basically the same thing.' Subsequently the band have regularly been asked how they feel about the 1984 rockumentary, and routinely dismiss it as a hatchet job – even a 'horror film'. They consider themselves to have been stitched up by their fan Marty DiBergi, who chose to show only the bits that made them seem foolish. Nigel has likened his experience with *This Is Spinal Tap* to the way the stars of *Who's Afraid of Virginia Woolf?* must have felt on seeing the film: 'Imagine how embarrassed Liz Taylor was to see her marriage portrayed like that.'

'TONIGHT I'M GONNA ROCK YOU TONIGHT'

I'd probably work with children.
– Derek on what he would do were it not for Spinal Tap

'Tonight I'm Gonna Rock You Tonight' is the track from *Intravenus de Milo* that opens and closes *This Is Spinal Tap* and so is the song with which the world first came to know the band. It is a classic heavy rock paean to an under-aged object of desire, with the evergreen lyrics:

> You're sweet but you're just four feet
> And you still got your baby teeth,
> You're too young, and I'm too well hung but
> Tonight I'm gonna rock ya.

A reminder of the generous endowment of the group's lead duo, with a precedent in David Bowie's song of his alter ego 'Ziggie Stardust':

> He came on so loaded, man
> Well hung, snow white tan

There is a history – almost a rich tradition – of pop and rock music stars being sexually drawn to jail-bait – a heritage that began with pioneers such as Jerry Lee Lewis and Elvis Presley and spread across the Atlantic to Jimmy Page and Bill Wyman. 'Tonight I'm Gonna Rock You Tonight' has entered the canon that contains such dodgy classics as 'Young Girl' ('You're much too young girl'), 'Thank Heaven for Little Girls', 'Clare', 'Save Your Kisses for Me' and 'I'm on Fire' and lends a retrospectively disturbing subtext to the group's celebrity photo-schmooze with Gary Glitter.

TORMÉ, MEL (1925–1999)

Old crooner, born in Chicago and popularly known as 'The Velvet Fog'. Tormé, who worked with Duke Ellington, Count Basie and Bing Crosby, appears in *The Return of Spinal Tap* sitting in a diner and singing a snatch from 'Big Bottom' to Tufnel. He asks: 'Does that get to you at all?' Tufnel, overwhelmed, responds: 'I'm wet.'

TREATMENT

The 1981 treatment for the film provides a synopsis for the prospective project:

> In the late fall of 1981, Spinal Tap, a veteran heavy metal English rock band embarked on what the rock world and many of the Third World nations hoped would be the last of a series of pathetic demonstrations of musical near competence. It was heralded (the poster said) as Spinal Tap's final tour.
>
> Through fifteen years and seventeen albums, from the now collector's item *Silent But Deadly* to the current *Smell the Glove*, Spinal Tap earned a place as one of Britain's loudest bands.
>
> Film-maker Marty DiBroma, best known for his award-nominated Figurine commercials, and a life-long Tap fan, decided to document what he thought could be a legendary seven weeks in rock'n'roll history.
>
> The tour began with a sold-out concert at New York's Beacon Theater, followed by what the band's record company (Parallel Records) hoped would seem like a lavish send-off party at Patsy's Clam House (a tradition in seafood since 1921).
>
> Presiding at the party was the distinguished homosexual and chairman of the board of Parallel Records, Sir Denis Eton-Hogg. Also populating the desperately festive occasion were Tap's latest manager, the pugnacious and tone-deaf Ian Faith; the female record company publicist assigned to accompany the tour, the short and coked-up Bobbi Flekman (who shows up at various places along the tour only

when it suits her needs); assorted groupies, reporters, obscure rock magazines and various drugged-out hangers-on.

From New York, the band limousined to Philadelphia to begin an East Coast swing, driven by Tommy Rispoli, a limo chauffeur who dreams of growing up to become Frank Sinatra -- or at least driving him some place. By their second performance, the shady optimism of New York was replaced by the grim realities of Philadelphia. The opening act on the bill, a high-tech all-girl all-new-wave band called "The Dose", not only blew Tap off the stage of Liberty Hall, but blew several members into semi-private rooms at Temple University Clinic for the venereally diseased.

Heavy metal music has never fared particularly well in Washington, and Tap's appearance there for a crowd heavily papered [sic] with winners of a ticket giveaway was no exception. Later that night, at a hotel-room party commerating [sic] the end of the East Coast swing, the band wavered between destroying the room and getting Tommy, the limo driver, high. They decided to get Tommy high and have him destroy the hotel room. With that, they bid a fond farewell to our nation's capital.

On arrival in Atlanta, Ian Faith, in what was to be one of his last and least articulate conversations with Sir Denis Easton-Hogg [sic], got some bad news. The cover of the band's current *Smell the Glove* was too controversial for release in America. Women's groups called it sexist. Tap members couldn't understand what was sexist about a naked heavily-oiled blonde posed on all fours, a dog collar around her neck, being forced to smell a suspicious-looking glove. This set in motion a crucial chain of events. Without a record to promote, record company support would be slowly withdrawn. Promoters along the tour started to threaten to cancel concert dates. In the face of the obvious, the band refused to change the cover and plodded on through the South.

At Ian's insistence, the band flew to Memphis where hundreds of drunk disc jockeys and record promoters were attending the annual national record marketing convention. The band was dragged through countless liquor and bad deli hospitality suites where they were forced to stand still and schmooze.

The band tried to cure it's [sic] collective hangover with a pilgrimage to Graceland to pay homage to the King, Elvis Presley. It was a tender moment filled with inarticulate sentiment and basic human stupidity.

With the spector [sic] of half-filled halls looming before them, the band assembled in its charted custom tour bus for a swing through the Midwest; joined now by David St Hubbins' live-in girlfriend, Janine [sic] Pettibone, a former model and current freelance astrologer. From her first day on the bus, Pettibone made herself an important and unwanted part of the band's business – from suggesting the group begin wearing clown-like stage make-up to preparing copies of an astrologically sound set-list. In Dayton, Tap re-encountered and spent a day trying to avoid Artie Fufkin, one of the 500 promo men they pretended to meet at the Atlanta convention.

During Mick Shrimpton's interminable drum solo at the Dayton Civic Auditorium concern [sic], Derek received a call from his lawyer informing him that his ex-wife-to-be had made her proposal for a property settlement public in a full-page ad in *New Musical Express*, Nigel was trapped in a dressing-room with Artie Fufkin, some girls and an over-sized vial of badly cut cocaine; and David was sitting backstage getting a much needed haircut and partial leg waxing. They all arrived backstage in time to see Mick fake his usual collapse and finish their show to a standing ovation.

On Interstate 40 heading towards Chicago, Derek introduced Mick to the complex joys of cooking and smoking free-base cocaine. At a sudden stop, the boiling liquid splatters on to the polyurethane carpeting of the bus, which becomes a temporary inferno on wheels, billows of black smoke curling out from the rear of the once luxurious vehicle.

Tempers flared in Chicago when Tap held a stormy band meeting at the legendary Southside pizzaria [sic] 'Two Guys Named Joey'. During the meeting, David made a number of suggestions to make the band's last half of the tour somewhat less of a nightmare; suggestions which everyone present knew had originated with Janine, who sat quietly at the end of the table eating a spinach and mushroom calzone. Finally, after taking a lot more of this medling [sic] by proxy than he could possibly stomach, Ian delivered a shouting ultimatum to everyone, 'Either she goes or I go.' David stormed out with Janine, Derek took advantage of his celebrityhood by accompanying one of Joey's less unattractive waitresses to a nearby soft spot in a local alleyway, and Nigel decided to visit a lifelong idol of his, the famous old blues great Blind Bubba Cheeks, who was performing in town.

The result of Ian's ulitimatium [sic] was: Ian stayed. Janine stayed, everyone agreed things were resolved and things got worse. They flew to Denver to appear at the Mile High Jam and while there David's son, ten-year-old, purple-haired, cigarette-smoking, sullen punker, David Jr showed up backstage. The tender father–son reunion climaxed with David telling his son to rinse that shit out of his hair and let it grow out like a man. From Denver, the band went to Caribou, an extremely expensive studio high in the Colorado Rockies to begin recording the remaining album of a three-record commitment. Recording is a slow and tedious process, especially when carried out by musicians of limited ability. To relieve the tedium, Ian and Janine spent a few hours in a nearby lodge conducting a semi-torrid affair.

The final leg of the tour began on the West Coast with performances at the suddenly scaled-down venues in Seattle and San Francisco. In Los Angeles, the tour's last concert ended when an attempt to revive the band's onetime over-theatrical epic rock classic 'Stonehenge' dismally misfired.

Remaining in LA until the last promoter's check [sic] cleared, amidst depression, despondency and talk of breaking up, the band learned that one of the cuts from the *Smell the Glove* album, which had been released in Japan, was played on the air continuously for forty-eight hours by a deranged Tokyo DJ and had become a Top Ten single. Ian quickly arranged for a Japanese tour and the band was given a new sublet on life.

In addition to documenting this tour, the film will also include: extensive interviews with the band members, individually and as a group, in which they talk about their history, their philosophy of rock'n'roll and life and their views on tax incentives and female genitalia.

We also see the continuation of a friendship between David and Nigel that goes back to their days as schoolboys in the Squatney section of London, a friendship which is tested during the course of the tour.

Footage of the band's appearances on the British *Popbeat* and the American *Bopshebop* TV shows.

Live concert footage from various stops on the tour and footage of the band members in England and Lictenstein [*sic*] at their impossibly overblown and under-restored castles, purchased with early royalties.

See screenplay.

TROGGS TAPES

The British pop band, led by millionaire crop-circle enthusiast Reg Presley and famous for 'Wild Thing' and 'Love is All Around' became the subject of cult fame with the *Troggs Tapes*. These recordings, available on bootleg tapes, were made during a session and display, according to *The Penguin Encyclopaedia of Popular Music*: 'instrumental incompetence, mutual recrimination and much foul language.' These tapes directly inspired the sequence in which Tufnell and St Hubbins have their row in the Rainbow Trout Recording Studio as Derek and the rest of the band and their entourage sit next door at the mixing desk.

In an out-take Nigel screams at David: 'Just fucking tell me something, why can't you play this? Just tell me that. [*To Derek*] Have you been listening to what we're doing out here? I've been playing the fucking part and he can't even fucking do it.' Nigel shouts his belief that the root of the problem is Jeanine: 'It's the fucking girl. It's the fucking bird in the hotel ... It's fucking Jeanine. It's fucking Jeanine. It's not me, it's Jeanine. It's fucking Jeanine, that is it. It's fucking Jeanine.' He walks off.

Derek and Nigel go off to a side-room and continue the discussion in which they agree that Jeanine is the problem. Derek returns to David with a parting shot from Nigel: 'Tell him to fuck himself.' David is lying down in the studio. Having told Nigel that everyone knows that he is the 'heart and soul of the fuckin' group', Derek tells David: 'Look, everyone knows you're the fuckin' heart and soul of the fuckin' band, right.'

The scene is marred by Derek referring to Nigel as David.

TUFNEL, NIGEL (1948—)

Character description from 1981 treatment: 'lead guitar in the band. One of the co-founders of Spinal Tap, whose composing style leans toward the pompous, overwritten and pseudo-important. His musical homage to the United States, "If I Were King of America", was written on the plane to New York, and serves as the underscoring for a pretentious DiBroma filmic montage.'

Tufnel was born in the Squatney district of London's East End on or around 1 March 1948, just a few weeks after Christopher Guest. He attended St Scubbins school along with St Hubbins. His first job as a child was to clean the chewing-gum from Bakerloo Station, for which he would be paid a farthing. His second job was working for Marks & Spencer, for whom he would work behind the scenes, marking the boxes of imperfect goods with a '2'. He recalls: 'I only had that job for a week, 'cause I kept forgetting the number. If you write a three or something, it goes to another department and gets all confused.' Another early job was working on a helter skelter at Battersea Amusement Park, where he would brush out the pieces of carpet that the children would sit on as they slid down: 'It was grotesque, I had to wear a nose pin, especially in the summer.'

Tufnel first picked up a guitar at around the age of seven. In the climax to the film, he is asked by DiBergi what he would do if he weren't a rock star. He replies: 'I'd like to open a *chapeau* shop.' In *Merseysound*, the newly successful Beatles are interviewed about their reactions to their first taste of pop glory. Asked what his life ambition is, Ringo replies: 'Well, I've always wanted to open a posh ladies' hairdressers, perhaps a chain of them.'

In *The Return of Spinal Tap*, we discover that between the disastrous collapse of the band's 1982 Japanese tour and their 1992 reunion Tufnel had busied himself in his inventing shed in Brinsby, Kent. His inventions include a folding wine-glass, from which wine conspicuously leaks because the rubber hinges being made in China haven't yet arrived. His other creation is the 'amplifier CAPO'. Instead of the obstruction to his hand caused by having the implement on the guitar neck, he places a vast one on his amp. Tufnel also reveals himself as an animal activist. He established a group called TFA (Travel for Animals). Helped by Tufnel's preternatural ability to communicate with animals, the organisation arranges holidays for animals and provides them with tiny passports. We learn that Trevor the ferret travels light, packing only tiny mints for when his ears pop in planes.

Tufnel claims never to have heard a Uriah Heep record.

See Uriah Heep.

U

USS *CORAL SEA*

The name of the ship on Marty's cap. The production team were informed that they were not allowed to use the name in the film, so producer Karen Murphy disguised the cap by some hand-stitching which rendered the name as the meaningless USS *OORAL SEA*.

U2

See 'Rock and Roll Creation'.

UPHAM, DENNY

Band's keyboardist fired in 1968 after the release of their second album, *We Are All Flower People*.

URIAH HEEP

One of key bands who inspired the Tap, the long-lived and resolutely unfashionable Heep were formed in 1968 by David Byron (vocals),★ Mick Box (guitar/vocals), Ken Hensley (guitar/keyboards/vocals), Paul Newton (bass) and Keith Baker (drums). Over the next thirty years the band enjoyed commercial success, especially in America, and plodded on despite critical indifference or scorn, enduring more than thirty changes in personnel (having a particular problem with drummers) and two deaths (Byron and bassist/vocalist Gary Thain).

John Sinclair, the original keyboardist with Spinal Tap, had to leave the band when the negotiations for the film were taking too long. Instead he went on tour with Uriah Heep. When he returned to the project to contribute to the album, he was of further use by telling the band

---

★ It could perhaps be that this was the Byron that Smalls had in mind when he likened Tufnel and St Hubbins to the great romantic poets. That might mean that the Shelley he was thinking of was Pete from the Buzzcocks.

the story of Uriah Heep being booked to play an air force base. While Tufnel insists that he has never even heard a Heep recording, Derek says that his favourite is: '"Abominog", mainly because I like it the way it's said backwards: "Gonimoba".'

V

VD

In an out-take, having fallen victim to a dose of herpes courtesy of the lead singer of The Dose, Derek eyes himself in a backstage mirror and judges: 'Well, Derek's out of circulation, isn't he?'

See Dose, The.

VAN DER KVELK, JAN

The keyboardist that proto-Tap band The Thamesmen hooked up with during their tour of the Benelux countries after the release of their first single, 'Gimme Some Money'. It was on their return from this tour that The Thamesmen briefly became The Dutchmen.

VAN HALEN

Hard rock group formed in California in 1973 by Eddie Van Halen (guitar and keyboards), Alex Van Halen (drums), Michael Anthony (bass) and David Lee Roth (vocals). The band went under the name Mammoth and considered calling themselves Rat Salade before settling on Van Halen. Their demo was produced by Gene Simmons of Kiss, and Eddie Van Halen has played with, among others, Michael Jackson and Tap-collaborator Steve Lukather. 'The Endless Party', a *Rolling Stone* article about Van Halen, inspired Tufnel's hysterical outburst about the backstage refreshments. Van Halen were said to have a backstage rider demanding that M&Ms be served but with all the brown ones removed. In Q magazine in May 1999, Orbital claimed that one of their backstage requests was for forty Topic bars with the hazelnuts taken out. Eddie Van Halen is reputed to have been the first rock guitarist to be inspired by *This Is Spinal Tap* and request a customised amp with dials going up to eleven.

VANDERMINT AUDITORIUM

Venue in Chapel Hill, North Carolina, at the backstage of which Nigel has his problems with the catering and where the band perform 'Hell Hole'.

VANSTON, C. J.

Keyboardist for the band in *The Return of Spinal Tap*.

VINYL TAP

One of the many strands of the involved back-story of Spinal Tap is the tale of the men who posed as Spinal Tap. In the story reported in the fake *Screem* magazine in 1977, it was revealed that Larry Barth, a theatrical agent who runs the booking agency Creative International Artists (CIA), and Manny Gorecki, the lead singer of the fake band, had conspired to defraud the Tap by offering venues the opportunity to book them. The band's attorney, Roger Grade, was quoted in the *New York Daily News*: 'A lot of people really thought they were the real Spinal Tap, although many others said "They sound better than they used to."'

Vinyl Tap is billed as 'The UK's only classic rock covers band dedicated to the sights, sounds and smells of the hardest working, longest lasting and loudest heavy metal band, Spinal Tap.' Vinyl Tap is indeed that inevitable phenomenon – the Spinal Tap tribute band. Formed in the spring of 1996, the line-up consists of Eddie Van Rental (lead vocals, bass), Randy Thodes (lead guitar, vocals), Ric Pastitt (rhythm guitar, vocals) and Ian Paicemaker (lead vocals, drums). Their regular set includes the Tap numbers 'Big Bottom' and 'Stonehenge' as well as heavy rock classics such as 'Smoke on the Water', 'Paranoid' and 'Ace of Spades'. The band's declared manifesto is 'for the band and the people who come along to see them to have a laugh and a good time'. You assume they mean to have a laugh and a good time all the time. The predecessors of the Tap, The Rutles, were themselves spoofed in an enterprise that would require a degree in irony to fully comprehend its cultural meaning. The album *Rutles Highway Revisited* consists of the tracks on the Rutles' album of parodic Beatles music being covered by an assortment of artists signed to New York's Shimmy Disc label. We await the Tap tribute albums *This Isn't Spinal Tap* and *Like, Break like the Wind*.

VOMIT

Eric 'Stumpy Joe' Childs, the band's second drummer, died in 1974 by choking on vomit – although it has never emerged on whose vomit it was that he choked and, as Nigel pointed out: 'You can't really dust for vomit.' AC/DC's lead singer Bon Scott died this way. There is also the case of Mama Cass Elliot, lead singer of The Mamas and the Papas, who started life in the mid-sixties with Tap-like name changes moving through the New Journeymen and 2 Journeymen. After the break-up of the band in 1968, Cass launched herself as a solo performer. On the night of 29 June 1974, after a live performance at the London Palladium, she died, her body being discovered the following morning. The coroner eventually recorded that she died from a heart attack brought about by her obesity, while there was a rumour that she died as the result of a heroin overdose. But there has been a persistent rumour, reputedly coming from the coroner's office itself, that the cause of Cass's death was in fact a ham sandwich. It is said that a morsel of the sandwich lodged in her windpipe and she died by inhaling her own vomit.

The greatest victim of death by choking on vomit is of course Jimi Hendrix, friend of Tap collaborator Jeff Beck. Hendrix died in his sleep on 8 September 1970 in the London flat of his girlfriend, Monika Danneman. The immediate inspiration for Stumpy Joe's death is certainly John Bonham, the drummer of Led Zeppelin. Led Zeppelin were famous for their debauched behaviour on tour, and Jimmy Page's dabbling with satanism lent the band a reputation for dangerous, dark excess. A succession of accidents, culminating in the tragic death of Robert Plant's young son Karac in 1977, led to the popular belief that the band were the victims of a curse. On the afternoon of 24 September 1980, Bonham started a drinking binge that continued until midnight when he passed out and was carried to bed. The following afternoon one of his assistants went to rouse him and found him dead. The coroner reported that he had consumed around forty shots of vodka, suffered alcohol poisoning and choked on his vomit in his sleep.

In early plans for *This Is Spinal Tap* there was to have been a longer chat on the theme of Eric and his death, with Derek concluding on the strange funeral arrangements: 'Stumpy died in his own vomit, we felt he should be buried in his own vomit.'

W

WAINWRIGHT III, LOUDON

In early incarnations of the band, including their first broadcast appearance on *The TV Show*, Loudon Wainwright III appeared as Spinal Tap's keyboard player. Born on 5 September 1946 in Chapel Hill, North Carolina, the singer-songwriter emerged from the folk scene in the late 1960s. He has remained a cult figure, hampered by the first label attached to him of the new Dylan and the second of novelty comedy/folk act which has stuck with him since his early hit 'Dead Skunk'.

Wainwright played a singing surgeon in several episodes of the TV series *M*A*S*H*, and acted on stage in *The Birthday Party*, *Owners* and *Pump Boys and Dinettes*, and in the film *Jacknife* (1988). He has also performed his comedy numbers on Jasper Carrot's TV show.

WE ARE ALL FLOWER PEOPLE

The band's second album, released in 1968, of which it has been noted: 'Sales, when they occurred, were disappointing.' Includes songs 'We Are All Flower People', 'The Incredible Flight of Icarus P. Anybody' (not to be confused with Iron Maiden's 1977 number 'The Flight of Icarus'), 'To Fly', 'I Am Flight' and 'Get Me Away from the Ground'. Re-released in 1969 without the title track as *The Incredible Flight of Icarus P. Anybody*. Derek has said: 'It was a very, very early concept album about a man who decided, like Icarus, that he would put on wings and fly – but that he would be a jet airliner and that he would sell seats on himself to pay for the project. You know, it was very acid-influenced.'

WESTERN MUSIC

In the out-take in which Nigel discusses his musical experimentation, he talks of his interest in the music of America's West of the 1860s and 1870s, cowboy campfire songs, and their little known connection to his other passion – Indonesian folk music. He demonstrates the kind of jolly cowboy song that people associate with Gene Autry and Roy Rogers, and then plays the authentic sound of the West – in fact the same two notes, as Marty notices: 'It is very similar to the Indonesian . . . It's almost exactly like the Indonesian.'

'WHERE ARE THEY NOW?'

Just after David has found out, and told Nigel, that Jeanine is going to join the tour in Milwaukee, Derek tells them to come into the next room to hear a piece of their history. 'Cups and Cakes' is playing on the radio. As the song finishes, the DJ says: 'They're currently residing in the "Where are they now?" file.' In an out-take we see that the post-scene depression concluded with Ian Faith coming into the room and explaining that what they should be doing is smashing up their hotel room, which he proceeds to do with his cricket bat.

In similar vein, shortly after the release of *This Is Spinal Tap*, David was in more sanguine mood about the band's shifting popularity and selective appeal as he contemplated a future comeback tour and possible live album: 'A comeback has to start with "Whatever-happened-to . . . ?" And if you don't really remember *who* it happened to, whatever it was, then you're not gonna want a comeback. Even a journey like a comeback starts with a single step, y'know?'

'WHOLE LOTTA LORD'

The Lambsblood single that owed a certain debt to Led Zeppelin's 'Whole Lotta Love'. The track features Derek Smalls on bass, and an extract from a live performance can be seen in *The Return of Spinal Tap*.

WILLARD, FRED (1939—)

The actor who plays Lieutenant Hookstratten at Lindbergh air force base. Willard's group, The Ace Trucking Company, toured on the same bill as The Credibility Gap. Willard has appeared in dozens of comedy films and TV sitcoms, and has collaborated with various members of Spinal Tap in *The History of White People in America: Vol II* (1986) and *Waiting for Guffman* (1996) as well as reprising his role as Lieutenant Hookstratten in *The Return of Spinal Tap*.

WOODSTOCK

Era-defining three-day music festival of August 1969 with appearances from

The Who, Jimi Hendrix, The Grateful Dead, The Band, Santana, Janis Joplin, Arlo Guthrie, Sly and the Family Stone, Joe Cocker, Crosby, Stills, Nash and Young, Jefferson Airplane, Joan Baez, Tim Hardin and Richie Havens, among others. In a special competition-winners interview, one fan asked the members of Spinal Tap if the organisers didn't ask them to perform. Derek replied: 'They did, but we were busy at the time.' Nigel offered further clarification: 'That's been raised a million times, that question. And the answer is, I think it was lost in the mail. I think they *did* invite us, and I think we just didn't get the letter.'

WRITERS

As the film was improvised by all the performers, Reiner, Guest, McKean and Shearer went to the Writers' Guild hoping to give proper credit to everyone. The Board of Directors voted fifteen to none that the credit should stay as it was – including only the four of them.

X

XANADU STAR THEATRE

The venue in Cleveland, Ohio (the sequence was filmed at the Embassy Auditorium in LA) where the band get lost backstage. In his commentary for the Criterion laser disc edition, Christopher Guest recalls the inspiration for the scene: 'We saw a tape of Tom Petty playing somewhere in Germany, where he's walking backstage and a door's opened and he ends up on an indoor tennis court and there's just this moment of stunned, you know, "Where am I?" and then he continues looking for the stage.'

Harry Shearer recalls that a similar thing happened to a friend of his, Harry Rifkin, occasional manager of The Grateful Dead. Wandering around backstage trying to find his way to the stage, he opened the wrong door and found himself walking in on a boxing match.

See *Don't Look Back.*

X-RAYS

See zucchini.

Y

YES

Steven Soderbergh, esteemed director of *Sex, Lies and Videotape* (1989) and *Out of Sight* (1998), made a documentary profile of Brit prog-rock band Yes in the mid-1980s called *9012 Live*. In his interview with Soderbergh in the *Observer* on 29 November 1998, Andrew Anthony asked incredulously if the film was made after *This Is Spinal Tap*. Soderbergh replied: 'Yeah. I took Jon Anderson to see it and he came back and told the rest of the guys about it. They started watching it, like, every day because it was so their world.'

YES I CAN

It is a copy of this book being read by a groupie in the back of his limo that inspires Tommy the chauffeur to talk about his love of Frank Sinatra. The book, published in 1965, was the first volume of Sammy Davis Jr's autobiography, co-written with his friend the journalist Burt Boyar.

YIN AND YANG

In the *Independent* profile of the band in February 1992, St Hubbins said of their internationally selective appeal: 'We always sold well in the Benelux nations, which almost made up for the complete lack of interest anywhere else. These days when we're in England we say we're big in America and when we're in America we say we're big in the UK. It's a balanced existence.'

Tufnel suggested: 'It's like yin and, er, the other one.'

YOKO PLOT, THE

See Pettibone, Jeanine.

Z

ZAMBONI, MARCO
Italian film director and one-time collaborator with Derek Smalls.

See *Roma '79*.

ZAPPA, DWEEZIL
Son of Frank, with whom he occasionally collaborated. Dweezil became a proficient rock guitarist in his own right and contributed a solo to 'Diva Fever' on *Break like the Wind*.

ZAPPA, FRANK (1940–93)
Legendary prolific, jazz- and classical-influenced, weirdness-tinged, drug-hating, groupie-loving, humorous/serious, experimental rock personage, the burning of whose equipment at a concert in Montreux in 1971 was immortalised in Deep Purple's 'Smoke on the Water'. In one of several instances of creative synchronicity, Zappa's composition 'Be in My Video' (from his album *Them or Us*), which mocks the pretentiousness of the video generation, as exemplified by David Bowie, includes the lines:

> Wear a leather collar
> And a dagger in your ear
> I will make you smell the glove
> And try to look sincere

ZUCCHINI
In the May 1999 edition of *Mojo* magazine there is a photo report of the video of Garbage's single 'You Look So Fine'. Singer Shirley Manson is pictured stroking a man lying on his back with a highly visible bulge in his trousers. The caption reads: 'The hunk impersonating the cucumber from Spinal Tap is Pamela Anderson's new beau, Kelly Slater.'

This is another of the instantly recognisable elements of the film. A large penis or the semblance of a large penis is essential to success in heavy rock. For men, at least. David declares himself to be 'too well hung' in 'Tonight I'm Gonna Rock You Tonight' and Nigel has talked of the armadillos that the band have down their trousers which scare sensitive young female fans. To prove their credentials, David and Nigel have been photographed with comically enhanced crotches. The scene in which Derek is caught with a foil-wrapped zucchini down his pants was filmed at the Imperial Terminal at LA airport. In the out-takes that can be seen in Criterion's special edition laser-disc version of *This Is Spinal Tap*, there is a lengthy prelude to this scene, which is interesting for fans to see. But, of course, had it in fact appeared in the completed film it would have blown one of the best gags. The whole sequence evolved from Derek being told in a band meeting that he had to remedy his 'downstairs problem'. Michael McKean recalls David's suggestion to Derek: 'You got to reach out into the audience a bit more.' Guest talks of how Tufnel attempted to clarify the matter: 'The fruit basket's a little light.'

In the out-take scene that survives, the band are on the tour-bus and for the benefit of Marty Derek plays a video of *Roma '79*, the *Song Remains the Same*-style fantasy/vanity project in which he plays a supposedly super-cool kind of hit man who is shown in a pre-credit sequence assembling a futuristic gun. As the video is playing, Nigel and David, who have seen it many times, take Derek aside to discuss a sensitive band issue.

David: 'We wanted a word with you about your stage appearance, specifically the costuming during your performance, sort of look. Maybe something may be missing in terms of . . .'

Nigel helps: '. . . thrust.'

David: '. . . of thrust. Specifically, more specifically, below the waist trouser area of the look.'

Nigel: 'Power zone.'

David: 'The power zone, exactly. We've noticed a sort of drape where maybe there should be a sort of a bit of a projection.'

Nigel: 'There's sort of a canyon where there should be a mountain.'

David: 'I mean, just a touch more in the power zone.'

David asks him to think about it as the pre-credit sequence of the film ends with the death of Derek's character. He has to admit to Marty that the film is about the man who comes in to shoot him.

There follows a scene in which the film's cult character, the band's roadie,

Moke, with Derek's advice, prepares the zucchini in the foil. He rolls one up, but Derek suggests a rather larger one which he thinks might work better. They discuss the importance of stability: 'Because I don't want it crawling down the old trouser leg. I don't want it landing on the shoes with a plop.' Derek insists that he dresses on the left: 'It's my good side. I think you need to make it more symmetrical to make it believable, because credibility's part of what we're going after here.'

In early drafts the increase was affected by five pounds of lead shot wrapped in leather. In the promo reel *Spinal Tap – The Final Tour*, the package is a bunch of rings wrapped up in a hanky.

In his profile of the band in the *Independent*, Jim White noted that after the complex room-service demands of Tufnel and St Hubbins, Smalls' request was much simpler: 'Just a banana.' Smalls has confided in recent interviews that to avoid a repeat of the LAX embarrassment, the zucchini he now uses is wrapped in the same material used to make the Stealth bomber.

The Tap keep on going. Derek Smalls says: 'Rock and roll is not a matter of age, it's a matter of volume. We're definitely old enough to play loud, the louder the better. Turn it up!'

Select Bibliography

BOOKS

AC/DC – The World's Heaviest Rock by Martin Huxley (Boxtree, 1996)

The Beatles by Hunter Davies (Heinemann, 1985)

Collins Encyclopaedia of Music by Sir Jack Westrup and F.L.I. Harrison, revised by Conrad Wilson (Chancellor Press, 1984)

The Great Rock Discography by M.C. Strong (Canongate, 1995)

Hammer of the Gods – The Led Zeppelin Saga by Stephen Davis (Sidgwick & Jackson, 1985)

Inside Spinal Tap by Peter Occhiogrosso (Abacus, 1992)

Keith Richards by Victor Bockris (Penguin, 1993)

Lost in Music by Giles Smith (Picador, 1995)

The NME *Guide to Rock Cinema* by Fred Dellar (Hamlyn, 1981)

The New Guide to Classical Music by Jan Swafford (Vintage, 1992)

No One Here Gets Out Alive by Jerry Hopkins and Danny Sugarman (Plexus, 1980)

The Penguin Encyclopaedia of Popular Music edited by Donald Clarke (Penguin, 1998)

Reading Jazz edited by Robert Gottlieb (Bloomsbury, 1997)

Rock 'n' Roll Confidential by Penny Stallings (Vermillion, 1984)

The Rolling Stone *Illustrated History of Rock & Roll* edited by Jim Miller (Picador, 1980)

Rotten: No Irish, No Blacks, No Dogs – The Authorised Autobiography by John Lydon with Keith and Kent Zimmerman (Hodder and Stoughton, 1994)

Shots from the Hip by Charles Shaar Murray, edited by Neil Spencer (Penguin, 1991)

The Stones by Philip Norman (Corgi, 1984)

Twenty Years of Rolling Stone – *What a Long, Strange Trip It's Been* edited by Jann S. Wenner (Straight Arrow, 1987)

The Virgin Encyclopaedia of Heavy Rock by Colin Larkin (Virgin, 1999)

The Virgin Illustrated Encyclopaedia of Rock editorial director Lucinda Hawksley, adapter Nick Wells (Virgin, 1998)

The Warner Guide to UK & US Hit Singles by Dave McAleer (Little Brown, 1996)

Wired – The Short Life and Fast Times of John Belushi by Bob Woodward (Faber and Faber, 1985)

ARTICLES

'The Spinal Solution' by Cynthia Rose (*NME*, 8 September 1984)

'Spinal Column' by Adam Sweeting (*NME*, 15 September 1984)

'Rock Diary' by Andy Kershaw (*Independent*, 17 November 1989)

'Rock Follies' by Charles Shaar Murray (*Guardian*, 4 August 1990)

'With No Holds Barred' by Mark Wareham (*Independent*, 27 December 1991)

'The Spinal Frontier' by Jim White (*Independent*, 24 February 1992)

'Tap: the Search for a Drummer' by Mark Wareham (*Independent*, 9 April 1992)

'The Three Wise Men' by Adrian Deevoy (*Q* magazine, April 1992)

'Top Hat and Tales' by Andy Gill (*Independent*, 23 May 1992)

'Ian Faith Lives!' by Chick Hadrian (*Spy* magazine, July/August 1992)

'Ian Gillan Interview' (*Mojo* magazine, December 1994)

'Hollywood Online Chat' (30 May 1996)

'Tap into the Future' by Jim White and Edward Helmore (*Independent*, 1 June 1996)

'That's One Big Bono Up There' by Shawn Ohler (*Music Writer*, 13 June 1997)

'Welcome Back, My Friends' by Jack Boulware (*The Nose*, Issue 12 1998)

'Try Not to Trash the Place' by Michael Collins (*Independent*, 18 July 1988)

'Talent on Tap' by Jonathan Bernstein (*Guardian*, 15 November 1998)

'Interview with Christopher Guest' by Scott Dikkers (*The Onion*, 1999)

'Rock – a Hard Place' by Stuart Jeffries (*Guardian*, 16 April 1999)

INTERNET

The Spinal Tap Fan Page – http://www.chiprowe.com

The Internet Movie Database – http://www.imdb.com

Spinal Tap Official Website – http:www.spinaltap.com

THE FILM

The Criterion Collection laser disc Special Edition, incorporating commentary tracks by Christopher Guest, Michael McKean and Harry Shearer/-Kent Beyda, Robert Leighton, Karen Murphy and Rob Reiner.

ACKNOWLEDGEMENTS

First of all I would like to thank Christopher Guest for sparing the time to respond to my various inquiries. The greatest help in the project came from Zak Reddan, who tirelessly supplied advice, help and invaluable research. As well as Fiona and my family, I would like to thank the following for their assistance and advice: Mary Fawcett, Paul Deighton, Fred Deakin, Ian Mortimer, Harriet Yudkin. Thanks to everyone at Bloomsbury, especially Matthew Hamilton and also Jocasta Brownlee, Mike Jones, Monica Macdonald and Elizabeth O'Malley.

The publisher would like to thank: the band members: Mike McKean, Christopher Guest, Harry Shearer; the band's management: Harriet Sternberg; Ron Halpen and Studiocanal; Karl French; Chip Rowe; Pascal Carris; Rob Reiner's office; Castle Rock Entertainment; MGM and Optimum Releasing.

A NOTE ON THE AUTHOR

Karl French is the co-author of *The French Brothers' Film Quiz Book* and the editor of *The Collected Marx Brothers' Screenplays*. He also edited the controversial and highly successful *Screen Violence* anthology, published by Bloomsbury. He is the author of the Movie Guide *Apocalypse Now*.

DISCOGRAPHY

Discography

Break like the Wind
(Dead Faith/MCA, 1992)
Songs: Bitch School (2.51), The Majesty of Rock (3.55), Diva Fever (3.06), Just Begin Again (4.53), Cash On Delivery (3.04), The Sun Never Sweats (4.24), Rainy Day Sun (3.42), Break like the Wind (4.35), Stinkin' Up the Great Outdoors (2.50), Springtime (4.02), Clam Caravan (3.37), Christmas With the Devil (4.33), Let Him Go (2.08), All the Way Home (2.09).
Notes: A version of the album on vinyl picture disc was issued in the US as a promotion and sold in the UK. One side contains the artwork from the album cover, the other shows a Spinal Tap logo and song list. The album also was released as a nonfunctioning promotional 8-track.

Spinal Tap – The Original Soundtrack Recording from the Motion Picture *This Is Spinal Tap*
(Polymer/Polydor, 1984)
Songs: Hell Hole (3.06), Tonight I'm Gonna Rock You Tonight (2.35), Heavy Duty (4.26), Rock and Roll Creation (4.06), America (3.29), Cups and Cakes (1.31), Big Bottom (3.31), Sex Farm (3.19), Stonehenge (4.36), Gimme Some Money (2.24), (Listen to the) Flower People (2.33).
Notes: Not to be confused with *Smell the Glove*, their 1982 release. (They have similar covers.)

Bitch School
(MCA Records UK, 1992)
Songs: Bitch School (2.52), Springtime (4.05), Talk With Tap Part 1 (2.06).
Notes: Stonehenge-shaped 12-inch LP with poster

Bitch School
(MCA Records UK, 1992)

Songs: Bitch School (2.52), Springtime (4.05), Talk With Tap Part 2 (1.59)

Notes: Picture sleeve, compact disc, 7-inch promo with picture sleeve

The Majesty of Rock
(MCA Records UK, 1992)

Songs: The Majesty of Rock (3.59), Stinkin' Up the Great Outdoors (2.53), Talk With Tap Part 3 (5.03)

Notes: Picture sleeve, compact disk; 12-inch purple vinyl 'Special Etched Disc', with roast beef scratch and sniff sticker, does not include Talk with Tap but a matte on gloss Spinal Tap heraldic crest.

The Majesty of Rock
(MCA Records, 1992)

Songs: The Majesty of Rock (3.59)

Notes: Promo CD single with inserts.

Christmas with the Devil b/w Christmas with the Devil (scratch mix)
(Enigma Records, 1984, picture sleeve, and limited edition)

Notes: This is a different recording to the song released on *Break like the Wind* and includes a message from the band as the song fades: 'This is Spinal Tap, wishing you and yours the most joyous of holiday seasons. God bless us everyone.' The scratch mix begins with the sound of a needle scratching across record grooves and does not include the holiday message. Scott Sookman of *Vinyl Hell* magazine writes: 'This was the only release of this song, which the band performed in May 1984 on 'Saturday Night Live', until a version appeared on *Break like the Wind* in 1992. Since it was released as a promotional item to radio stations, it contains the same song on both sides. It was issued in a black-and-white sleeve with the Spinal Tap logo and devil artwork. This version of 'Christmas with the Devil' also appears on the compact disc *Rarities Volume 8 (Christmas)* issued by the Westwood One Radio Company in 1991.'

Hard Rock Cafe: '80s Heavy Metal
(Rhino Records, 1998)

Notes: Collection of sixteen metal classics, including Tap's 'Big Bottom'.

Holiday Collection Volume 3
(MCA Special Products Division, Hand Records, 1993)
Song: We Three Kings (1:19)
Notes: Sold as Christmas promotional item by Nordstrom department stores to benefit children's hospitals. The song also appears on another compilation album, *Share the Wonder* (Star Systems, 1993).

TAP'S OTHER ALBUMS ARE OUT OF PRINT:

Spinal Tap Sings '(Listen to the) Flower People' and Other Favorites
(Megaphone, 1967)
Songs: (Listen to the) Flower People (2.33), Have a Nice Death
Notes: Released in England as *Spinal Tap*

We Are All Flower People
(Megaphone, 1968)
Songs: We Are All Flower People, To Fly, I Am Flight, Get Me Away From the Ground, The Incredible Flight of Icarus P. Anybody
Notes: Re-released in 1969 without title track as *The Incredible Flight of Icarus P. Anybody*

Silent But Deadly
(Megaphone, 1969)
Songs: Short 'n' Easy (18.37), Breakfast of Evil, Silent But Deadly
Notes: Live album

Brainhammer
(Megaphone, 1970)
Songs: Big Bottom (3.31), Lie Back and Take It, Swallow My Love, Brainhammer

Nerve Damage
(Megaphone, 1971)

Blood to Let
(Megaphone, 1972)

Songs: Blood to Let

Intravenus de Milo
(Megaphone, 1974)
Songs: Tonight I'm Gonna Rock You Tonight (2.35), Saliva of the
  Fittest

The Sun Never Sweats
(Megaphone, 1975)
Songs: Daze of Knights of Old, The Princess and the Unicorn, The Obelisk,
  The Sun Never Sweats (4.24); Stonehenge (4.36)

Jap Habit
(Megaphone, 1975)
Songs: Nice 'n' Stinky, Devil Take the Hindmost, Nocturnal Mission
  (instrumental)
Notes: Live triple album; US release was double album

Bent for the Rent
(Megaphone, 1976)
Songs: When a Man Looks Like a Woman, High Heels, Hot Wheels,
  Heavy Duty (4.26), Bent for the Rent

Tap Dancing
(Megaphone, 1976)

Rock and Roll Creation
(Megaphone, 1977)
Songs: Young, Smug and Famous, Rock and Roll Creation (4:06)
Notes: Also known as *The Gospel According to Spinal Tap*

Shark Sandwich
(Polymer, 1980)
Songs: No Place Like Nowhere, Throb Detector, Sex Farm (3.19)

Smell The Glove
(Polymer, 1982)

Songs: Hell Hole (3.06)

Heavy Metal Memories
(Metalhouse, 1983)
Songs: Sex Farm (3.19), Stonehenge (4.36), The Incredible Flight of Icarus
P. Anybody, Blood to Let, Big Bottom (3.31), Brainhammer, Silent But
Deadly, Bent for the Rent, Tonight I'm Gonna Rock You Tonight
(2.35), Break like the Wind (4.35), Cups and Cakes (1.31), Rainy Day
Sun (3.42), (Listen to the) Flower People (2.33), Heavy Duty (4.26),
The Sun Never Sweats (4.24), (Again with the) Flower People, Nice 'n'
Stinky, Rock and Roll Creation (4.06), Gimme Some Money (2.24)

Unreleased Albums: *Flak Packet, Here's More Tap, Lusty Lorry*
Bootlegs: *Audible Death, Live at Budokkan, Got Thamesnen on Tap, It's a
Dub World, Openfaced Mako*

THE END?

David: 'I don't really think that the end can be assessed as of itself as being the end because what does the end feel like? It's like saying when you try and extrapolate the end of the universe, you say the end, the universe is indeed infinite, then, how, what does that mean? How far is all the way? And then, if it stops, what's stopping it? And what's behind what's stopping it? So "What's the end?" is my question to you.'